Basics of Microsoft® Internet Explorer 5, Outlook® 2000, and FrontPage® 2000

Basics of Microsoft® Internet Explorer 5, Outlook® 2000, and FrontPage® 2000

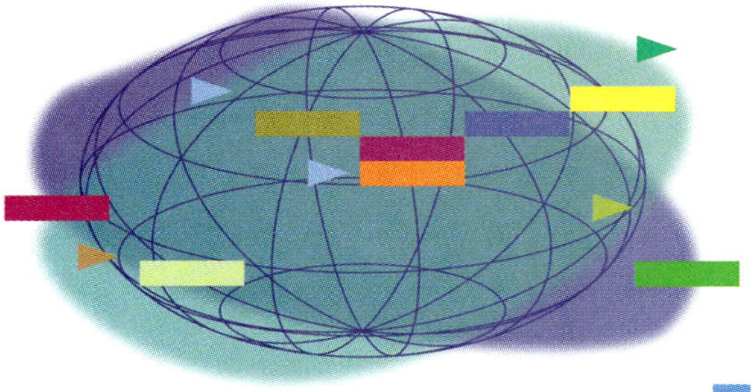

Tim Duffy

Prentice Hall
Upper Saddle River
New Jersey 07458

To Wendy and Michael,
the two most important people in my life

Editor-in-Chief: Mickey Cox
Executive Editor: Alex von Rosenberg
Acquisitions Editor: Anita Devine
Editorial Assistant: Jennifer Surich
Marketing Manager: Kris King
Managing Editor: Deanna Storey
Project Manager: Lynne Breitfeller
Project Management and Text Design: Elm Street Publishing Services, Inc.
Senior Manufacturing Supervisor: Paul Smolenski
Manufacturing Manager: Vincent Scelta
Production Manager: Gail Steier de Acevedo
Design Manager: Patricia Smythe
Interior Design: Brian Salisbury
Cover Design: Joan Connor
Cover Illustration: Brian Salisbury
Composition: Gillian Hall, The Aardvark Group

0-201-45920-5

Prentice-Hall International (UK) Limited, London
Prentice-Hall of Australia Pty. Limited, Sydney
Prentice-Hall Canada, Inc., Toronto
Prentice-Hall Hispanoamericana, S.A., Mexico
Prentice-Hall of India Private Limited, New Delhi
Prentice-Hall of Japan, Inc., Tokyo
Editora Prentice-Hall do Brasil, Ltda., Rio de Janeiro

Printed in the United States of America

10 9 8 7 6 5 4 3 2 1

Contents

PREFACE

Welcome to the *Microsoft Office User Specialist (MOUS) Certified Edition of Basics of Microsoft® Internet Explorer 5, Outlook®2000, and FrontPage®2000* by Tim Duffy. After completing the projects in this book, students will be prepared to take the core exams for Outlook. Successful completion of these exams gives students measurable, marketable skills.

NEW TO MICROSOFT® OFFICE 2000 PROFESSIONAL

New Text Design. As you open the pages of *Basics of Internet Explorer 5, Outlook®2000, and FrontPage®2000*, you will immediately notice the clear, easy to follow interior design. The clean page layout includes ample white space for note taking and a wealth of visual aids to guide students through each project.

Web Tools. Connectivity is paramount in computing and business. Today's students are required, more than ever, to know how to use the World Wide Web and Web develoment tools. *Basics of Internet Explorer 5, Outlook®2000, and FrontPage®2000* by Tim Duffy has changed with the technology and features all the latest in Microsoft Office Web development and connectivity tools including Internet Explorer 5, Outlook®2000, FrontPage®2000, and the Web-integrated operating system of Windows®98.

Interdisciplinary Exercises. Learning Microsoft® Office applications does not happen in a vacuum. In addition to learning the fundamentals of each application, students must also be able to take their experience using software applications and apply it to their other courses and experiences. In addition to the wealth of business-oriented exercises in this book, Tim Duffy has added interdisciplinary exercises that show students how to use software applications in other fields as well as for personal use.

AN AUTHOR YOU CAN COUNT ON

For more than two decades, Tim Duffy has been teaching and writing. As a teacher, he has taught introductory computer courses to thousands of Illinois State University students. As an author, he has introduced the very same computing concepts and skills to millions of students worldwide through his highly successful series.

In both his classes and his books, Duffy achieves a perfect balance between concept and skill—the why and the how—of computing. The "why" is the foundation of computing. Learn the concept and why that concept is important, and you can implement any skill. Because he teaches introductory computing throughout the school year, Duffy knows first-hand the conceptual information and techniques students need and want to learn and the best way to present the material. Duffy knows what works in the classroom and what works in the computer labs. He knows where students have difficulty and designs his book to help present concepts clearly. He has developed examples, assignments, and exercises that illuminate concepts and uses techniques to teach each application effectively.

Duffy teaches what he writes and writes what he teaches. In his books, he brings his classroom teaching experience directly to you with the most innovative, up-to-date material available anywhere. His pedagogy is classroom-tried and tested.

BUILDING KNOWLEDGE

For Duffy, learning is like building knowledge. A concept is presented, a feature or task is briefly described, and then students work with it. They complete an exercise or practice a task. Once that task is learned, they add a little more, building on what they are learning. After completing a small group of such tasks, each within its own context, students are presented with projects that unify concepts and skills. To achieve this natural balance between concepts and skills, there is constant reinforcement and evaluation throughout the book, including:

- *Unifying Features.* **Common Features of Office 2000** applications and tasks/features common to those applications give students an overview of how to use an integrated suite.
- *Active Learning.* **Hands-On Exercises** apply software commands and features of each Office 2000 application program to a specific problem, reinforcing skills described in the text.
- **Running Case.** Everyday problems are presented with just enough information to challenge the students. The Running Case teaches critical thinking while reinforcing the basic skills that students have learned to that point.
- **Document to Web Presentation.** This shows students how to transform an ordinary document into a professional presentation. They will be effectively guided through the process of enhancing the original, putting it on the Web, and then, finally, improving the Web page so as to produce a professional electronic document.
- *Task Steps and Reference.* **Reinforcing the Exercise** sections provide students with summary information on how a task is performed to reinforce learning and to provide a reference for the future.
- *Self-Learning.* **On Your Own** boxes allow students to gain additional mastery of features as they explore Office 2000 applications on their own.
- **Timely Tips.** Special notations tell students what potential traps they may encounter with a software tool, what can go wrong, and how to remedy the problem, as well as provide helpful hints on how to use a particular software feature.
- **Toolbar Button Reference.** Tables of toolbar buttons give students a central location to find summaries of buttons found on frequently used toolbars.
- **Keyboard and Toolbar Icons.** Task-specific icons appear frequently in headings and tables to help students identify and remember keystrokes or toolbar buttons required for accessing a particular software feature or performing a particular task.
- *Self-Evaluation.* **End-of-session exercises** offer reinforcement in multiple formats including true/false, multiple choice, short answer, and project-based questions.
- *Web Integration.* Web-based exercises appear at the end of each session in the **Internet Exercises** section. The Web site provides an interactive experience for students as they complete exercises in the text that send them to the site for information or files. In the Web exercises, Duffy teaches students how to view and save graphics, how to navigate on the Web, and how to download files; he even offers a guide to buying a personal computer and help on creating personal home pages.

Duffy takes advantage of the **Web-aware** tools provided with Office 2000 to help students translate their skills for use with the Internet and the Web.

Timely Tips inform students of helpful shortcuts, potential mistakes, or troubleshooting measures they can use with the text.

Interdisciplinary Exercises show students how to use software applications in other fields, such as social sciences, health sciences, and chemistry.

Reinforcing the Exercise

1. The Start button is the starting point for all Windows programs, documents, and settings.
2. When you open a window, an application button icon appears in the taskbar.
3. Documents you delete are stored in the Recycle Bin.
4. The My Computer window gives you information on the various resources of the computer, such as disk drives and printers.

CONTROLLING THE DESKTOP APPEARANCE

If your desktop looks different from that depicted so far in this text, your desktop has probably been configured differently. Windows 98 provides much more control over how your desktop appears and how you interact with that desktop. Windows now refers to the desktop as the **Active Desktop**. Certain features, like the appearance of the Internet Explorer Channel Bar, are automatically installed and included when Windows 98 is initially installed. Other features of the Active Desktop have to be specifically selected.

Displaying the Internet Explorer Channel Bar

The Internet Explorer Channel Bar appears in its own window when it is active. As a result, you can close the window by clicking the Close button in the upper right-hand corner of that window. The Close button appears when you position the mouse to the top of the Channel Bar. Use the commands in the following Hands-On exercise to redisplay the Channel Bar.

Web Options

You can also make your desktop function like World Wide Web applications. This means that each object appears underlined, like an HTML hyperlink, and can be accessed by just clicking the mouse. Web options can be applied using the Folder Options dialog box shown later in Figure 1.23.

Hands-On Exercise: Manipulating the Channel Bar

1. **Close the Channel Bar.**

   Position the mouse to the top of the Channel Bar (if it is present) and click the Close button of the Internet Explorer Channel Bar.

2. **Activate the Channel Bar.**

Right-click Right-click a blank area of the Desktop to invoke the context menu.

Active Desktop Choose Active Desktop from the context menu (Figure 1.17).

Customize my Desktop Click on this option to invoke the Display Properties dialog box (Figure 1.18). The dialog box should appear with the Web tab active and the two options shown in Figure 1.18 selected. (If the options

3. Use the Relationships command to relate the Paymast and Paytrans tables. Make certain that you specify referential integrity. Once the relationship is established, access the Paymast table. You should be able to access the corresponding Paytrans records using a subdatasheet.

Interdisciplinary Exercises

The following exercises require the Races and Movies databases used in Session I.

1. Open the Movies Database.
   a. Link the movies, actors, and directors tables.
   b. Open the Movies table.
   c. Add a field named MoneyGrossed, type currency, 0 decimals.
   d. Add an amount for each movie in the table. (If possible use real data).
   e. Make the default movietype "Comedy."
   f. Require DirectorCode to be upper case and A–Z only, and to be required.
   g. Require the length to be under 400 minutes.
   h. Require the release date to be after 1880 and before 2040.
   i. Make the only possible choices for MovieType to be Comedy, Drama, Western, Action, or Cartoon.
   j. Open the Directors table.
   k. Require DirectorCode to be upper case and A–Z only, and to be required.
   l. Open the Actors table.
   m. Make the movienumber and actorname be required.
   n. Use the Report Wizard to create and print a report for the Movie table.
   o. Create a multi-table query that relates the Movie and Actors tables. Generate a query. Print the query results. Save the query.
   p. Create a report for each table using a table Wizard. Save the reports. Print the reports.
2. Open the Races database.
   a. Open the Daily_log table.
   b. Delete the last two records.
   c. Use the Report Wizard to create and print a report.
   d. Move the comments field to the end of the table.
   e. Open the Races table.
   f. Make the default distance 5 and the default units "K".
   g. Make the Date and City required fields.
   h. Make the default state "AL" and require it to be uppercase and the letters A-Z.
   i. Generate a report for the races table.

Internet Exercises

1. Access Information about the Crosstab Query feature of Access.
   a. Get to the Web site for this text (http://www.prenhall.com/duffy).
   b. Access the Web page for advanced topical coverage and then get to the above page.
   c. You might want to print the Web page and then do the referenced hands-on exercise.
   d. The required disk file resides with your other student files.
   e. Print the dynaset.
2. Use the Access Assistance Library.
   a. Access the Microsoft Web page with your browser (http://www.microsoft.com).
   b. Click the Products button at the top of the Web page, and then choose Access 2000 for Windows from the list of products.
   c. Click the Visit the Microsoft® Access 2000 for Windows® Website link in the Contents pane on the left side of the page.
   d. Click the Enhancements and Assistance link.
   e. Click the Access 2000 Assistance link.
   f. Click the More Access Assistance link near the bottom of the page.
   g. Browse through the links displayed on the Microsoft Access 2000 Assistance Library page. Visit any links that relate to generating reports.
   h. Go back to the Assistance Library page.
   i. Print the Web page.

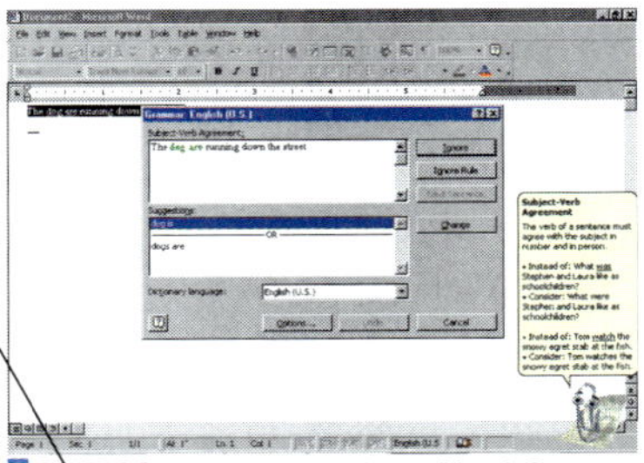

FIGURE 2.9 Additional help appears when you click on the Grammar option of the context menu.

Inserting Text

Office applications default to Insert mode. **Insert mode** moves existing text in a document to the right when new characters are added. **Overwrite mode** replaces existing characters with characters that you enter from the keyboard. Press the INS key to switch from insert to overwrite mode.

Timely Tip

Sometimes you will find that you are replacing text as you type. When this happens check the status line to see if the OVR indicator is on. Press the INS key to turn it off.

Deleting Text

You can delete text in all Office applications by first using the mouse to select the text to be deleted and then pressing DEL or BACKSPACE to delete the text. As you will see in the next part of this session, if you erroneously delete text, you can click the Undo button to restore the deleted text.

You can also delete text one character at a time. Use the DEL key to delete the character to the right of the insertion point. Use the BACKSPACE key to delete the character to the left of the insertion point.

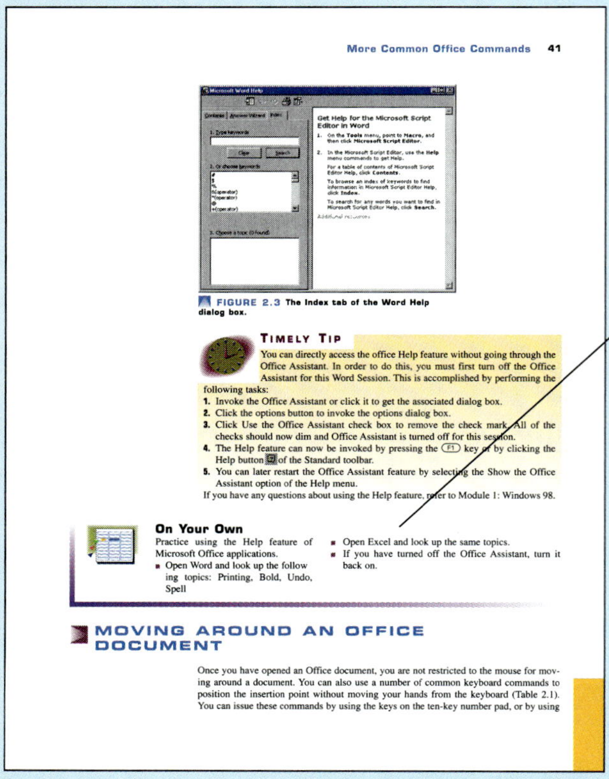

More Common Office Commands 41

FIGURE 2.3 The Index tab of the Word Help dialog box.

TIMELY TIP

You can directly access the office Help feature without going through the Office Assistant. In order to do this, you must first turn off the Office Assistant for this Word Session. This is accomplished by performing the following tasks:

1. Invoke the Office Assistant or click it to get the associated dialog box.
2. Click the options button to invoke the options dialog box.
3. Click Use the Office Assistant check box to remove the check mark. All of the checks should now dim and Office Assistant is turned off for this session.
4. The Help feature can now be invoked by pressing the F1 key or by clicking the Help button of the Standard toolbar.
5. You can later restart the Office Assistant feature by selecting the Show the Office Assistant option of the Help menu.

If you have any questions about using the Help feature, refer to Module 1: Windows 98.

On Your Own

Practice using the Help feature of Microsoft Office applications.

- Open Word and look up the follow ing topics: Printing, Bold, Undo, Spell
- Open Excel and look up the same topics.
- If you have turned off the Office Assistant, turn it back on.

MOVING AROUND AN OFFICE DOCUMENT

Once you have opened an Office document, you are not restricted to the mouse for moving around a document. You can also use a number of common keyboard commands to position the insertion point without moving your hands from the keyboard (Table 2.1). You can issue these commands by using the keys on the ten-key number pad, or by using

On Your Own boxes encourage students to explore the full range of features available in Office 2000 applications.

Hands-On Exercises, based on the Running Case, give step-by-step instructions for learning each application. Numerous screen captures and button icons show students exactly what they need to know.

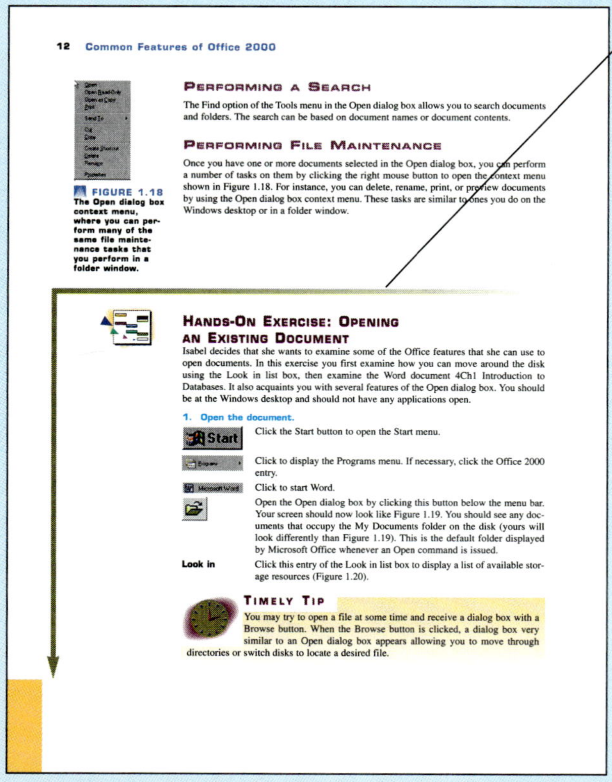

12 Common Features of Office 2000

FIGURE 1.18 The Open dialog box context menu, where you can perform many of the same file maintenance tasks that you perform in a folder window.

PERFORMING A SEARCH

The Find option of the Tools menu in the Open dialog box allows you to search documents and folders. The search can be based on document names or document contents.

PERFORMING FILE MAINTENANCE

Once you have one or more documents selected in the Open dialog box, you can perform a number of tasks on them by clicking the right mouse button to open the context menu shown in Figure 1.18. For instance, you can delete, rename, print, or preview documents by using the Open dialog box context menu. These tasks are similar to ones you do on the Windows desktop or in a folder window.

HANDS-ON EXERCISE: OPENING AN EXISTING DOCUMENT

Isabel decides that she wants to examine some of the Office features that she can use to open documents. In this exercise you first examine how you can move around the disk using the Look in list box, then examine the Word document 4Ch1 Introduction to Databases. It also acquaints you with several features of the Open dialog box. You should be at the Windows desktop and should not have any applications open.

1. Open the document.

Start — Click the Start button to open the Start menu.

Click to display the Programs menu. If necessary, click the Office 2000 entry.

Microsoft Word — Click to start Word.

Open the Open dialog box by clicking this button below the menu bar. Your screen should now look like Figure 1.19. You should see any documents that occupy the My Documents folder on the disk (yours will look differently than Figure 1.19). This is the default folder displayed by Microsoft Office whenever an Open command is issued.

Look in — Click this entry of the Look in list box to display a list of available storage resources (Figure 1.20).

TIMELY TIP

You may try to open a file at some time and receive a dialog box with a Browse button. When the Browse button is clicked, a dialog box very similar to an Open dialog box appears allowing you to move through directories or switch disks to locate a desired file.

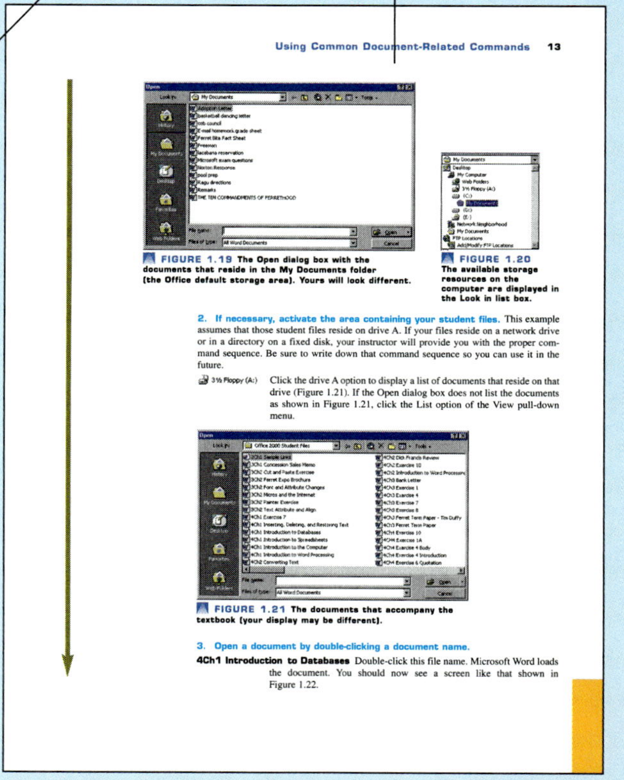

Using Common Document-Related Commands 13

FIGURE 1.19 The Open dialog box with the documents that reside in the My Documents folder (the Office default storage area). Yours will look different.

FIGURE 1.20 The available storage resources on the computer are displayed in the Look in list box.

2. If necessary, activate the area containing your student files. This example assumes that those student files reside on drive A. If your files reside on a network drive or in a directory on a fixed disk, your instructor will provide you with the proper command sequence. Be sure to write down that command sequence so you can use it in the future.

3½ Floppy (A:) — Click the drive A option to display a list of documents that reside on that drive (Figure 1.21). If the Open dialog box does not list the documents as shown in Figure 1.21, click the List option of the View pull-down menu.

FIGURE 1.21 The documents that accompany the textbook (your display may be different).

3. Open a document by double-clicking a document name.

4Ch1 Introduction to Databases — Double-click this file name. Microsoft Word loads the document. You should now see a screen like that shown in Figure 1.22.

Reinforcing the Exercise

1. You use the Look in list box to examine files that reside on various computer drives and resources.
2. The Up One Level button allows you to move up one level in a folder hierarchy.
3. The Preview button allows you to examine the contents of an Office document.
4. You can perform a search using the Open dialog box.
5. The Properties button allows you to see the name of the designated author of a document.

CLOSING A DOCUMENT File, Close or X

Once you have opened a document and made changes to it, you must close it before you can close the application. In addition, you may want to close a document before you move to another document or application. You can close any Office application document by clicking on that document's Close button. The Close button for a maximized document window is always located at the right end of the menu bar. If you have made changes to a document or you have not saved the document before, a dialog box like that shown in Figure 1.30 appears, prompting you about saving the file. Click the Yes button to save changes to the document and clear the document window. Click the No button to clear the screen without saving the document. Click the Cancel button to return to the document.

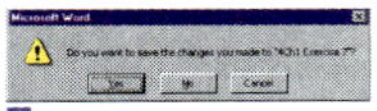

FIGURE 1.30 The dialog box for saving a document that appears after you have issued the Close command.

FIGURE 1.31 The Office Assistant querying about saving a changed file.

If the Office Assistant is present when you close a document, your screen will appear with the Assistant depicted in Figure 1.31.

If you are working with an unnamed document that you've never saved before and decide to close it, a Save As dialog box appears, prompting you for a filename. The Save As dialog box is discussed in detail later in this session.

After you close a document, you can open another document or start a new application.

EXITING AN APPLICATION File, Exit, or X

Once you decide to exit an application program, you have several alternatives. You can issue a File, Exit command sequence or click the Close button on that application's title bar. Make certain that you click the Close button on the title bar and not the Close button on the menu bar or the document title bar (that will only close the open document).

If you have not previously saved the document, a dialog box like that shown in Figure 1.30 or Figure 1.31 appears, prompting you about saving the file. If you are working with an unnamed document and decide to save it, a Save As dialog box appears prompting you for the new filename. The Save As dialog box is discussed in detail later in this session.

Reinforcing the Exercise sections help students recall and refer to the work they have completed.

Tables of keyboard or **toolbar icons and symbols** provide students with quick reference to the conventions and uses of Office 2000 applications.

MANIPULATING THE PREVIEWED DOCUMENT

A number of buttons appear at the top of the Preview window that you can use to manipulate the previewed document. These buttons are summarized in Table 1.5. The menu bar also appears in the Preview window, so you can issue commands from it to change the appearance of the previewed document. You can also make any changes to the text of the document that are required while in Print Preview mode.

TABLE 1.5 Preview Window Buttons

BUTTON	NAME OF BUTTON	FUNCTION
	Print	Sends the document immediately to the printer. No Print dialog box is displayed.
	Magnifier	Changes the pointer to a magnifying glass. Click the part of the document you want magnified. Click that part again to return it to its original size.
	One Page	Displays one page of the document at a time.
	Multiple Pages	Displays a menu that allows you to determine the number of pages to be displayed at one time.
19%	Zoom	Controls the size of the simulated text displayed in the Preview window. The Office default setting is typically used for this button.
	View Ruler	Activates the ruler for the previewed document. The ruler shows where the left and right margins are, along with any tab stops that have been included in the document.
	Shrink to Fit	Reduces the number of pages in a document by one by slightly changing the size of type used in the document.
	Full Screen	Hides most of the screen elements (menus, toolbars, and so forth) so that more of the document can be previewed.
Close	Close Preview	Closes the Preview window and returns to the application window.
	Context Sensitive Help	Click this to turn the pointer into a big question mark. When you now click a button or object, a help bubble appears explaining that item.

HANDS-ON EXERCISE: PREVIEWING AN OFFICE DOCUMENT

Isabel wants to use the Print Preview feature to demonstrate to several of the secretaries how easy it is to see exactly how a file will print. She also wants to demonstrate the effects of several of the Preview window buttons.

This exercise examines the Print Preview feature by using the Word document 4Ch1 Introduction to Word Processing. It assumes that you have Word started.

1. **Open the document.**

Open the Open dialog box by clicking this toolbar button. If necessary, select the drive and/or folder in the Look in list that contains your student files.

COMPANION WEB SITE

The Companion Web Site is an on-line learning environment for instructors and students. The range of activities available in Companion Web Sites includes:

- *On-line Study Guide*—different types of self-assessment exercises including multiple choice, true/false, and fill-in-the-blank questions, with instant feedback available at the click of button.
- *Internet Exercises*—take the text feature one step further by providing the links in the exercises. The Companion Web Site extends the exercises by providing an interactive experience for students as they complete exercises in the text that send them to the site for information or files. The textbook uses this feature to introduce a number of advanced software topics and provides the same type of topical coverage, Hands-On Exercises, and Reinforcing the Exercise found in the regular textbook.
- *Password Protected Faculty Resources*—ancillary materials accessible for instant download, syllabus creation, and management tools are integrated into the Companion Web Site, including PowerPoint slides written by Tim Duffy, as well as a text art library.
- *Student Data Files*—The student data files required for hands-on exercises and end of session exercises can be downloaded from this location.
- *Syllabus Manager*—an online syllabus creation and management utility. Syllabus Manager™ provides instructors with an easy, step-by-step process to create and revise syllabi, with direct links into Companion Web Site and other online content. Students access Syllabus Manager™ directly from within the Companion Web Site, providing quick access to course assignments.

TEST MANAGER

Test Manager™ is a comprehensive suite of tools for testing and assessment. Test Manager™ allows educators to easily create and distribute tests for their courses, either by printing and distributing through traditional methods or by on-line delivery via a Local Area Network (LAN) server. Four question formats are available: multiple choice, true/false, matching, and completion exercises. Answer keys and page references for test questions are provided.

PRINTED INSTRUCTOR'S MANUAL BY BILL DALEY AND TIM DUFFY

The printed Instructor's Manual includes a Test Bank and Transparency Masters for each project in the student text. The Test Bank contains tests with answers and consists of multiple choice, true/false, and fill-in questions that refer to pages in the student text. Transparency Masters illustrate key concepts and screen captures from the text. The Instructor's Manual also offers teaching notes to help integrate current technology (such as the text Web site) into a modern course on Office 2000; objectives and outline for each session; and grading tips.

INSTRUCTOR'S CD-ROM

Instructors get extra support for this text from supplemental materials. The Instructor's Resource CD-ROM contains screen captures, diagrams and tables from the text, as well as files that correspond to key figures in the book. These can be incorporated into PowerPoint electronic slides that professors can create for their classes. Screen-by-screen steps in a project can be displayed in class or reviewed by students in the computer lab. The Instructor's Resource CD-ROM includes the entire Instructor's Manual with Test Bank in Microsoft Word. It also includes text-based PowerPoint presentation slides that support classroom lectures for each session. Six slides can be printed per page and distributed to students to facilitate notetaking. A Computerized Test Bank is included to create printed tests or network tests. Student data files and completed data files are also on the Instructor's Resource CD-ROM. All the electronic files can be found on the instructor's password protected Web site at http://www.prenhall.com/duffy. Contact your Sales Representative for your ID and password.

STUDENT SUPPLEMENTS

SKILLCHECK Assessment Software is a network-based skills assessment-testing program available through the Prentice Hall Point Program. SKILLCHECK measures student proficiency with Word 2000, Excel 2000, Access 2000, and PowerPoint 2000. Through a completely customizable set of test options or by using the pre-loaded MOUS certification review exams, professors select the tasks to be tested and receive student results immediately. The test is taken in a simulated software environment, which enables the software to run on network or individual computers. On-screen instructions require students to perform tasks as though they were using the actual application. The program automatically records responses, assesses student accuracy, and reports the resulting score in a printout or disk file as well as to the instructor's grade book. Results can also be downloaded as an Excel file.

COURSE KITS

The Duffy Office 2000 applications texts are available separately or in a single *Microsoft® Office 2000 Professional* volume. The Office 2000 Professional suite includes Common Features of Office 2000, Windows®98, Internet Explorer 5, Word 2000, Access 2000, Excel 2000, PowerPoint 2000, Outlook®2000, and FrontPage®2000. Available as a separate module is Web Collaboration Tools, which includes Outlook®2000, FrontPage®2000, and Internet Explorer 5. Whether you package the entire Office 2000 suite with our concepts books or the individual modules, your students will receive a significant discount.

PRENTICE HALL POINTS PROGRAM

As a publisher, we are aware of the need to have the most current software application programs available to students in introductory computer courses. We are pleased to partner with colleges and universities to achieve this goal through our Prentice Hall Points Program.

By adopting our text and lab books, your school may qualify for free software programs and site licenses to be used by your students in your school's computer lab.

ACKNOWLEDGMENTS

I am amazed that seventeen years have passed since I started the first edition of Four Software Tools. At that time, I was completely unaware of the time-consuming efforts needed to produce a college-level textbook. Since then, however, I have developed a sincere appreciation of what is required to make a successful text. The success formula includes family, friends, colleagues, and many individuals in the publishing business. I remain deeply indebted to my wife, Wendy, who encouraged me to write the original version of Four Software Tools. Without her encouragement, the original text never would have been finished, and without her continued support, these projects would be impossible to accomplish.

Keith Hallmark at Calhoun Community College helped draft the interdisciplinary exercises, and Bill Daley from the University of Oregon wrote the Companion Web Site student study guide questions—many thanks for a job well done. I also want to express my sincere appreciation to the reviewers of this manuscript:

Michael Barrett, *Clarion University*
Jill Betts, *Tyler Junior College*
Bill Daley, *University of Oregon*
Kathryn A. Drexel, *Drexel Associates*
Peter Drexel, *Plymouth State College*
Keith Hallmark, *Calhoun Community College*
Albert L. Harris, *Appalachian State University*
Seth Hock, *Columbus State Community College*
Cynthia Johnson, *University of Central Florida*
Marie McCooey, *Bryant College*
Randall J. Molmen, *Baldwin–Wallace College*
Vincent J. Motto, *Asnuntuck Community–Technical College*
Stephen C. Solosky, *Nassau Community College*
Donald M. Stasiw, *Utica College of Syracuse University*
Barbara Z. Taylor, *Elon College*
Melinda C. White, *Santa Fe Community College*
Bob Williams, *Clinton Community College*
Dr. Andrew Yang, *Southern Connecticut State*

Individuals at the publishing company also play an important role. Addison Wesley Longman's editorial staff is superb. With warm feelings, I would like to acknowledge Anita Devine and Ed Moura. Maureen Allaire initially signed this book, and over the years she has had much to do with many of my books. I am pleased to have worked with Anita Devine, who brings a wealth of editorial experience in microcomputer texts. Ed Moura, Editor-in-Chief, brought a number of excellent ideas to this project. Holly Rioux, Assistant Editor, made certain that everything was moving on an even keel. Deanna Storey's attention to detail and the review process helped shape this project and make this edition happen. Martha Johnson, Emily Kim, and Ann Sargent's copyedits and technical edits helped to assure internal consistency of the text. This is the first time I have worked with Michele Heinz and Elm Street Publishing Services—they have been wonderful to work with.

A dedication is not complete without including my son, Michael. Michael continues to make any writing project a challenge. His requests to go biking, golfing, swimming, or pursuing a new interest are much appreciated. Michael especially likes to surf the Web to complete homework assignments and has become a twelve-year-old master at ferreting out information from the Web.

BASICS OF MICROSOFT® INTERNET EXPLORER 5, OUTLOOK® 2000, AND FRONTPAGE® 2000

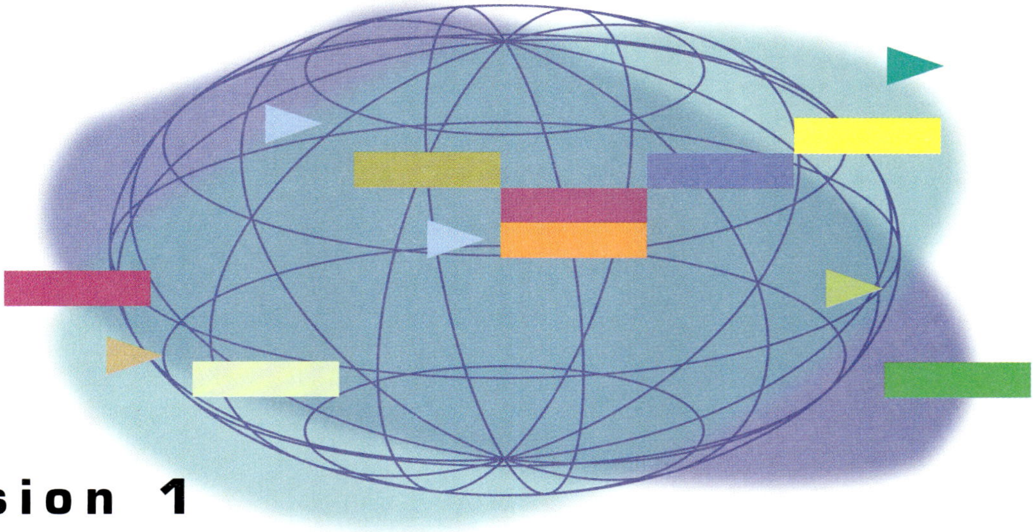

Session 1
INTRODUCTION TO THE INTERNET

After completing this session, you should be able to:

- Develop an understanding of the Internet
- Use an Internet address/account
- Understand various Internet services
- Use a Web browser
- Visit various Web sites
- Send E-mail messages

If you are taking a course dealing with software use for microcomputers in a college or university setting, the computer you are using is probably hooked up with other computers in a network. A **network** is a set of hardware and software components that supports several people working together and allows these individuals to share hardware, software, and information with one another.

INTRODUCTION TO THE INTERNET

One of the major sources of communication and information access today is the Internet. The **Internet** is a network of networks that allows you to communicate with people anywhere in the world as well as access information that you desire any time of the day or night. All you need is a computer and a communication connection.

The Internet allows you to access enormous amounts of information, from weather reports to stats on your favorite sports team, from movie reviews to updates on your favorite TV show. It is a valuable source of information for your term papers and research for classes. Businesses can use the Internet to advertise their products, and individuals can send written communications to anyone who has Internet access.

The Internet was started in the 1960s as a joint effort by government and education to provide continuing linked computer support in case of a nuclear attack. In its early days it was referred to as ARPAnet (Advanced Research Projects Agency Network). It quickly evolved to be an important tool for sharing research-related information between these groups. As the Internet matured, communication methods were developed that allowed just about any computer to be hooked up to the Internet.

Today's Internet allows millions of people around the world to communicate with one another and access information from any location. One of the major reasons for the explosive growth of the Internet was the development of the World Wide Web (WWW or Web) in the early 1990s. The Web makes it easy to use text and graphics to publish information that others can access easily via the Internet.

To access the Web, you need a Web browser. A **Web browser** is software that communicates with other Web sites and transfers text, graphics, and even sound to your computer screen or speakers and displays and plays this data correctly. There are numerous Web browsers on the market today. Two of the most popular browsers are Netscape (Figure 1.1) and Internet Explorer (Figure 1.2). Internet Explorer will be covered in more detail later in this module.

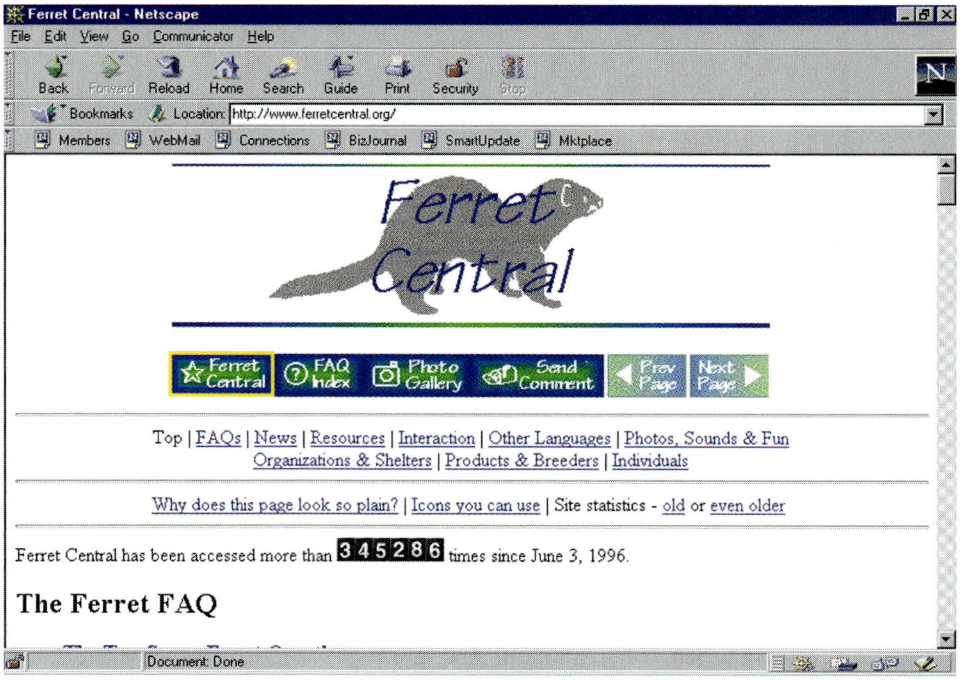

FIGURE 1.1 The Netscape browser accessing a Web site related to ferrets.

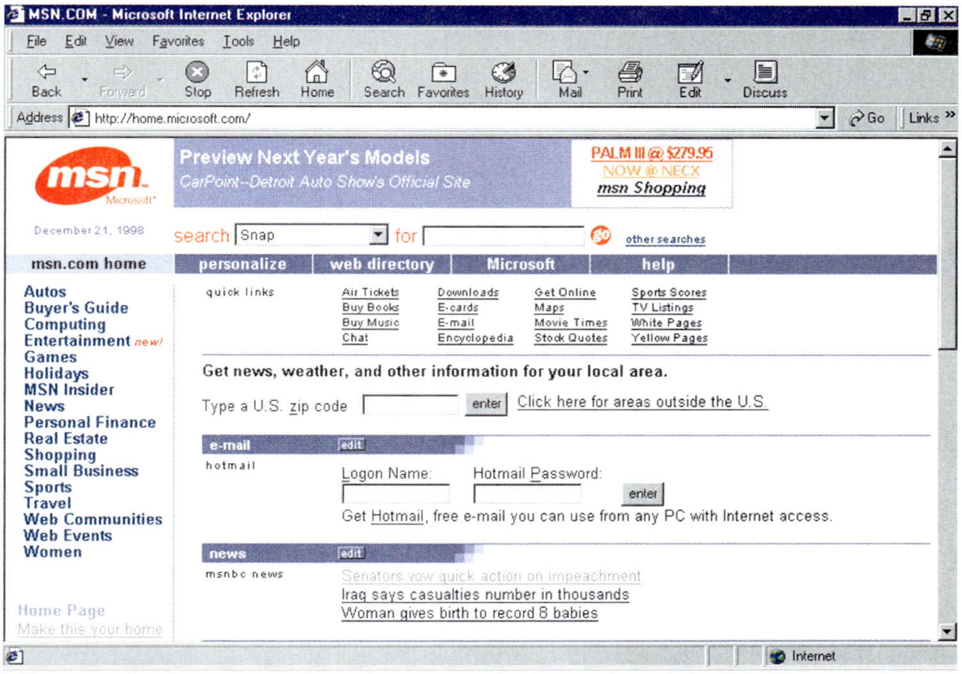

FIGURE 1.2 Microsoft's Internet Explorer browser accessing the Microsoft Web site.

Connecting to the Internet

Before you can communicate with someone on the Internet, your computer must have the communications capability to access it. This capability has at least three components: communications capability using a modem or network hookup, an Internet account, and access to the Internet using an Internet service provider (ISP).

If you are using a home computer, your computer must have a modem. A **modem** (short for modulation/demodulation) changes computer digital symbols to sound for transmission across telephone hookups. The receiving computer's modem then changes the sounds back to binary symbols (Figure 1.3).

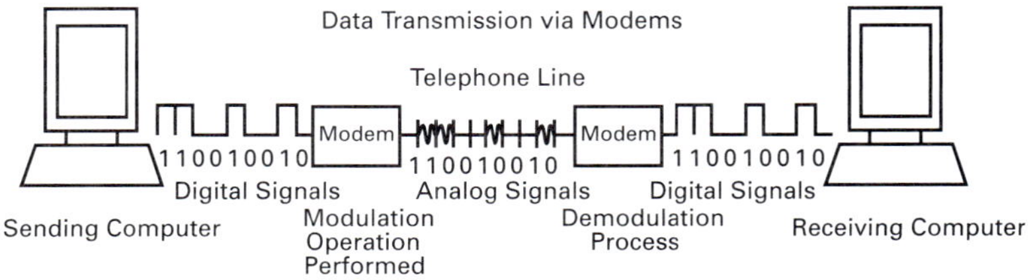

FIGURE 1.3 Sending and receiving computer data across telephone lines require converting digital signals to analog (sound) and back again.

If you are using a computer at school to access the Internet, your computer will probably be hooked to a network that has access to the Internet via its own communications hardware.

The Internet service provider at an educational institution is probably the school itself. You receive an account that allows you to send messages and obtain information using the Internet.

For your home computer, you can obtain access to the Internet by using a commercial Internet service provider, such as America Online (AOL), Microsoft Network (MSN), or Prodigy. You can also access the Internet by using a local provider. Historically, both types of providers have allocated a basic amount of time you could use to access the provider's services. After you had used that time, you were charged on a per-hour basis for connect time. In the past few years many providers have begun to allow unlimited access at one price per month.

If you are currently a student at a college or university and want to use your home computer to access the Internet, you can probably use your school account and your school's dial-up capability to access the Internet from your home.

The Internet Account/Address

To communicate with someone on the Internet, you must know that person's account/address information (Figure 1.4). The **account** is the individual's unique identifier at a particular location. Only one person can have a specific account at a location. The **address** is the location where the individual receives messages. The account and address are separated by the at sign (@).

FIGURE 1.4 To communicate with someone over the Internet, you need to know that person's account and address.

An Internet address has two main parts separated by periods: the subdomain and the topdomain. The **subdomain** indicates the name of the location and possibly the name of the server to which the message is to be sent. The **topdomain** specifies the type of organization that is to receive the message (Table 1.1). There are currently only six topdomains, but soon there may be more because the .com topdomain is reaching the maximum available capacity.

To send a message to another country, you use a topdomain consisting of a two-character signifier preceded by the **country (co) indicator**. For example the Internet address `xxxxxxx@futurenet.co.uk` would connect with the specified user at the futurenet site in Great Britain.

Once you have an account set up, you are ready to access the Internet. If you are accessing the Internet from home or from school, you usually have to go through a login procedure. This **login** procedure identifies you to the host computer (your school or commercial provider). A typical login procedure requires you to enter your account information along with a password. A **password** is a series of characters that verifies to the computer that you are indeed a valid user. Asterisks typically appear on-screen when you enter your password information. Be sure not to give this password to any other persons because they could misuse your identity or do something undesirable that could be falsely traced back to you.

Your Internet account gives you access to the many services of the Internet, including accessing other computers, locating information, and communicating with other users. Some of these services might be built into your browser or are available using a different software package.

Electronic Mail

Electronic mail (E-mail) consists of messages you can send and receive by using the computer. Several software packages have been designed specifically for E-mail. Figure 1.5 shows the opening window of one such package, Microsoft's Outlook Express.

TABLE 1.1 Standardized Internet Domains

Current Topdomain Name	Type of Organization
.com	Commercial or business
.edu	Educational
.gov	U.S. government
.mil	U.S. military
.net	Network
.org	Private or nonprofit
Proposed New Topdomain Name	**Type of Organization**
.firm	Business or firm
.store	Business offering goods for purchase
.web	Web-based entity
.arts	Cultural or entertainment activity
.rec	Recreational or entertainment entity
.info	Information services entity
.nom	Individual or personal

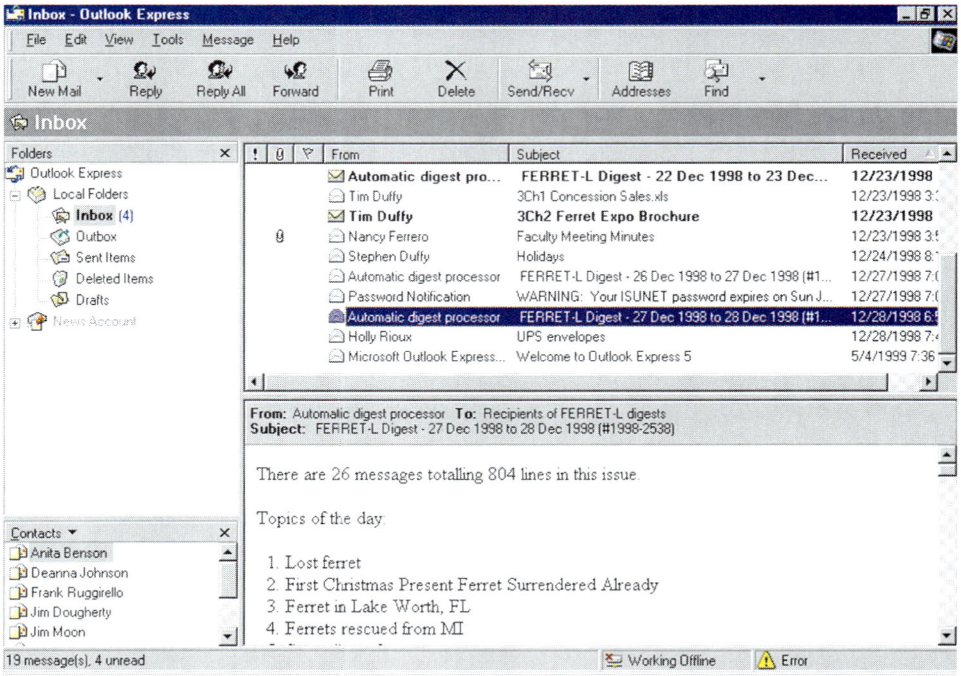

FIGURE 1.5 With Microsoft's Outlook Express, you can read electronic mail that people send you.

You send an E-mail message to a person's mailbox (that is, that person's Internet account/address designation), and the individual who knows the correct password for that account can read the message.

Notice that the sender, subject, and date received (as you scroll to the right) are displayed in the upper right-hand box of the window, and the first few lines of the message are displayed in the lower right-hand box. A message with an open envelope indicates that a message has already been read, while a closed envelope indicates an unread message. You can read a message by clicking the desired message and then scrolling through it in the bottom box. You can also double-click the entry for the message to display a message window like that shown in Figure 1.6.

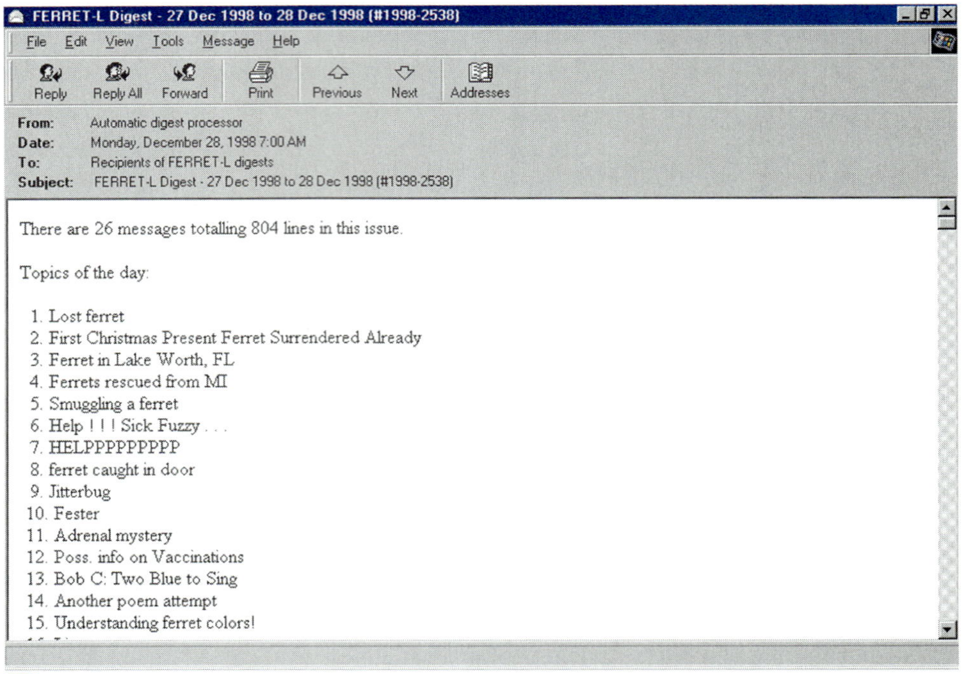

FIGURE 1.6 The Outlook Express message window, which appears when you double-click a message listed in the Outlook Express window.

You can send an E-mail message to someone in the same organization or anywhere in the world where that individual has an E-mail address. If you want several people to receive the same message, you don't need to type a message for each person. A single message can have one or many recipients. You use the message window shown in Figure 1.7 to send an E-mail message to one or more recipients.

The To portion of the window contains the Internet address of the recipient(s). If your message has more than one recipient, you must separate the addresses with commas(,) or semicolons (;). As a courtesy, the Cc (carbon copy) entry indicates who else is receiving a copy of the message and is dimmed if not used. The Bcc (blind carbon copy) differs from Cc in that recipients are not listed. Recipients included in Bcc will not be known to others. The Subject entry tells the recipient the purpose of the message. The text of the message is contained in the bottom box. When you have completed the message, you can click the Send button (the addressed envelope icon labeled Send, at the far left on the toolbar) to send the message.

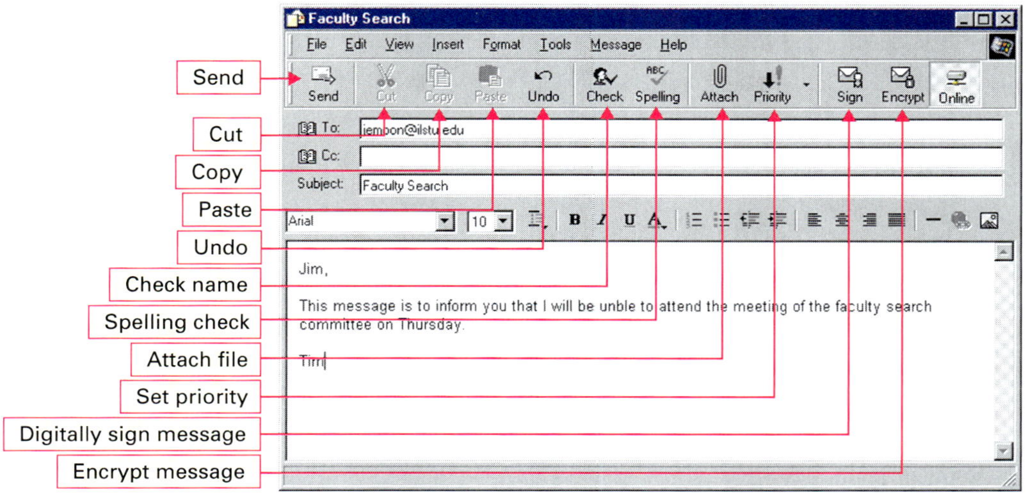

FIGURE 1.7 The New Message window you use to send a message.

E-mail is used extensively in business, education, and government. It is currently one of the fastest growing message media in the world. One problem with E-mail is that it is so easy to use that people often send messages without reading them over carefully. A recent magazine article estimated that 70 percent of most E-mail messages are so badly written that further messages must be sent to clarify them.

Another problem with E-mail is that some people become verbally violent. **Flaming** refers to sending a nasty message, or flame, to an individual on the Internet. Many times flames are sent by people who don't take the time to cool down before sending their messages. In a paper-based environment, a letter may sit in an out box for several hours before it is picked up by the mail service. This gives the person sending the message time to rethink and maybe retrieve the message. In an electronic environment, a message is sent by simply clicking a Send button. Once such a message is sent, it can only be retrieved if the recipient has not opened it (if your E-mail system has this retrieval capability).

Written communications experts have developed some guidelines for using E-mail:

- Keep the message brief and concise.
- Don't send confidential information or messages that might be embarrassing.
- The messages belong to the organization; therefore, someone in a supervisory capacity may be reading them.
- Don't send copies to people who don't really need to see the message.
- Don't type your messages in all uppercase letters. This is equivalent to shouting and is discouraged. At the same time, using all lowercase letters is equivalent to mumbling.
- Always include a salutation and signature line in your communication. Use proper punctuation and grammar. Be certain to personalize your letters rather than depending on computer-generated address fields.
- Always check the To: and Cc: fields to make certain that you are sending the message to the correct individual(s).

The preceding guidelines on brevity have resulted in the evolution of an **E-mail shorthand** frequently used in E-mail messages and Internet chat sessions (Table 1.2). This online shorthand can help to keep messages short and make communication easier and quicker (as long as you know the shorthand).

TABLE 1.2 E-mail Shorthand

ABBREVIATION	MEANING	ABBREVIATION	MEANING
AAMOF	As a matter of fact	OIC	Oh! I see
BTW	By the way	ROTFL	Rolling on the floor laughing
BYKT	But you knew that	SO	Significant other
CMIIW	Correct me if I'm wrong	TIC	Tongue in cheek
EOL	End of lecture	TTFN	Ta ta for now
FITB	Fill in the blank	TYVM	Thank you very much
IAC	In any case	<G>	Grinning
IMHO	In my humble opinion	<L>	Laughing
LJBF	Let's just be friends	<J>	Joking
LOL	Laughing out loud	<S>	Smiling

One problem with using E-mail as a communications medium is that there is no face-to-face contact. The message recipient cannot see any visual clues you may be providing—your "body language."

To help show their emotions, many people use **emoticons**, or **smileys**, that they create by using keyboard characters (Table 1.3). (The emoticons found in Table 1.3 are from CompuServe's SMILEY.TXT file.) For example, indicating that you are currently smiling or that something is humorous, use the :-) emoticon.

TABLE 1.3 Commonly Used Emoticons

:-)	Smile	:-/	Undecided
;-)	Winking	:-C	Bummed out
:-(	Frowning	;-e	Disappointed
:-|	Indifferent	:-o	Surprised
:->	Sarcastic	>:-<	Mad
>:->	Devilish	:-O	Uh oh
:'-(	Crying	:-D	Laughing
:'-)	Happy and crying	:-/	Skeptical
:-@	Screaming	<:-|	Dunce
:-&	Tongue tied	:-S	Incoherent

You should always avoid any type of gossip or impropriety using E-mail. Never send a message over e-mail that you would not mind everyone in the world reading. Remember, E-mail messages do not belong to you; rather, case law dictates that they belong solely to the company operating the E-mail system. E-mail messages do not have the same protected legal status as mail delivered by the United States Postal Service.

Office 2000 has two E-mail packages that allow you to send messages. The Outlook 2000 software package provides many different E-mail features that are covered later in this textbook. It allows you to do such things as keep an electronic calendar, maintain contacts in an electronic Rolodex file, maintain an electronic to do list, keep electronic notes, set up an electronic journal, as well as other tasks. It is a truly feature-rich software package.

Outlook Express version 5 is a less feature-rich E-mail package. Internet Explorer comes bundled with Outlook Express. It assumes that you want to send messages over a standard Internet communications link. Besides providing E-mail support, it also allows you to communicate with newsgroups or send messages over a local area network. Outlook Express is the E-mail package that will be discussed in this chapter.

Usenet and Newsgroups

Usenet started out as a bulletin board system and expanded to include thousands of computer sites providing services to people all over the world. **Newsgroups** are interactive discussions that can occur via Usenet and cover a wide variety of topics. You can read or add information to the newsgroup via a **posting**, which is a message you send or receive by using E-mail software. A set of postings related to a specific topic within a newsgroup is called a **thread**. You read a thread by using newsgroup software such as Agent and MS Outlook Express.

While no one person controls a newsgroup, newsgroups are controlled at each Usenet site by an administrator. This person is responsible for determining how long postings can stay on that site before they are deleted. For example, if the expiration date is 15 days, any posting over 15 days old gets deleted from the site.

Information in a newsgroup is arranged by topic or by areas of interest. A newsgroup name contains information about the topic followed by other sections that further describe the newsgroup. The group name and any sections are separated by periods. Table 1.4 lists some sample newsgroups.

TABLE 1.4 Sample Newsgroups

Newsgroup	Purpose
comp	Computer hardware, software, and related topics. Example: comp.mail.eudora.ms-windows
misc	Topics that don't really fit a category. Example: misc.consumers.house
rec	Recreational activities, hobbies, art, and so forth. Example: rec.arts.disney.parks or rec.models.railroad
sci	Research in a number of scientific areas. Example: sci.anthropology.paleo
soc	Social, cultural, and political discussions. Example: soc.culture.arabic
talk	Discussion forums for politics, philosophy, or other areas that may be controversial. Example: talk.religion.buddhism

You can participate in a newsgroup in a number of ways. Figure 1.8 shows one type of shareware or freeware software (Free Agent, which you can obtain) specially designed for doing this. You can also use Outlook Express to interact with newsgroups.

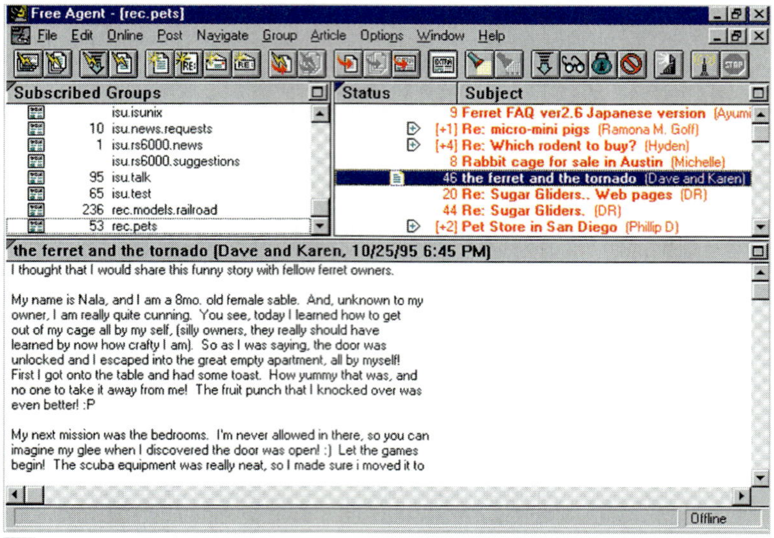

FIGURE 1.8 Newsgroup-oriented software like Free Agent allows you to interact with newsgroups.

Microsoft's Outlook Express provides communication with newsgroups. If you click the plus sign (+) to the left of the the newsgroup icon in the left-hand box, you will see newsgroups to which you have subscribed (Figure 1.9). Once the subscribed newsgroups are visible, you click the one you want to read in the left-hand box. The various postings for that newsgroup appear in the upper right-hand box. Click the message that you want to read and the first lines of content appear in the bottom box. You can now use the scroll bar to scroll through the message (Figure 1.10). You can also double-click a message to place that message in a separate window. Notice that any links associated with the World Wide Web are in blue and underlined. When you click any of these blue links, the browser software is activated to access that site.

If you click on the News Account icon, the window displayed in in Figure 1.11 appears on your screen. This window allows you to synchronize the various newsgroups to which you have subscribed. This synchronization requires Outlook to access your news server to see if any new messages have arrived for each of your subscribed newsgroups. If new messages have arrived, Outlook will automatically load those messages to the appropriate newsgroup. Once any new messages have been loaded, you can access those messages using the steps cited above.

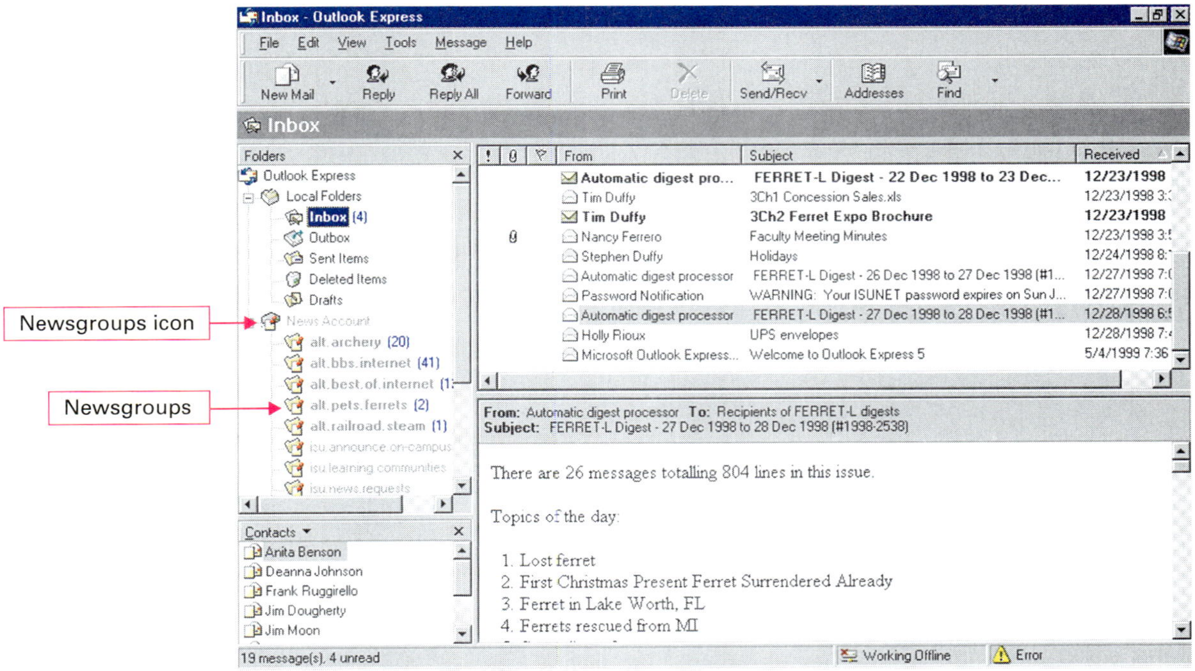

FIGURE 1.9 The left-hand box of Outlook Express contains the Newsgroups icon (in this case labeled news.ilstu.edu), which allows you to access newsgroups on your news server (in this case, news.ilstu.edu) to which you have subscribed.

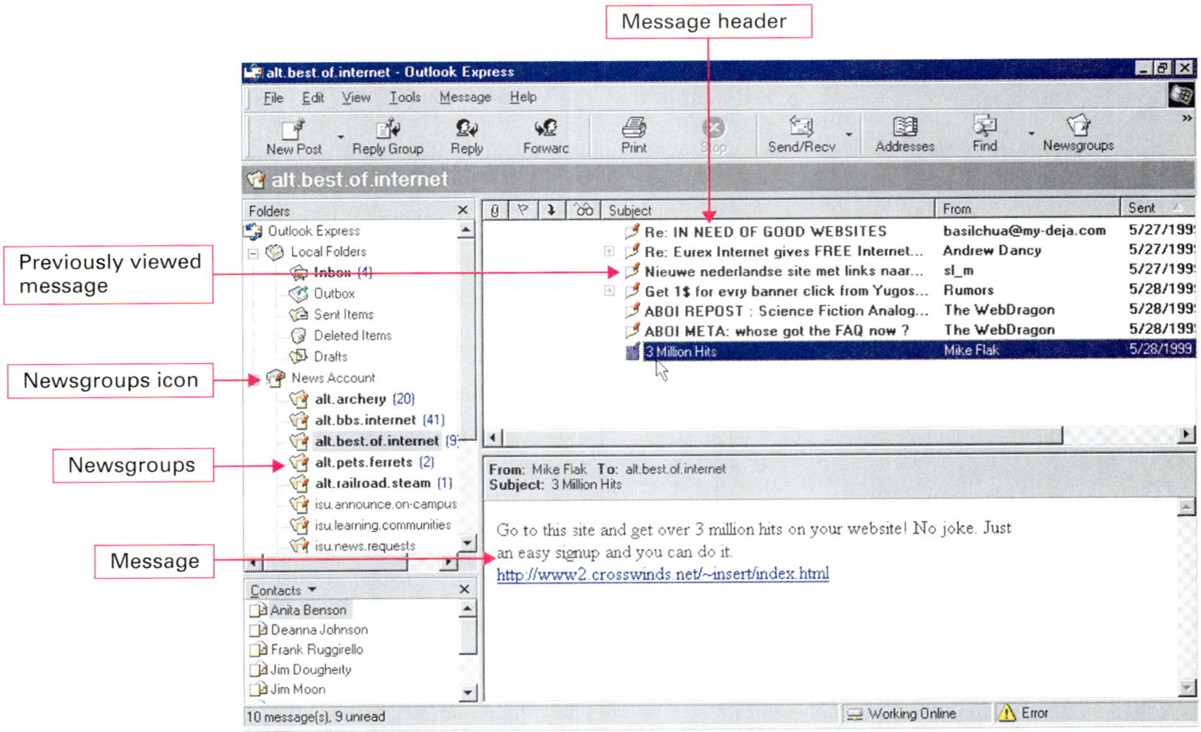

FIGURE 1.10 The subscribed newsgroups are listed in the left-hand box (rec.pets is selected). The postings and content of the postings for the rec.pets newsgroup are shown in the right-hand portion of the Outlook Express window.

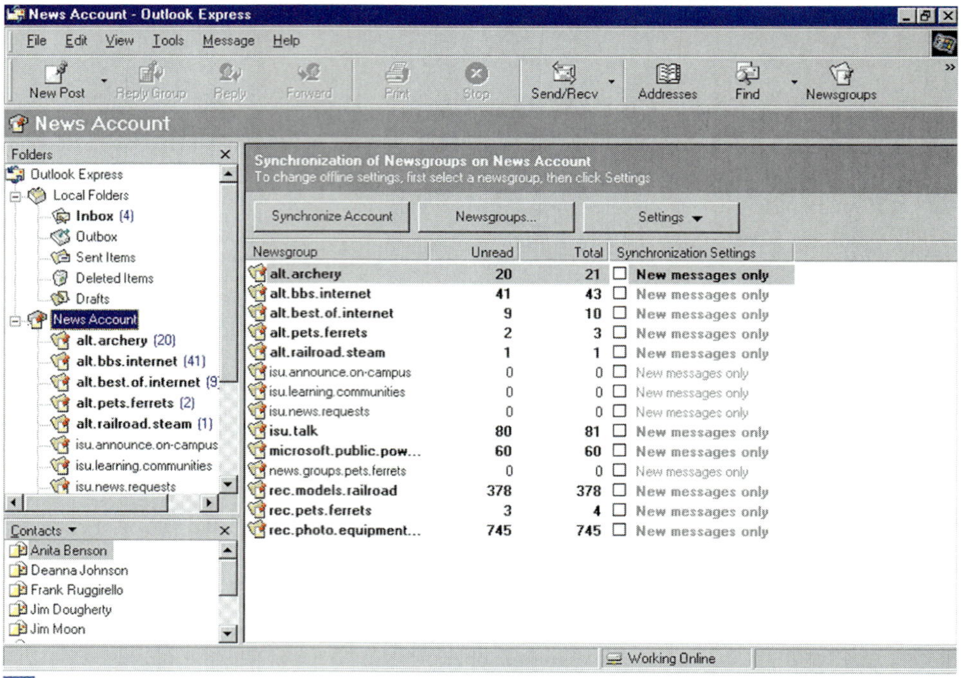

FIGURE 1.11 **The Synchronization of Newsgroups on News Account window allows you to access any messages that have arrived for your newsgroups.**

To see which newsgroups you have access to or have subscribed to, click the button labeled Newsgroups in the Outlook Express toolbar. The Newsgroup Subscriptions dialog box now appears. Click the Subscribed tab to see which Newsgroups can currently be accessed (Figure 1.12). You can use this dialog box to subscribe to new areas of interest or to cancel subscriptions to current groups.

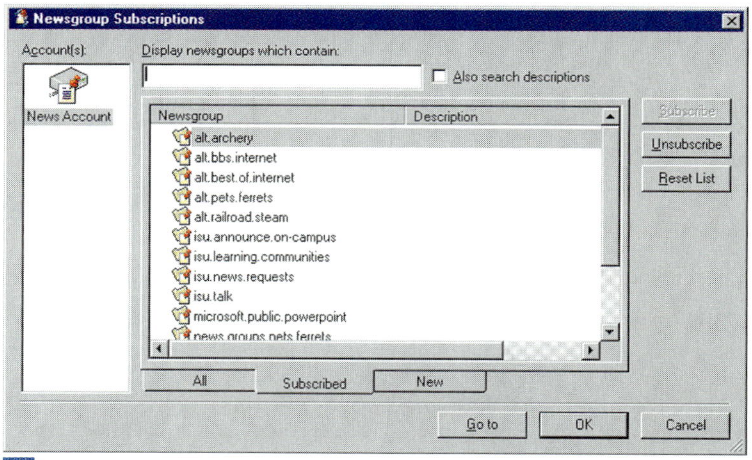

FIGURE 1.12 **The Newsgroup Subscription window allows you to determine which newsgroups you want to access as well as newsgroups to which you have subscribed.**

Here are some basic guidelines for joining a newsgroup:

- Before posting to a newsgroup, look for an **FAQ (frequently asked questions)** file. An FAQ contains guidelines for using the newsgroup as well as elementary information about that particular topic. Review or print the FAQ so that you are aware of the guidelines for that newsgroup. There is even a Web site (http://www.faq.org/) where you can obtain the FAQ files for just about any newsgroup.

- Review articles or postings from the last two or three weeks (whatever is available) to get a feeling for the newsgroup.
- Spend some time lurking. **Lurking** refers to the practice of spending a few days or weeks to see how the flow of the newsgroup progresses and to get an idea of the types of individuals participating in the group.
- Be careful in your first postings. If some of the participants feel that you are not using the proper etiquette for that newsgroup, they may send you E-mail flames.

One other document that is somewhat related to a newsgroup is a **listserv**. A listserv consists of all E-mail messages related to a topic at one time. It is sent out as an E-mail message to anyone who has subscribed. Each subscriber resides in a file called a mail list and is automatically included as a recipient when a copy of the listserv document is sent. This type of document, therefore, requires only E-mail software to read. You subscribe to a listserv by sending an E-mail message indicating that you want to subscribe.

The Ferret Mailing List (FML) is an example of a listserv. Each day Bill Gruber, the listserv moderator, sends out a 20- to 30-page document to ferret aficionados who have subscribed to this service. This listserv contains E-mail messages that have been posted by subscribers. Anyone who wants to respond to a listing sends an E-mail message to the listserv site.

File Transfer Protocol

File transfer protocol (FTP) is a method of using the Internet for copying a file from one computer to another. You can accomplish this process by using Unix commands, by using special FTP software like that shown in Figure 1.13, or by using browser software that supports FTP, such as Netscape or Internet Explorer.

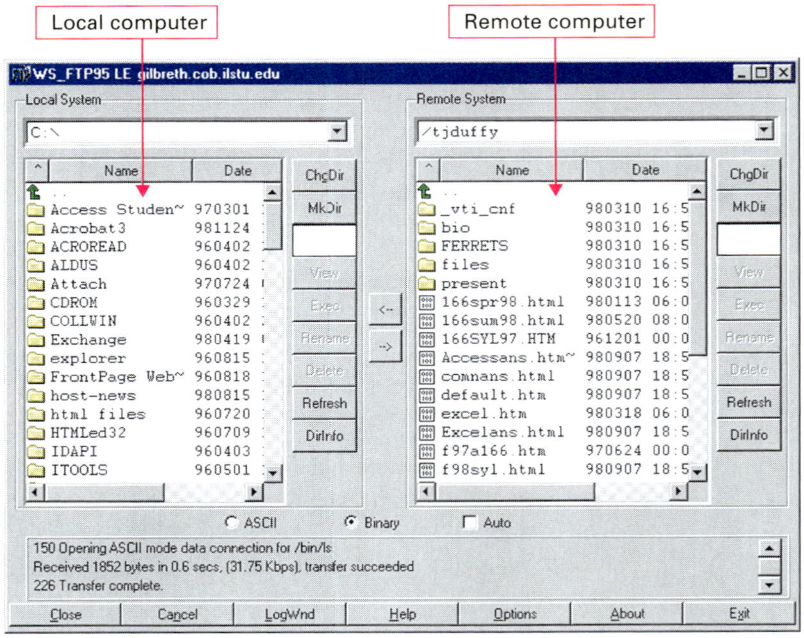

FIGURE 1.13 **You can use this FTP Client software package to copy a file from one computer to another.**

The process of using FTP software is often referred to as anonymous FTP because most people use anonymous as their user name when they are requesting files. Many software firms, for instance, allow you to log in to their computers and download software repairs or updates using this method.

TELNET

Telnet allows you to have remote access to another computer, for example, to access the card catalog of another university or college library. The computer that you are contacting must allow this type of public access. To access the Telnet feature (Figure 1.14), you must get to the Telnet window, which may be accessed via an icon in an Internet menu.

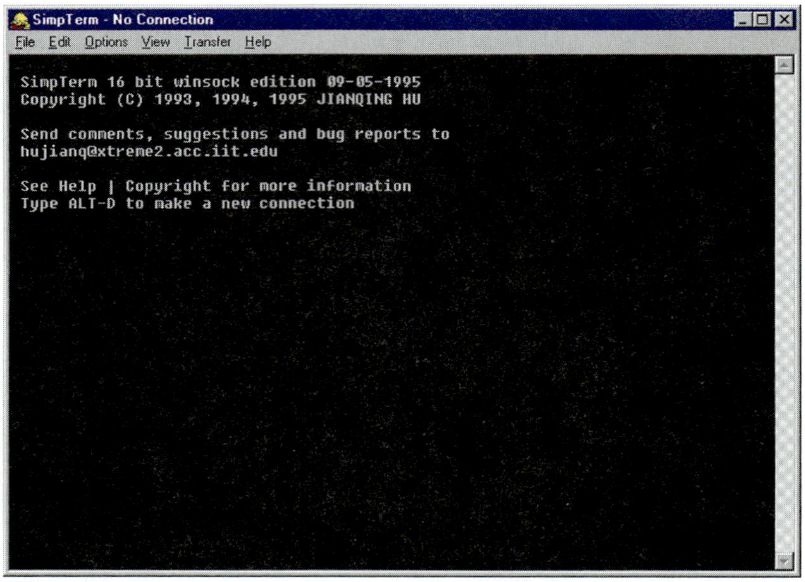

FIGURE 1.14 The Telnet screen that can be used for accessing another computer.

Once you are in the Telnet feature, you may have some difficulty contacting the computer you want to communicate with if the language it uses is different from what you are accustomed to using. You need to know how to invoke the Help feature of the new computer to get a listing of commands.

Telnet allows you to access information from other locations. Unlike FTP, it does not allow you to download files. You can use Telnet to access other libraries, get weather forecasts, or obtain any other information that you do not need to download.

GOPHER AND VERONICA

Gopher is a text-based, menu-driven program that allows you to access, view, and download files. It is the immediate precursor of the Web and is still used today, but has fewer users as more and more Internet sites convert to WWW format. It differs from the Web in that Gopher information is text-based rather than a combination of text, graphics, and sound. You can, however, use Gopher to download files that contain graphic images or sound.

Gopher provides a variety of services. Many people use Gopher to get weather information along with information about skiing conditions at their favorite resorts. Figure 1.15 shows the Gopher site from University of Illinois at Chicago accessed by using Internet Explorer. Notice that there are no graphic images.

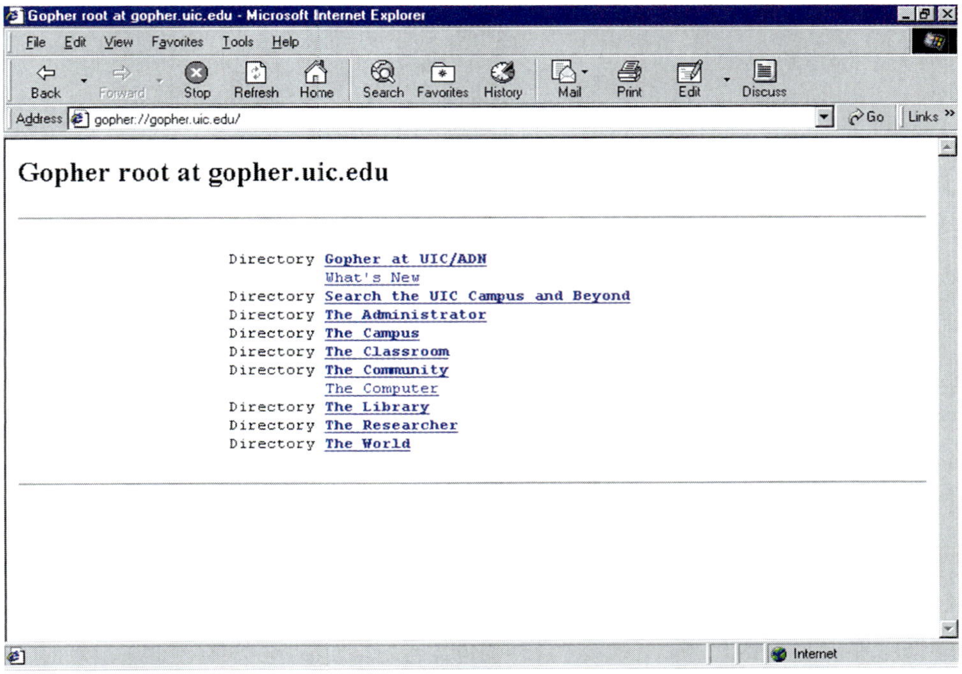

FIGURE 1.15 The text-based Gopher site at University of Illinois at Chicago.

Veronica is a service that allows you to perform searches easily by using multiple Gopher sites on the Internet. Once you have located files containing information that you want, you can use Gopher or FTP software to access and download the file contents.

Internet Relay Chat

Internet Relay Chat (IRC) permits you to communicate "live" with other Internet users. To use this type of Internet service, you first log in to a specific location and then enter an Internet location, called a chat room, that relates to a particular topic.

As you enter messages on the keyboard, they appear on any other computers that are hooked up to that chat room. Any number of people can be connected to your chat room and participate in the conversation.

If you want to participate in chat sessions, you can download a program called Comic Chat from Microsoft. This program represents each individual in the chat room as a comic-book-style character selected by that user (Figure 1.16). In addition to Comic Chat, there are a number of other chat engines. More information can be obtained at the IRC Central Web site (http://www.connected-media.com/IRC/).

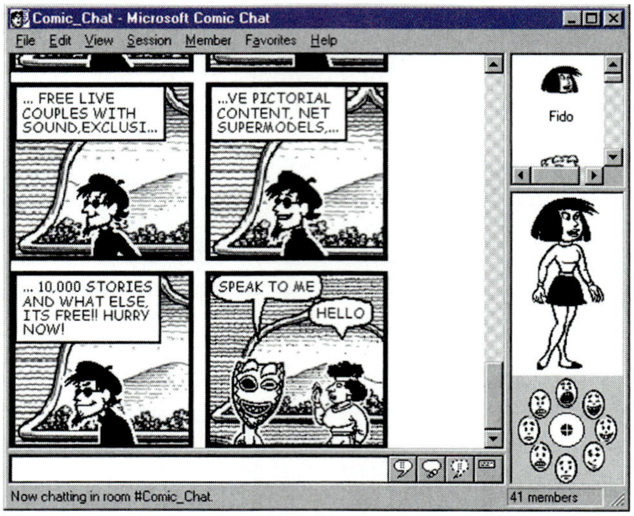

FIGURE 1.16 The Comic Internet Relay Chat screen used to chat with others on the Internet.

World Wide Web

The **World Wide Web (WWW or Web)** was designed in 1989 by a computer scientist, Tim Berners-Lee, while working in Switzerland. Berners-Lee designed the Web to simplify telecommunications technology used for international research collaboration. Since its inception, the Web has grown to tens of thousands of sites. Web site addresses now commonly appear in TV commercials and printed advertisements. Just about any business of any size has a Web site today.

The Web makes extensive use of hypertext and hypermedia. In **hypertext**, you use pointers or links to jump to other parts of the document or to other files or Web sites. You can search through multiple layers of data and find your way forward or backward through those layers. **Hypermedia** makes it possible to add other items to text documents, including images, animation, and sound.

To build a Web address or Web page, you use an easy-to-understand hypertext language called **HTML (Hypertext Markup Language)**. This language controls the appearance of the Web page. You also need a Web server—a system that transfers files using a version of FTP software called **HTTP (Hypertext Transfer Protocol)**. The server can send files through the World Wide Web to any other Web server on the Internet.

Each location, as well as each file at a location, has a specific address, or **URL (uniform resource locator)**. The URL gives the exact location of a resource, be it a server or a file, and is composed of the protocol, the host name, and the resource—the path of the indicated item including any directories/subdirectories along with the filename (Figure 1.17).

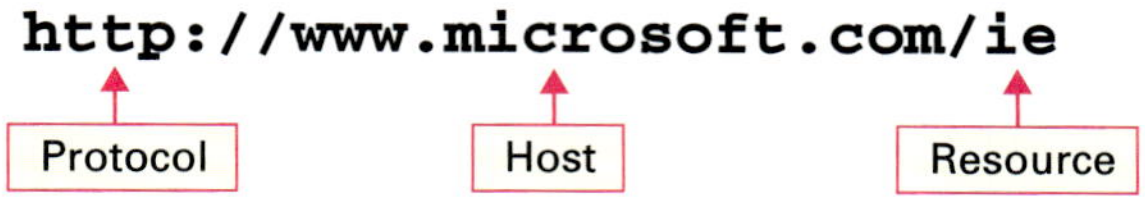

FIGURE 1.17 The parts of a World Wide Web URL.

Before you can access information on the Web, you need a browser, which is software that retrieves HTML documents using the HTTP protocol and formats them so you can see them on-screen. It is the browser that interprets the hyperlinks and loads the documents from the designated locations specified by the links. You can, therefore, see a document on-screen that consists of files from several different locations around the world.

A number of browsers are currently on the market, including Netscape Navigator (usually referred to as Netscape), Microsoft Internet Explorer (the browser bundled with Office 2000), and Mosaic. When you open a browser, you may see items displayed in a different color and underlined. That item is a link to data or other pages or locations, and when you click such an item, the browser loads the file from wherever it resides. The loaded file may reside on the same computer or on a computer on the other side of the world.

Timely Tip

Browsers indicate that the mouse pointer is positioned at a hyperlink by turning it into a hand with the index finger pointing upward. Click to activate the link.

Browser software will be discussed in more detail in the next section of this session.

Using Internet Explorer

Microsoft, at the time this book was written, bundled Internet Explorer with its Windows operating system as well as with Office 2000. Internet Explorer is the Web browser covered in this text.

Starting Internet Explorer

Depending on how your computer is configured, you can start Internet Explorer in one of the following ways:

- Double-click the Internet Explorer shortcut icon if it is present on the desktop of your screen.
- Click the Windows Start button, then Programs, then Internet Explorer.
- If you cannot find Internet Explorer using the above methods, consult with your instructor on how to access it.

The Internet Explorer Window

Once Internet Explorer is up and running, you will see the Internet Explorer window shown in Figure 1.18. When Explorer first starts operating, it tries to find the default start page. The **start** or **home page** is the first Web page that Explorer loads each time you start the program. Your start page will probably be one designed for your particular school.

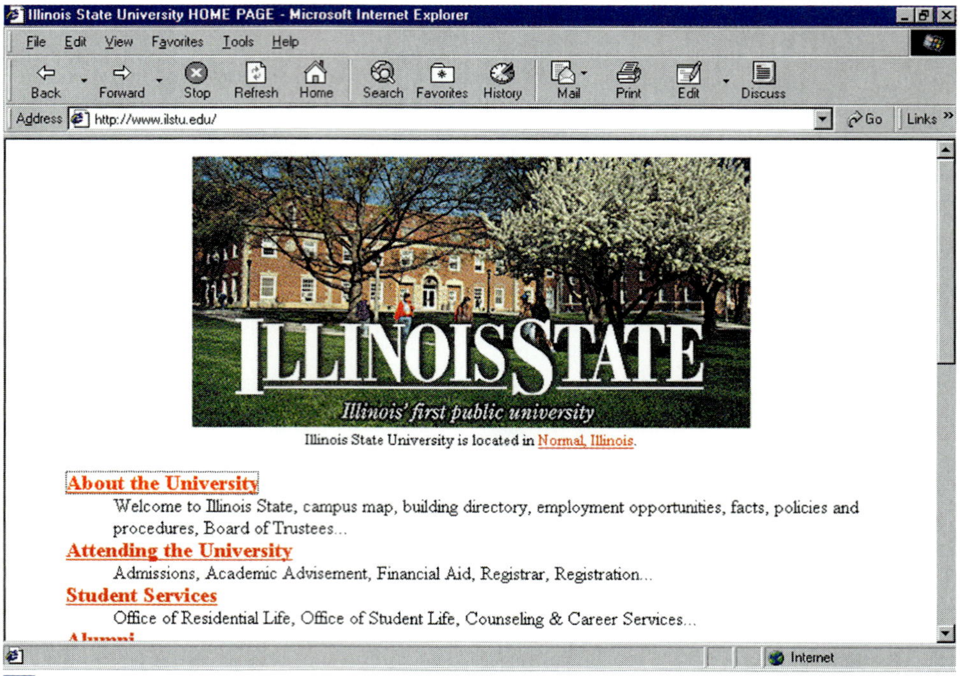

FIGURE 1.18 **The Internet Explorer application window displaying a default start page.**

Title Bar

At the top of the Explorer window is the title bar (Figure 1.19), where the name of the program and the title of the open Web page are displayed. The Minimize, Maximize, and Close buttons also appear here.

FIGURE 1.19 **The Internet Explorer title bar contains the application name, URL title, along with the Minimize, Maximize, and Close buttons.**

Menu Bar

The menu bar (Figure 1.20) contains menu options that activate pull-down menus. These menus and options follow standard Windows conventions.

FIGURE 1.20 **The Internet Explorer menu bar.**

Toolbar

With the **toolbar** (Figure 1.21), located beneath the menu bar, you can enter commands by clicking buttons, which is quicker than going through various menus. Table 1.5 shows each toolbar button, its name, and a description of its purpose.

FIGURE 1.21 **The Explorer standard toolbar and its component buttons.**

TIMELY TIP

If necessary, choose Toolbar from the View menu of Internet Explorer.

TABLE 1.5 The Explorer Toolbar

BUTTON	NAME	FUNCTION
	Back	Displays the previous Web page. If you click the down-arrow portion of the button, you get a listing of Web sites/pages that you have been to previously.
	Forward	Displays the next Web page in a series of previously displayed pages. Clicking the down-arrow portion of the button displays all of these sites/pages.
	Stop	Stops the page-loading process.
	Refresh	Tells Internet Explorer to reload the current page. This button is used to reload the page when the information at a Web site changes constantly. This ensures that you have the latest version of the Web page.
	Home	Displays your system's start page.
	Search	Creates a search bar to the left of the screen and loads information about the current default search engine specified by Microsoft. Allows you to enter characters to be used in a search process or select a topic displayed by scrolling down the frame (Figure 1.22). Clicking the Search button again turns off the search bar.
	Favorites	Displays Web pages that you have marked as favorites in a bar much like the Search option (Figure 1.23). These Favorite sites can also be seen in a pull-down menu (Figure 1.24). Any of these sites can be accessed by clicking the desired Web site.
	History	Displays a bar that lists sites that you have recently visited (Figure 1.25).
	Mail	Displays a pull-down menu that allows access to Outlook Express. Other options allow you to send a link or a Web page to someone via E-mail. You can also use Outlook to view any subscribed newsgroups.
	Print	Sends the current Web page to the Print Manager and prints the document.
	Edit	Allows you to invoke NotePad, Microsoft Word, or FrontPage Editor so that you can make changes to the Web page (only if you have access rights).
	Discuss	Allows you to embed comments in a Web document that is shared among a group of users in a project team. These comments can then be examined and viewed by other users in the group. You must have access rights to use this feature.

Internet Search bar

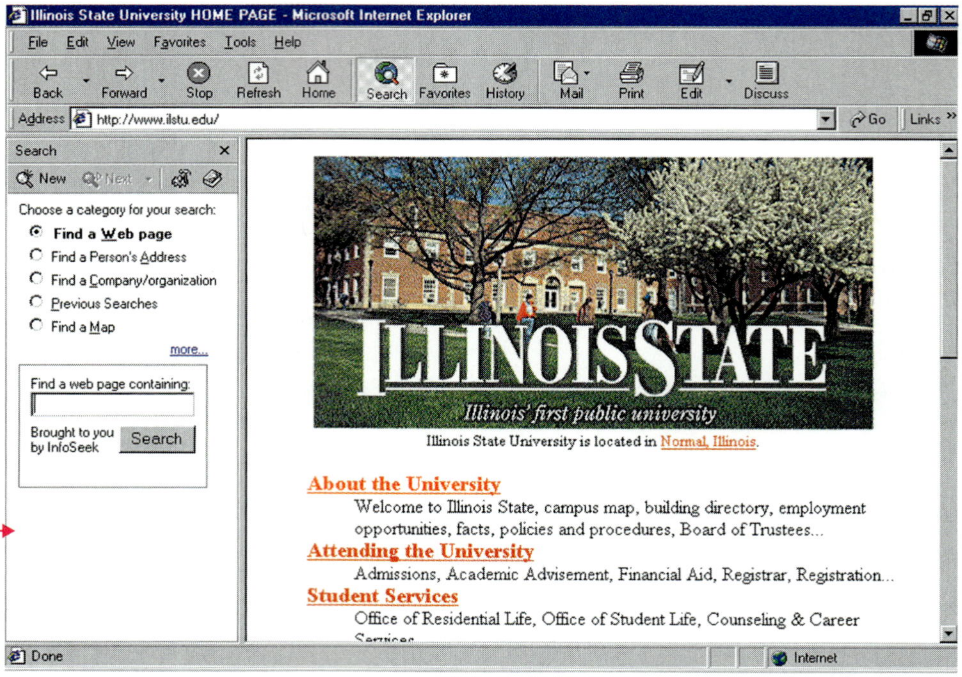

FIGURE 1.22 **The Explorer Search bar using the Infoseek search engine supported by Microsoft for conducting Web searches.**

Clicking a "favorite" loads that Web page

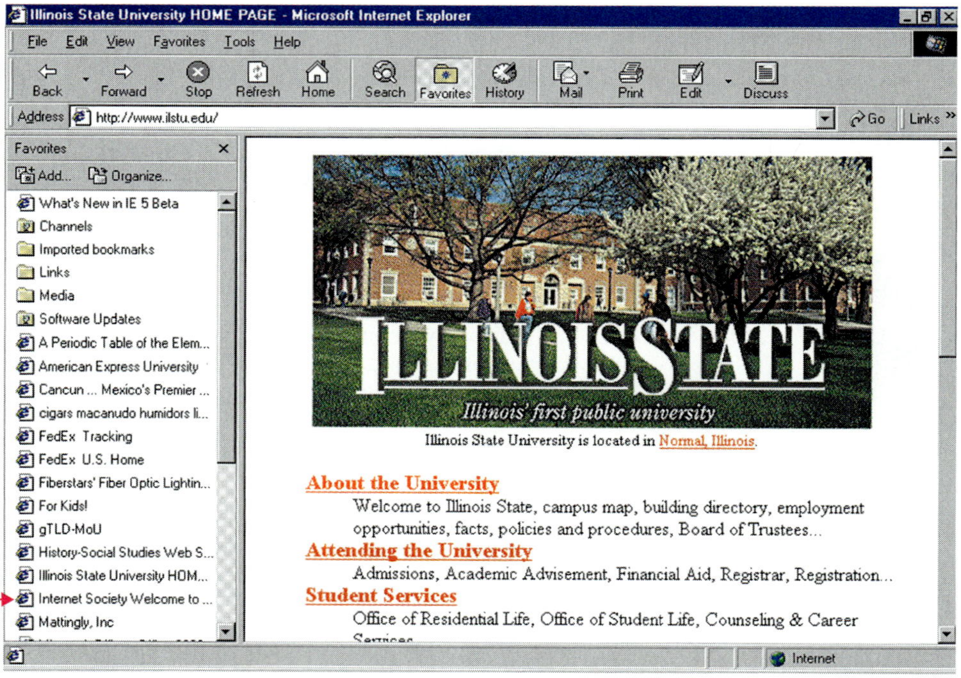

FIGURE 1.23 **The Favorites bar with sites that have been marked as favorites.**

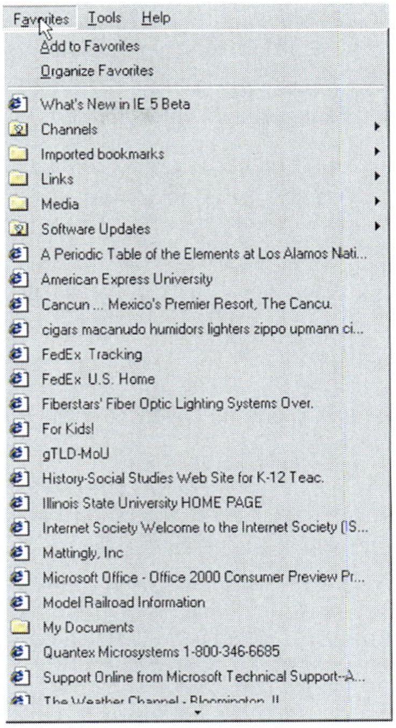

FIGURE 1.24 The pull-down menu with sites that have been marked as favorites.

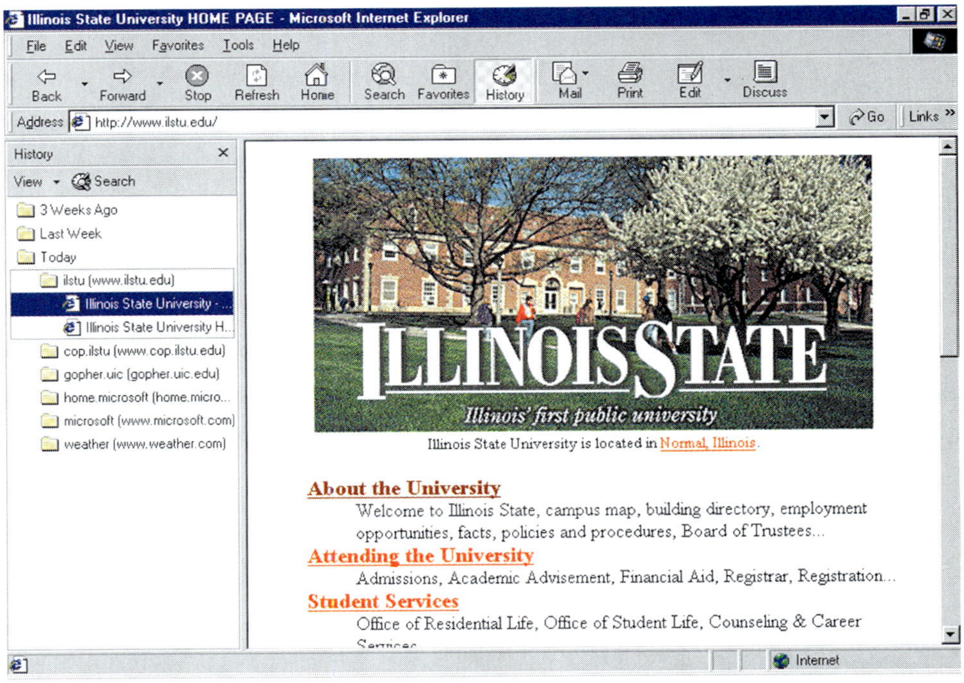

FIGURE 1.25 The Explorer bar displaying history information. When information will not fully display in the frame, you can see the complete name and link by positioning the mouse to that area in the frame.

Address Text Box

The Address text box (Figure 1.26) shows the URL of the current Web page. As you move from page to page, the entry in this box changes to reflect the new location. To go to a different location, click the current address, enter the new Web address, and then press Enter.

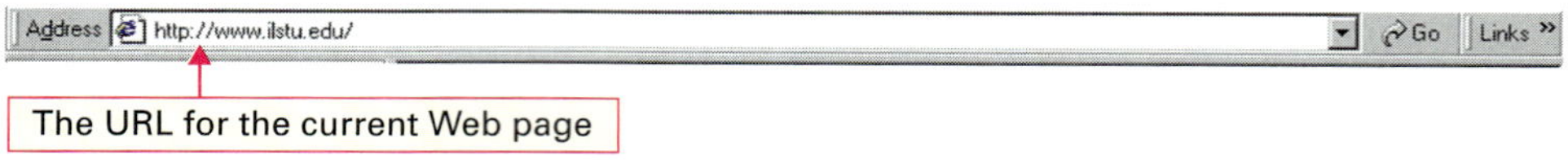

FIGURE 1.26 The Address text box contains the URL for the current Web page.

Clicking the down arrow button at the right end of the Address text box displays the sites you have recently visited. Clicking the Go button has the same effect as pressing the enter key after you have entered the Web address. Double-clicking the Links button changes the address bar to a series of Quick Links supported by Microsoft (Figure 1.27). Clicking the Best of the Web entry displays a Web page like that depicted in Figure 1.28, showing Web locations that Microsoft deems to be the most interesting.

To make the Address text box reappear, you double-click the Address button.

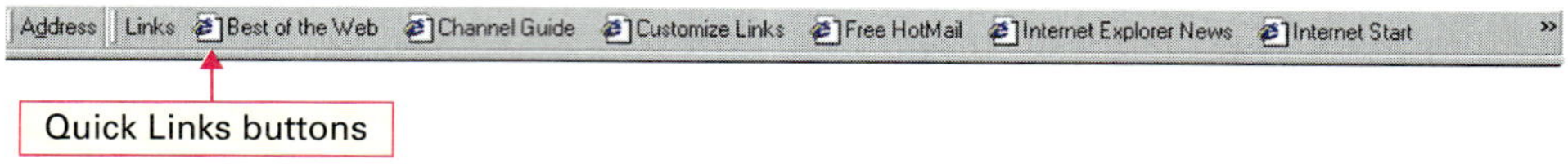

FIGURE 1.27 The Address bar changed to a series of links supported by Microsoft

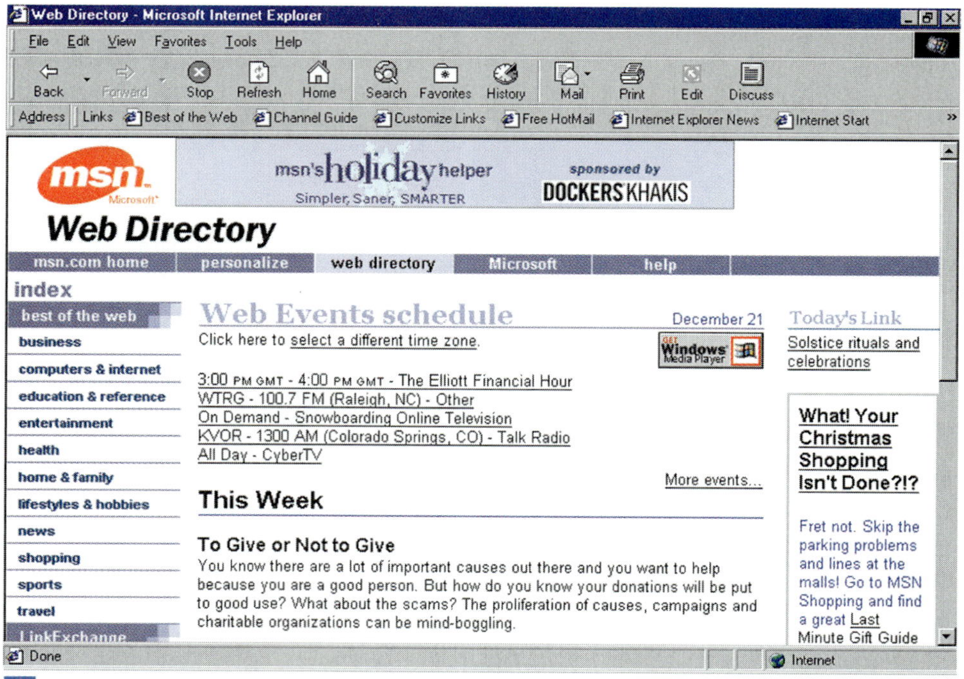

FIGURE 1.28 The Web page displayed by clicking the Best of the Web entry of the Address bar.

FIGURE 1.29 The Internet Explorer logo serves as the status indicator.

Status Indicator

The **status indicator** is the Internet Explorer logo (Figure 1.29). Activity on the logo indicates that Internet Explorer is in the process of loading information for a Web page. When the activity stops, the page has finished loading.

Document Window

The **document window** displays the current Web page. The start or home page is the first page to appear in the document window when you start Internet Explorer.

Scroll Bar

The horizontal and vertical scroll bars allow you to move quickly from left to right or up and down to view parts of a Web document. These bars have arrows on each end that you can click to move within the document; alternatively, you can drag the scroll box to jump quickly to the end or beginning of the document. They also show the relative position in the page.

Status Bar

The bar at the bottom of the Internet Explorer window is called the status bar. The left side of the status bar displays explanations about menu entries or displays the text address of a link. It also displays the information about what Explorer is trying to accomplish, such as the progress it has made downloading a large file.

Navigating Around a Web Page

Internet Explorer gives you several ways to move vertically within a Web page. You can use the ten-key pad or the mouse in conjunction with the scroll bar. Table 1.6 summarizes these methods.

TABLE 1.6 Internet Explorer Navigation Commands

Keys	Movement
↑, ↓	Up or down the Web page about 3/4 of an inch at a time
PGUP, PGDN	Up or down one window at a time or click above or below the scroll box
CTRL + HOME	To the beginning of the Web page
CTRL + END	To the bottom of the Web page

Hands-On Exercise: Using Internet Explorer

The following hands-on exercise introduces you to some rudimentary Internet Explorer features.

1. **Start Internet Explorer.** If necessary, click the Maximize button to enlarge the Internet Explorer window. You should see your home page. The home page for Illinois State University is shown in Figure 1.30. Make certain that the toolbar buttons are displayed.

Timely Tip

If your version of Internet Explorer doesn't show the toolbar, choose Toolbar from the View menu and select from the available toolbar choices.

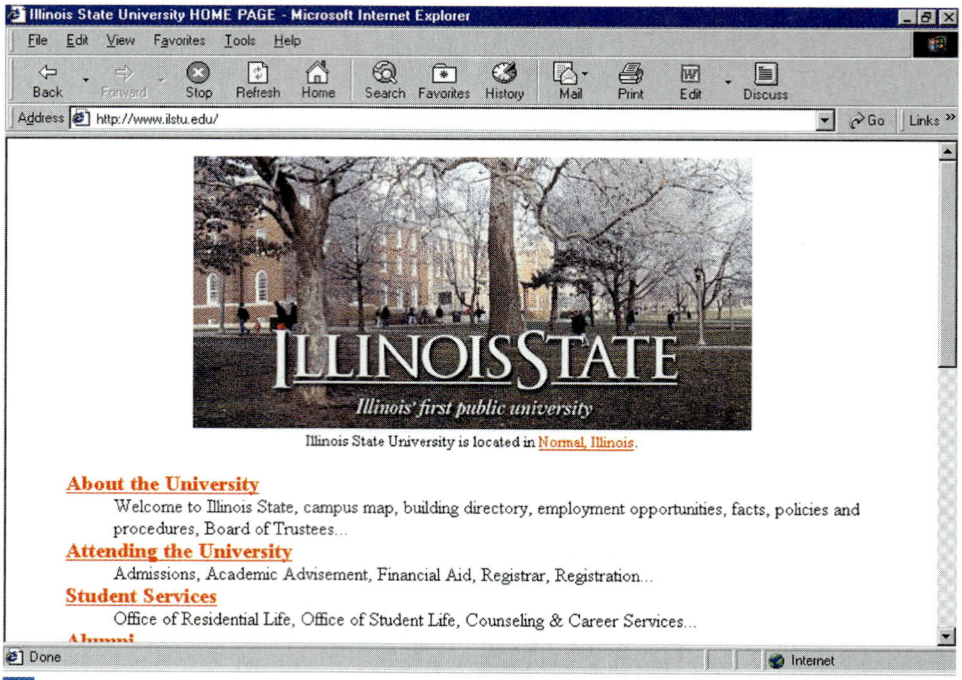

FIGURE 1.30 **The Illinois State University home page.**

2. Visit the Best of the Web site.

Double-click to invoke the Quick Links bar.

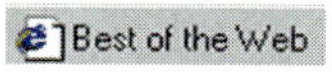

Click this Quick Link to invoke the Best of the Web page at Internet Explorer's corporate site (Figure 1.31).

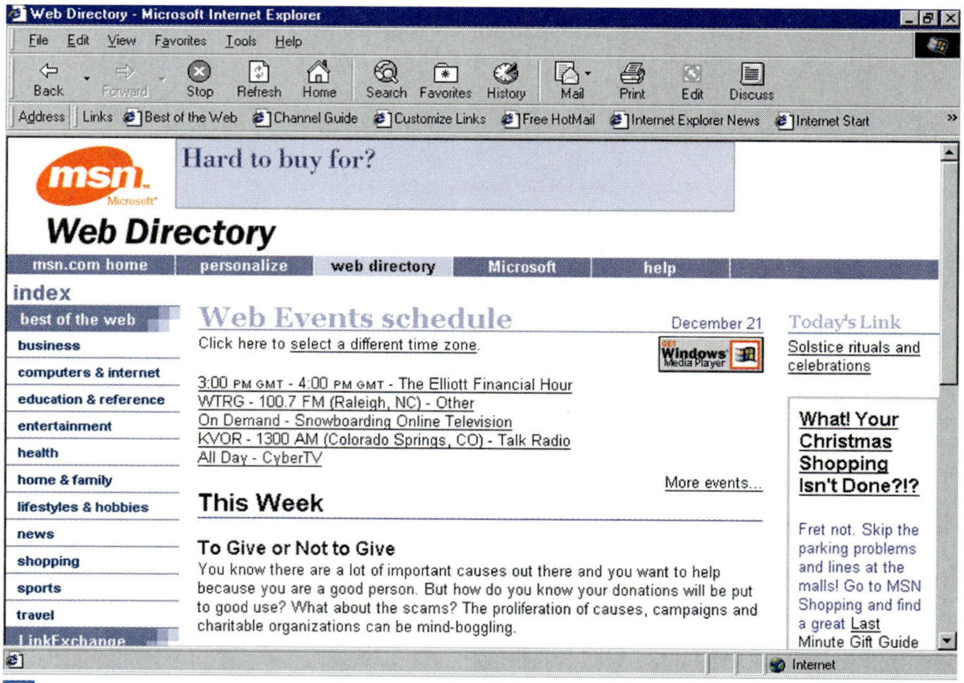

FIGURE 1.31 **The Best of the Web page contains new Web grouping classifications along the left-hand side of the window.**

Click If necessary, click the vertical scroll bar below the scroll box to move down until the Travel link appears.

Travel Click Travel. Examine that Web site, and click on any hyperlinks (where the mouse pointer turns into a hand with the index finger extended) that you want to see. Be sure to use the scroll bar or keyboard commands for examining each Web page.

Click to return to your home page.

Double-click to redisplay the large Address box.

3. Search the Web for Web pages related to a specific topic.

Click this toolbar button to invoke the Explorer Search bar shown in Figure 1.32. In this figure, the Infoseek search service is activated. Make certain that the Find a Web page entry is selected as in Figure 1.32.

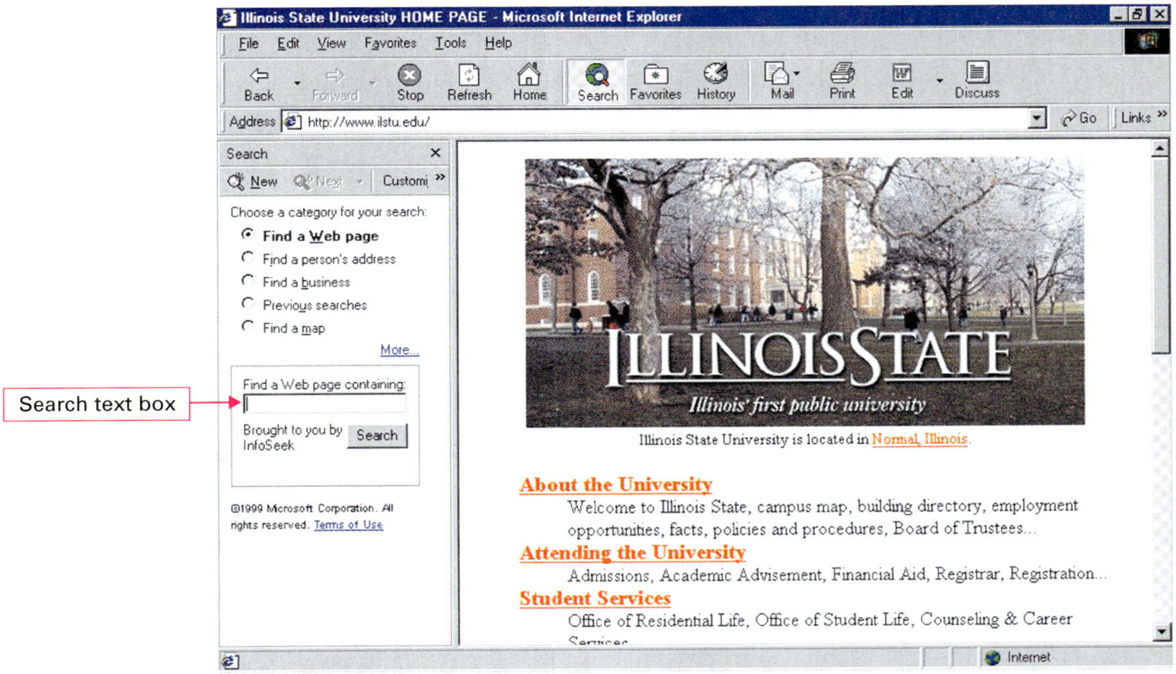

FIGURE 1.32 The Explorer Search bar with the default Infoseek search service activated.

Click Click in the Search text box to enter the topic you want to search the Web for.

Type: `ferrets` Enter the topic to be used for the search. We will be searching for any information related to ferrets.

Click to initiate the search process.

Click Click below the scroll box of the scroll bar to move down one window. You should see the first selections that match the search criteria. Figure 1.33 shows the first matches that appeared at the time this book was written.

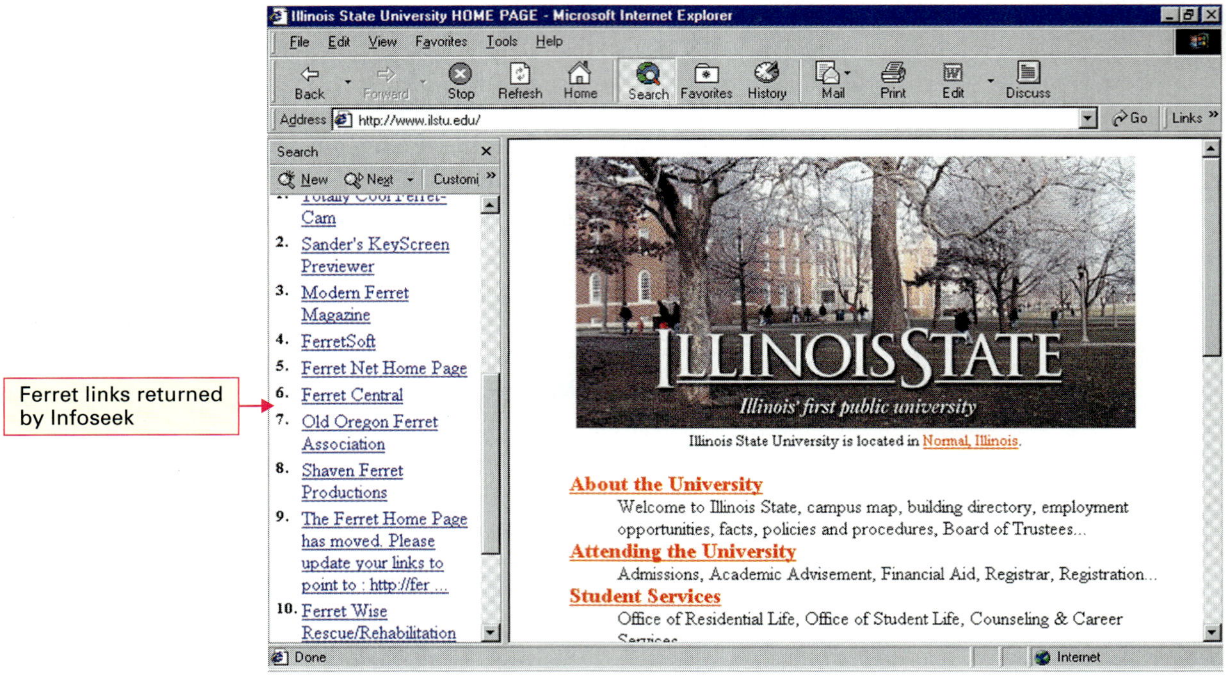

FIGURE 1.33 The screen returned with links about ferrets in the Explorer search bar.

Click Click the first underlined entry, and examine that Web page.

Click Scroll down the Explorer Search bar until you see the Next 10 link. This will take you to more Web sites on your topic (Figure 1.34).

Next 10 Click to get the next ten Web sites. Explore any of these Web sites.

Click to turn off the Explorer Search bar.

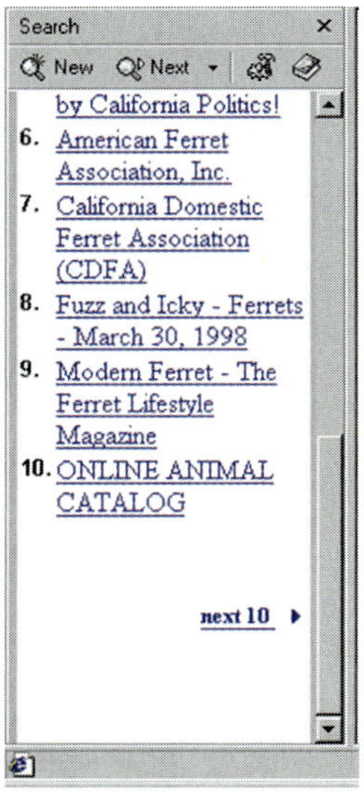

FIGURE 1.34 The prompt for the next ten documents in the Explorer Search bar allows you to get more Web pages related to your topic.

Timely Tip

The World Wide Web is a very volatile, fast-changing place. Many sites appear and disappear each day. Existing sites also may undergo extensive reconstruction. A site that you visited last week may not even look the same today, so Web site figures in this book may not correspond to what you see on your computer screen.

4. Use a search engine Web site to locate the Walt Disney World Web site.

A number of search engines like Yahoo, HotBot, Webcrawler, and Excite enable users to find information on the World Wide Web from their search sites.

Click the Address text box. All of the text in the box should be selected.

Type: `HotBot` Type the name of the search engine site that you wish to use, and press (ENTER). The .com topdomain, which has been automatically added by Internet Explorer, suddenly appears and a screen like Figure 1.35 should now appear on your monitor.

Click Click in the Search: The Web text box in preparation for entering the search criteria.

Type: `Walt Disney World Resort` Enter the information to be located.

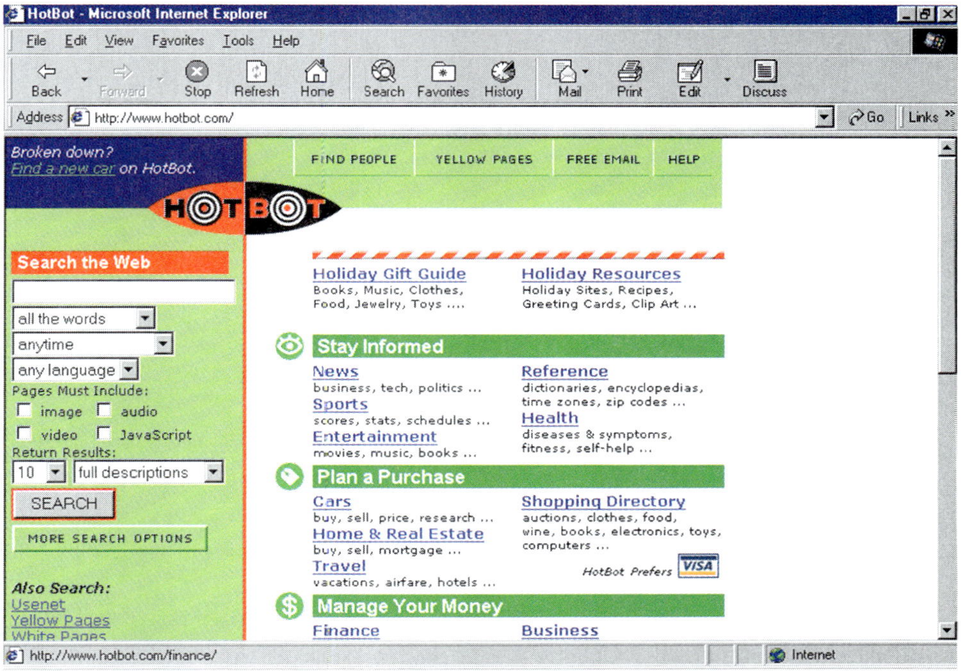

FIGURE 1.35 **The HotBot Search Center screen used to find sites with desired information on the Web. Your display might look different.**

Click the Search button on the HotBot page to find links to Walt Disney World Resort. A screen like that shown in Figure 1.36 should now appear with the first ten links that HotBot found that meet your search criteria. Notice that a number of advertisements appear.

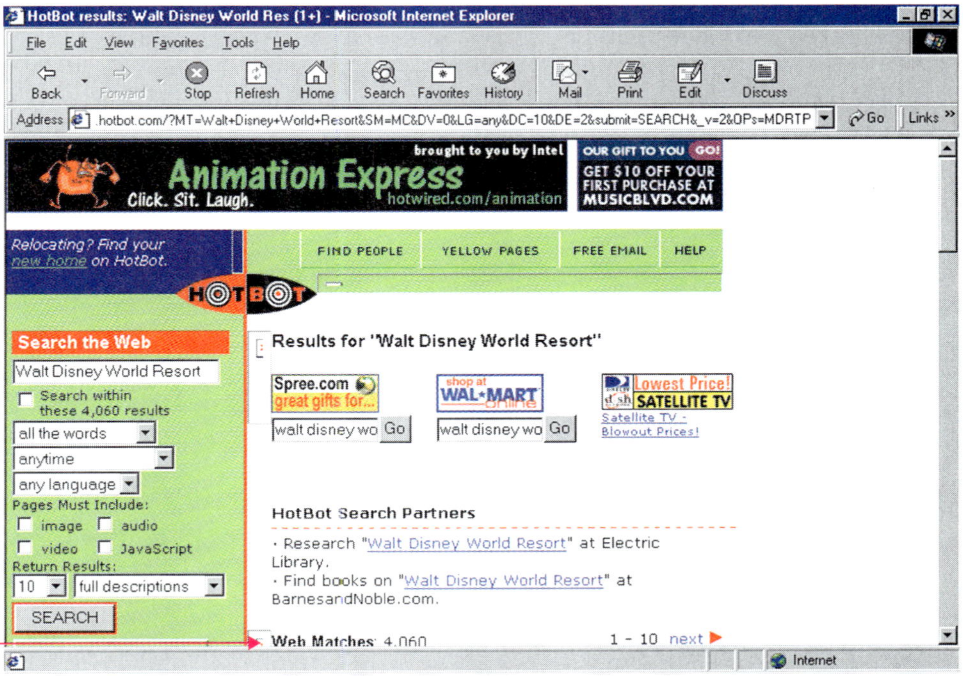

Search results summary

FIGURE 1.36 **The first string of the results window returned by HotBot. Notice that each word of the search string has the number of Web documents listed as well as the number of documents for the combined string.**

Click Click under the scroll box to scroll down a screen You should now see a screen containing a number of links to sites found by HotBot dealing with, in this case, Walt Disney World Resort (Figure 1.37).

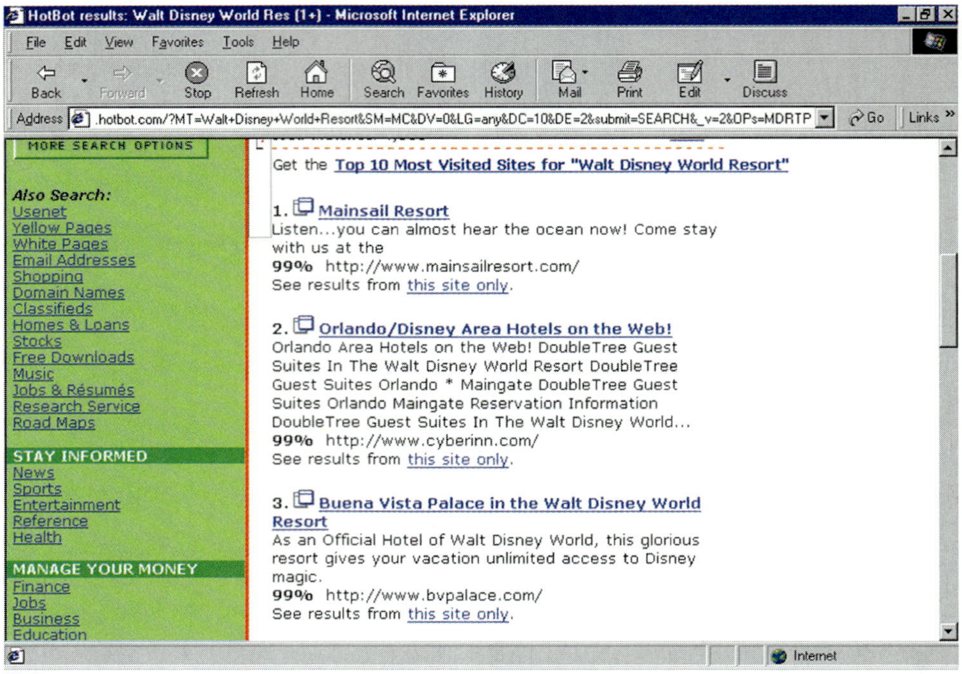

FIGURE 1.37 The HotBot screen with the first links to sites dealing with Walt Disney World Resort.

Click Click a link and explore that location. Use the Back button to return to the links page. Explore any other links that you find interesting.

Timely Tip

Internet Explorer has a feature called AutoComplete that remembers previous entries you've made for Web addresses. When you type information in the address field, AutoComplete may suggest possible matches. These matches can include folder and program names typed in the address bar as well as Web sites. When you are entering information in the address bar and you've typed a similar entry before, AutoComplete lists possible matches as you type. If a suggestion in the list matches what you want to enter into field, click the suggestion. If not, continue typing.

5. Open the Web site for Prentice Hall (the publisher of this textbook).

Click the Address text box to select all of the text.

Type: `http://www.prenhall.com/`

(ENTER) Enter this address to get the Prentice Hall home page (Figure 1.38).

FIGURE 1.38 **The Prentice Hall home page.**

6. Print the home page.

Click this button to print the Prentice Hall Web page.

7. Explore the various links of the Prentice Hall Web page.

8. Return to your home page.

Click to activate your home page.

TIMELY TIP

Instead of entering the complete address of a Web site, use the mouse in a drag operation to "highlight" the portion of the address that changes following www. portion of the address. You can then enter the portion that is different.

9. Explore the Weather Channel's Web page.

Click the Address text box.

Type: `http://www.weather.com` Enter this URL.

(ENTER) Invoke the Weather Channel's Web page (Figure 1.39).

FIGURE 1.39 The Weather Channel's Web page.

U.S. City Forecasts Starting with this link, enter the name of your city to obtain the current weather information for your location (Figure 1.40). You may have to scroll down the Web page to reach this link.

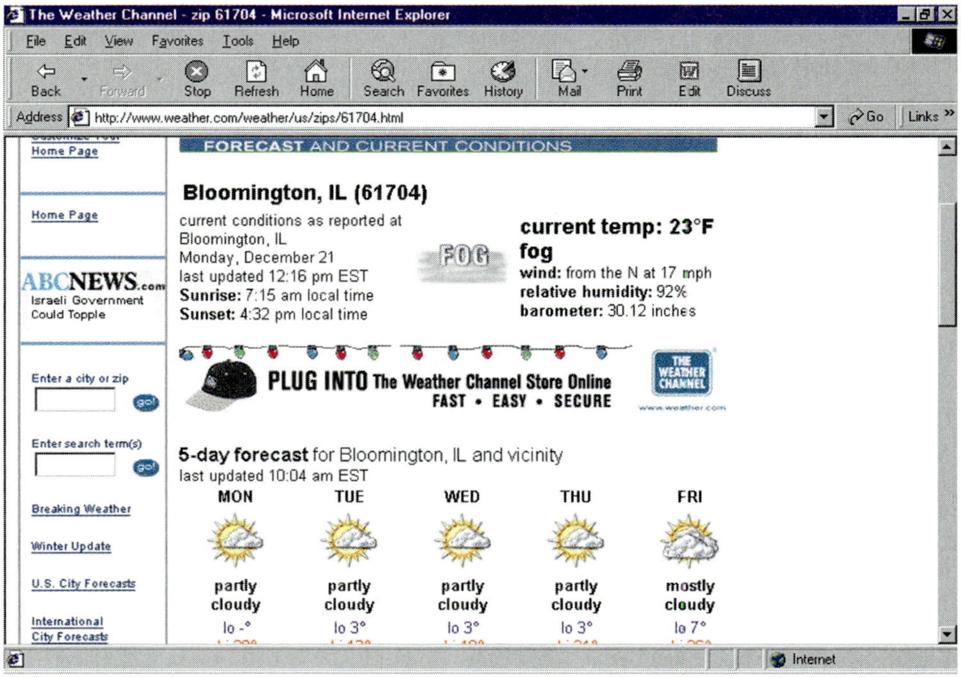

FIGURE 1.40 The Current Weather Conditions for Bloomington, IL.

10. Print your city's weather information.

Click to print the weather forecast Web page for your city.

11. Go back to the Weather Channel's home page.

Click until you get to the Weather Channel's home page, shown in Figure 1.39.

12. Record the Weather Channel Home Page as a favorite so that you can easily return to this site.

Favorites Click to invoke the Favorites submenu.

Add to Favorites . . . Click to add this site to your current favorites. The Add to Favorites dialog box appears (Figure 1.41), suggesting a title for this Web site.

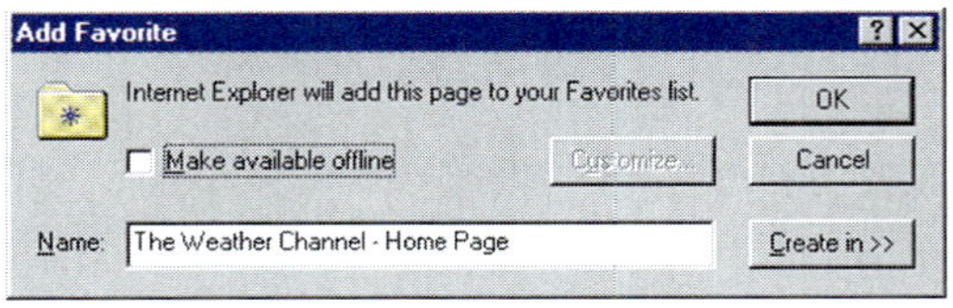

FIGURE 1.41 The Add to Favorites dialog box.

Click to add.

13. Examine a Web page in the Favorites entries.

Click to invoke the Favorites bar. You will probably see several entries.

Click Click one of the sites contained in the Favorites entries. You will now see that site's information. Go ahead and explore the new site.

14. Return to your home page, and if necessary, exit Internet Explorer.

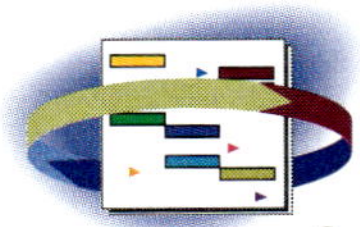

Reinforcing the Exercise

1. Enter a URL in the Address text box to open another Web site.
2. Standard links appear in blue underlined text and, when clicked take you to other information or another page on the Web.
3. Links can also be embedded in a graphic or text.
4. Links are visually indicated by the mouse pointer changing to a hand with the index finger extended.
5. The Back and Forward buttons move you through Web pages that you have already accessed.
6. Favorite entries allow you to move quickly to a Web page that you have "bookmarked" previously.

More Internet Explorer Topics

Once you have begun to use Internet Explorer and visit Web sites, you will probably want to: save information to a file for later retrieval; access, save, and print graphic images; E-mail a Web page; have access to more than one Web page at a time; or review some of the Web locations that you have visited.

Saving Web Pages

Many times you will access information on the Web that you want to use for further reference. One way to accomplish this is to print the desired information. What happens, however, if you want to save that information to disk for later access? In such a situation, you can save the contents of the entire Web page by choosing Save As from the File menu. Internet Explorer then displays the Save As dialog box shown in Figure 1.42. To save the Web page to a file on drive A, you activate that drive by clicking the Save In box, click drive A, and then click the Save button. If no filename appears, enter a name before you click the Save button.

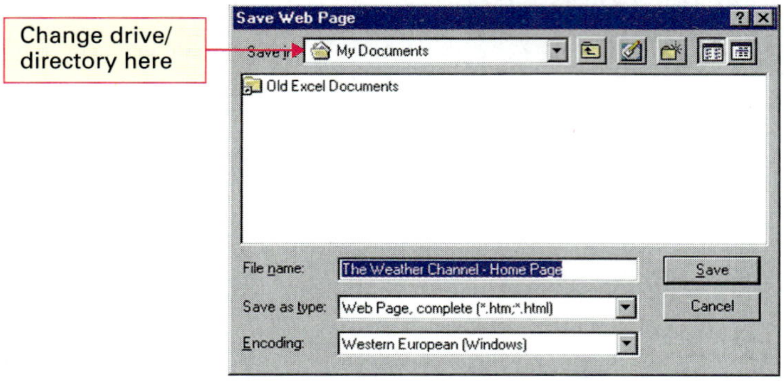

FIGURE 1.42 The Save As dialog box used for saving the text of a Web page to disk.

It should be noted that only the text of the Web page is saved to the disk as one file and the graphic images are saved to a correspondingly named folder. Any graphic images that appeared on the Web page are stored in that folder. To access the text in the saved file, choose Open from the File menu and the Open dialog box appears (Figure 1.43). Click the Browse button to select the appropriate drive and/or directory and the file (Figure 1.44), and then click the Open button to see the file's contents. Your copy of the Web page should appear just like the original. One difference will be that the address of the Web page includes the disk location to which it was previously saved. It should be noted that when a Web document with images is saved, a folder with the same file name is created to hold all of the image files for the original Web page on disk.

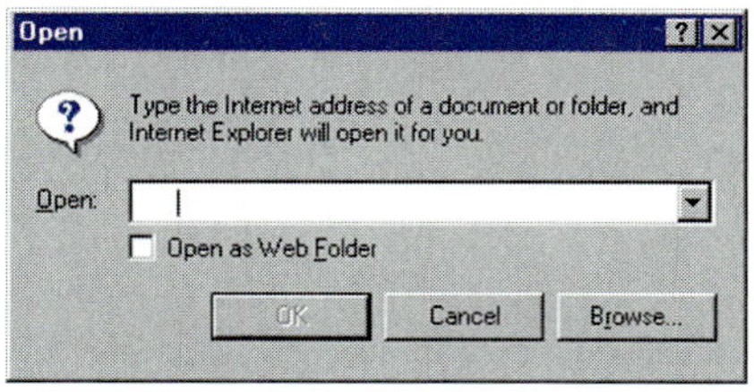

FIGURE 1.43 The Open dialog box used for accessing a Web page saved to disk.

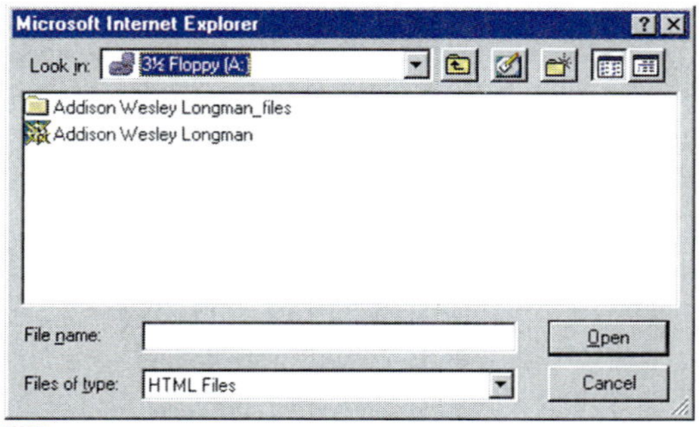

FIGURE 1.44 The Open dialog box containing the HTML file and folder with the stored image files for a saved Web page.

To see the underlying HTML statements used to display a Web page, choose Source from the View menu. The document is loaded into the Windows Notepad editor (Figure 1.45). You see a number of codes surrounded by greater than (>) and less than (<) symbols. These are the HTML codes that control the browser's display of the document.

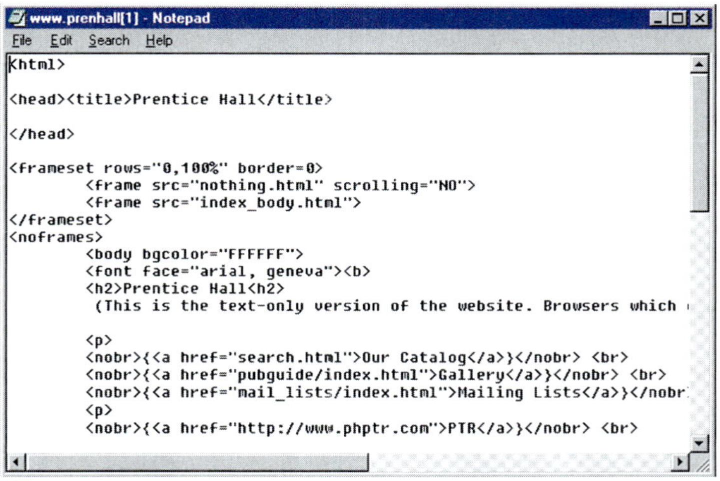

FIGURE 1.45 Windows Notepad editor displays the HTML statements for the previously displayed Prentice Hall Web page.

FIGURE 1.46 The Internet Explorer context menu.

Graphics

A Web page can be designed so that it automatically loads graphic images, or the Web page can be designed so the user can click icons or links to control when and if graphic images appear.

When an image is automatically loaded, you can save that image to disk as a file. To do this you simply right-click the desired image. A context menu appears (Figure 1.46).

Click Save Picture As to open the Save As dialog box. Once you have made any changes related to the filename or destination, click the Save button to save the image.

Send a Web Page via E-Mail

Internet Explorer provides the ability to send a Web page using your E-mail software. If you find a Web page that you want to send to someone else or send to yourself for later

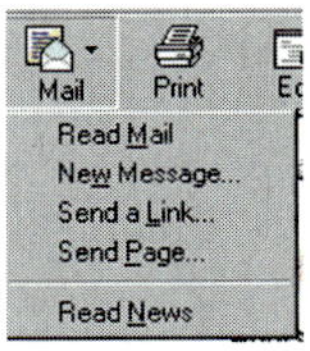

FIGURE 1.47 **The Mail menu options.**

perusal, click the Mail button on the Explorer toolbar (the first time you do this you may have to provide some E-mail server information to the browser). Clicking this button displays a menu of options from which you can select the Send Page option (Figure 1.47). The Send Page option activates default E-mail program. The E-mail program that has been configured for your system is now loaded (this might be different than Outlook Express) and a new message screen is displayed. Once your To address is entered, your E-mail message with the Web page appearing as the message content is ready to send (Figure 1.48). Click the Send button to send the message to the desired recipient. If you send the message to yourself, you can later access the Web page using your E-mail software.

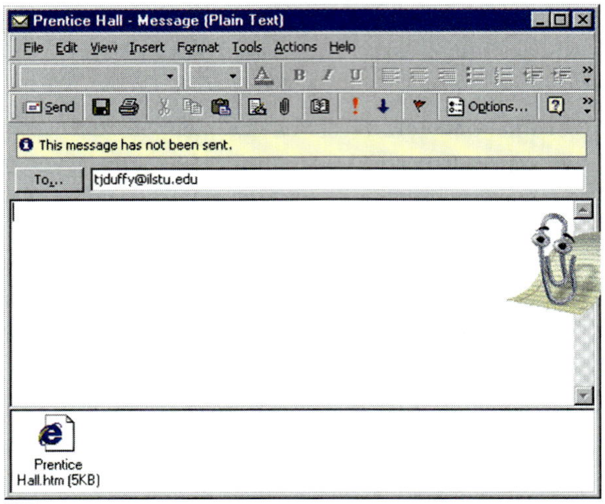

FIGURE 1.48 **The completed E-mail message with the Web page ready to send.**

Other Uses of the Context Menu

Using the context menu, you can access several Web pages at once. First choose Open Link in New Window from the context menu to open each Web page you want to access, then switch between these Web pages by simultaneously pressing an ALT + TAB, instead of using the Back and Forward buttons.

Timely Tip

For each new window you open, a new button appears on the taskbar at the bottom of the screen. Click the desired window's button to activate that window instead of pressing ALT + TAB.

History

You may be interested in the sites that you have visited during an Internet Explorer session. This information is available in the Explorer History bar (Figure 1.49), which you open by clicking the History button of the toolbar.

Click on any site to open its Web page.

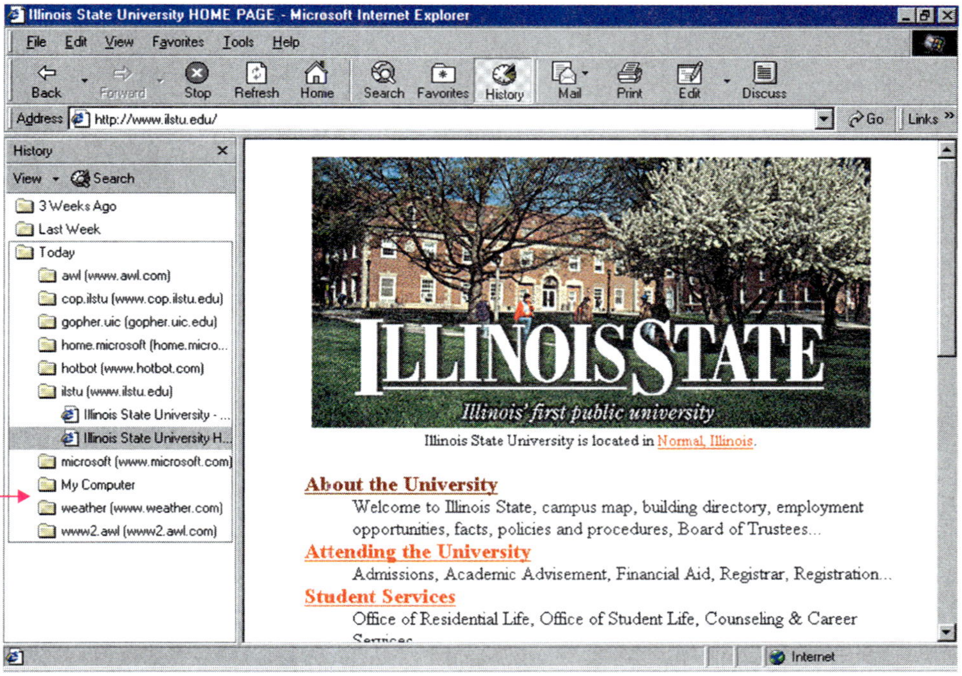

FIGURE 1.49 The History bar lists sites that you have visited recently.

Hands-On Exercise: Saving Pages and Files

The following exercise deals with a Web page that was created to accompany this textbook.

1. Access the Web page.

Click to activate the address box.

Type: **`http://www.prenhall.com/duffy`** Enter the URL for the Web page for this textbook.

(ENTER) Press to access the page shown in Figure 1.50.

2. Examine the logo.

Right-click Position the mouse pointer to the blue sky image and right-click for instructions. The context menu shown in Figure 1.46 appears. Save the image.

3. Click the edition of the book that you are using to get to that subpage.

Examine other parts of that Web page and any links that interest you.

If you have examined any links, use the Back button to return to the original Web page.

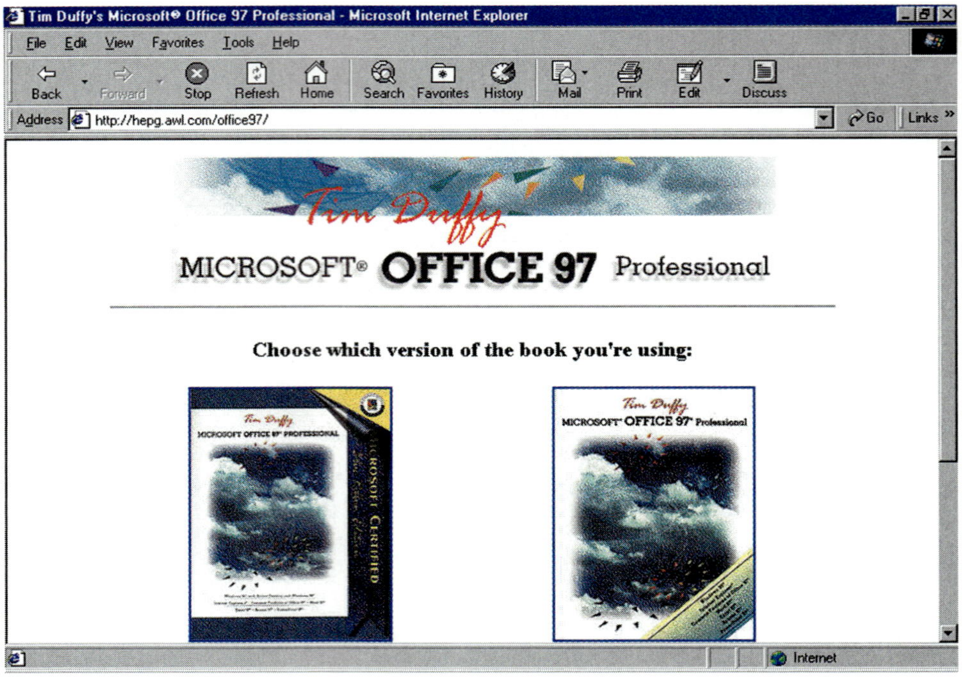

FIGURE 1.50. The Web site built specifically to accompany this textbook.

4. Examine a graphic reference.

Scroll Scroll down until the ferret appears on the screen (Figure 1.51).

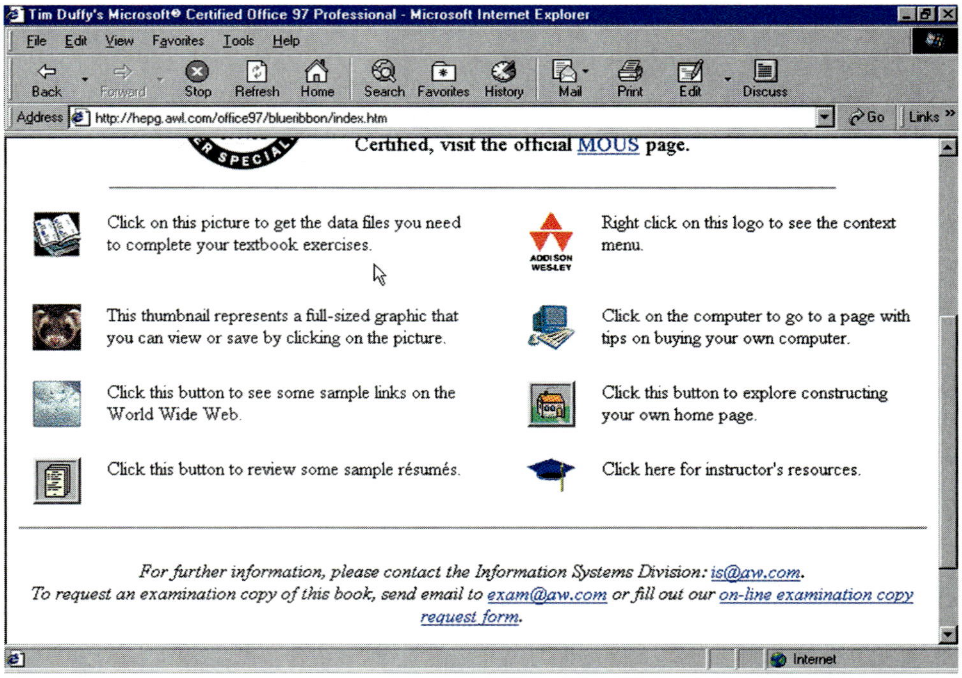

FIGURE 1.51 The ferret graphic icon indicates that the ferret graphic can be accessed by clicking this link.

5. Load the graphic.

Click Click the ferret link. The graphic is now loaded into Internet Explorer. It should look like the ferret graphic shown in Figure 1.52.

FIGURE 1.52 **The ferret graphic shown in Internet Explorer.**

6. Save the graphic image to a file on your disk.

Right-click Invoke the context menu.

Save Picture As . . . Click this option on the context menu to invoke the Save As dialog box.

Save in: Click the Save in selection box.

3½ Floppy (A:) Click to indicate that the file is to be saved to disk. Enter a file name.

Save Click to save the file to disk. Click the Back button to return to the opening page.

FIGURE 1.53 **The graphic used to link to the page dealing with tips on buying your own computer.**

7. Get to the Purchasing a Home Computer Web page via the graphic link shown in Figure 1.53. Save the opening page to a file on disk.

File Click this command from the menu bar to invoke the File menu.

Save As . . . Click to open the Save As dialog box.

Save in: Click the Save in selection box.

3½ Floppy (A:) Click to indicate that the file is to be saved to disk. Enter a file name.

Save Click to save the file to disk. Click the Back button to return to the opening page.

FIGURE 1.54 **The graphic used to link to the Sample Links document of the start page.**

8. Access another Web page without losing the information in this page. Use the graphic icon shown in Figure 1.54 to open the Sample Links document (Figure 1.55) of the start page and go to the Categories table.

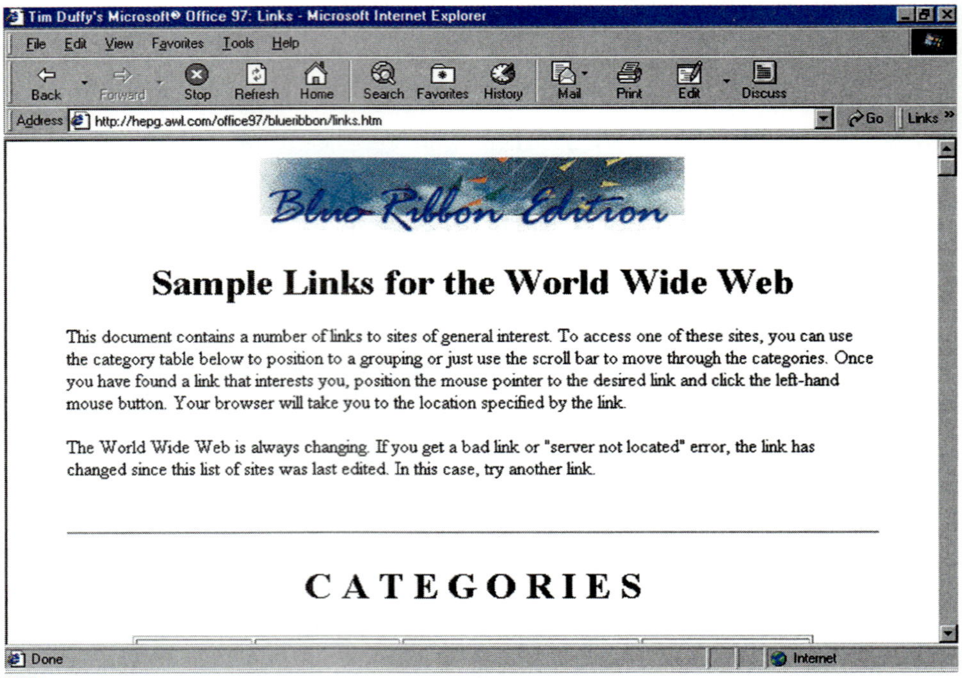

FIGURE 1.55 **Sample Links for the World Wide Web, the document used to access a number of sites on the Web.**

Scroll Scroll down the Sample Links document until you have the Categories Table depicted in Figure 1.56 displayed.

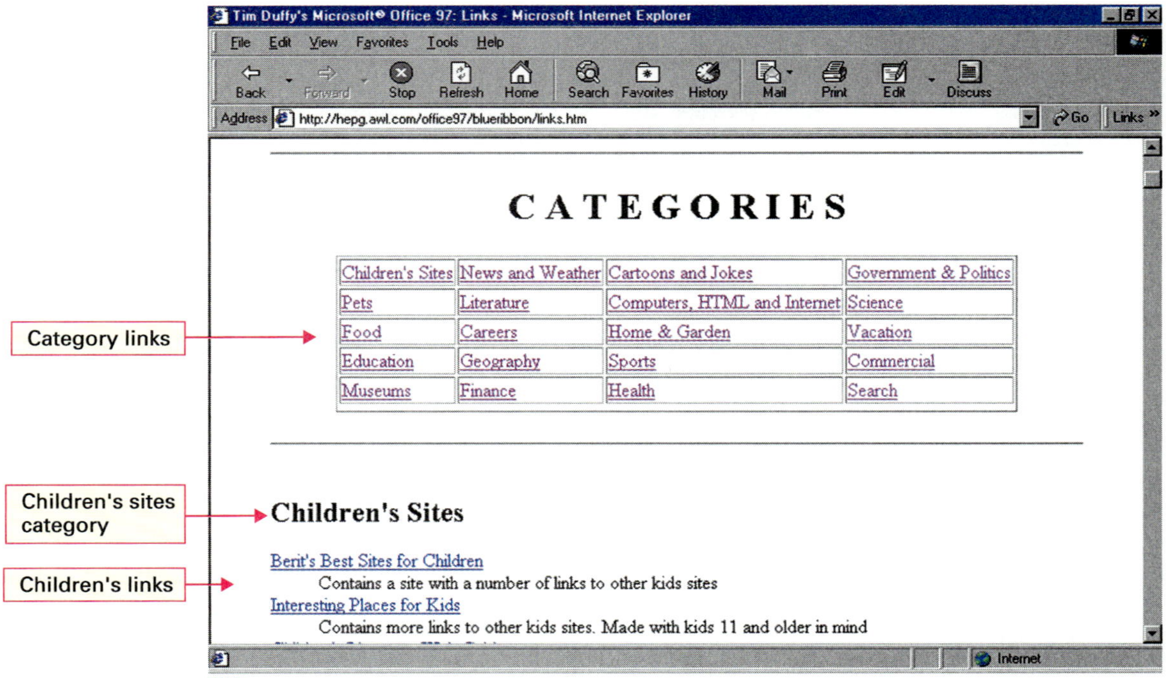

FIGURE 1.56 **The Categories table shows the various groupings of Web links that you can visit.**

Cartoons and Jokes Select this category.

Dilbert Zone Right-click this graphic link to open the context menu.

Open in New Window Click to open a different window and place the Dilbert Web site there.

9. Access still another Web page without losing the information in this page.

Dilbert Store Right-click this link to open the context menu.

Open Link in New Window Click to open a different window, and place the Dilbert Store Web site there.

10. Verify that you have several Web pages open at one time. Your Windows taskbar should have three different Internet Explorer buttons as shown in Figure 1.57.

FIGURE 1.57 The various sites that are open as Web pages can be seen as buttons on the Windows taskbar.

11. Close each of the just opened Page windows to return to the World Wide Web Sample Links document.

Click to close that Web page. Continue clicking this button until you have returned to the World Wide Web Sample Links document. Explore any more links that interest you in this document.

12. Visit the Walt Disney World link found in the Vacation category. Is this the same page that you visited in the previous exercise using the Search command? Depending on which sites were returned by the search engine, this may be an entirely different Web page. When you have finished examining any interesting links, click the Home button to return to your default start page.

13. Access the file that you saved in step 7. The file should have an .HTM file extension and should show the Microsoft's Internet Explorer icon. Choose Source from the View menu to examine the text file from the Web page that you saved to disk.

Reinforcing the Exercise

1. You can access and activate multiple home pages at once by using the Open in New Window command.
2. You can save the text from a Web page to disk as a text file.
3. You can save graphic images to disk using the context menu.
4. The History window displays a listing of all the sites you have visited.

On Your Own

Experiment with the Outlook Express program to examine any newsgroups that interest you.

- Activate the News feature by clicking the plus sign (+) of your News Account entry in the Outlook Express Window. Maximize the window, if necessary. If newsgroups and postings appear and you want to subscribe to a different newsgroup, click the Newsgroups button. (If you do not see a News entry, you may have to configure your newsgroup using the Tools, Accounts command sequence to activate the Internet Accounts dialog box, select the News tab, and then click the Add button to configure a news reader for your computer.)
- Open the All tab to see a list of all newsgroups available to your news server.
- Double-click any newsgroup you want to subscribe to. You know you are subscribed when an icon (a yellow folder with a sheet of paper attached to it using a push pin) appears to the left of the newsgroup.
- When you have finished subscribing to interesting newsgroups, click the Subscribed tab to see a list of the newsgroups you have subscribed to. Click the OK button to close the Newsgroups window.
- If you want to examine the postings on a topic, click the desired newsgroup.
- Double-click any posting that you want to examine in a separate window.
- Click the desired newsgroup. The unread articles appear with yellow pages in the top box (Figure 1.58). New postings appear as a yellow sheet of paper. Postings that have been read appear as a white sheet. Click any desired article. The text of that article appears in the bottom of the window. Double-click an article to make the message appear in a larger window.

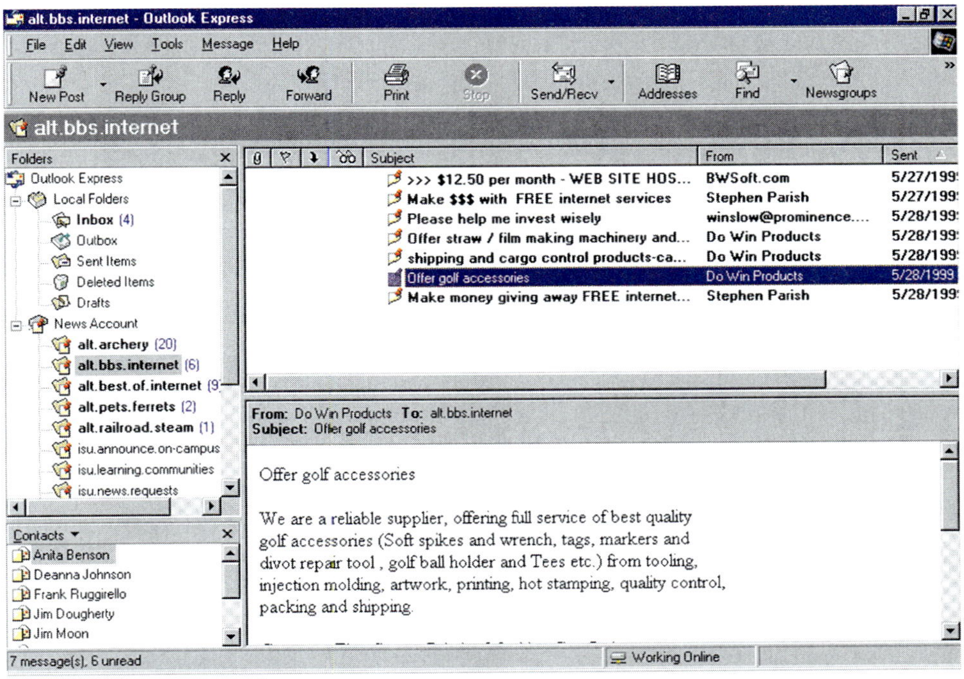

FIGURE 1.58 **The Outlook Express Newsgroups window displays the articles for the selected newsgroup (alt.bbs.internet) in the upper right-hand box.**

Using Outlook Express for E-mail

You can use Outlook Express to send and receive E-mail. Windows controls E-mail using preestablished identification information you enter when you start the Outlook Express program. Outlook Express saves this information so that when you send a message, your identifying information remains for the next person who uses the computer to see. While that person could not receive your mail, they could send out an E-mail message with your account information on it. For this reason, if you are using a school lab computer, you or the computing staff must make some changes so that you have an individual E-mail disk or an area of a networked disk that has been assigned for your specific use. A disk is not necessary if you have your own copy of Outlook Express on your home computer.

You may want to see any Web pages that you have sent yourself during a session with Internet Explorer. Figure 1.59 shows the Web page that was sent from the Prentice Hall Web site as an attachment. Double-click the message to open a separate message window (Figure 1.60).

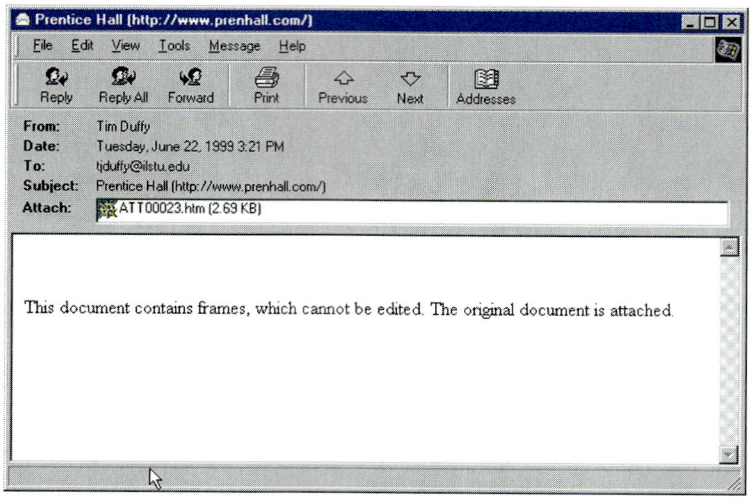

FIGURE 1.59 The E-mailed Web page appearing in the lower right-hand pane.

FIGURE 1.60 The message window with the E-mailed Web page.

You can send an E-mail message by clicking the New Mail button in the Outlook Express window (Figure 1.61). This action invokes the Outlook Express New Message window (Figure 1.62). The toolbar buttons for this window are discussed in Table 1.7.

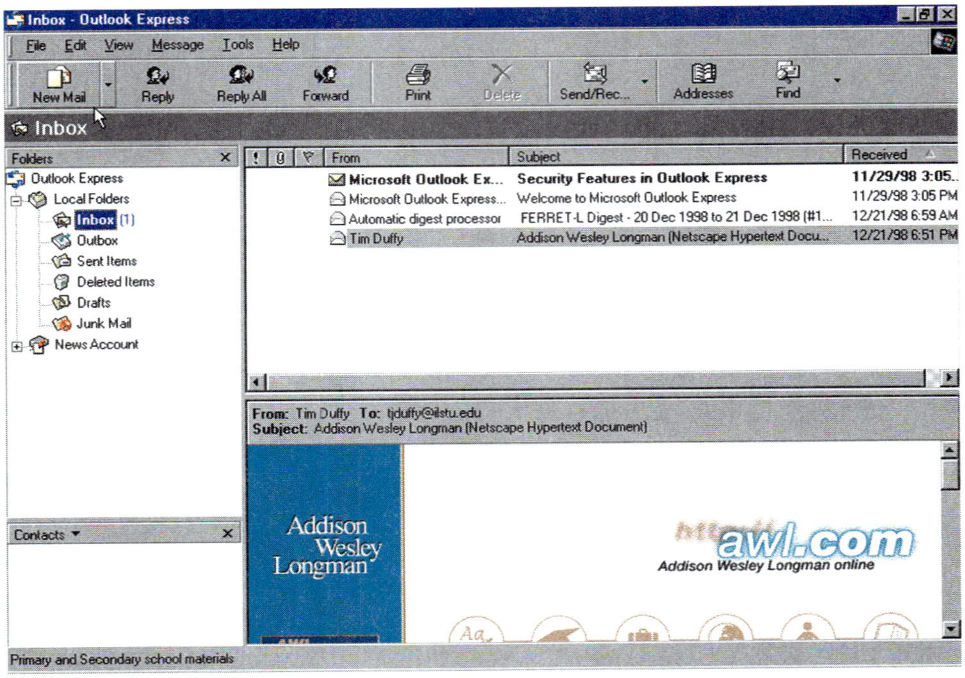

FIGURE 1.61 The Outlook Express window toolbar handles mail-related tasks.

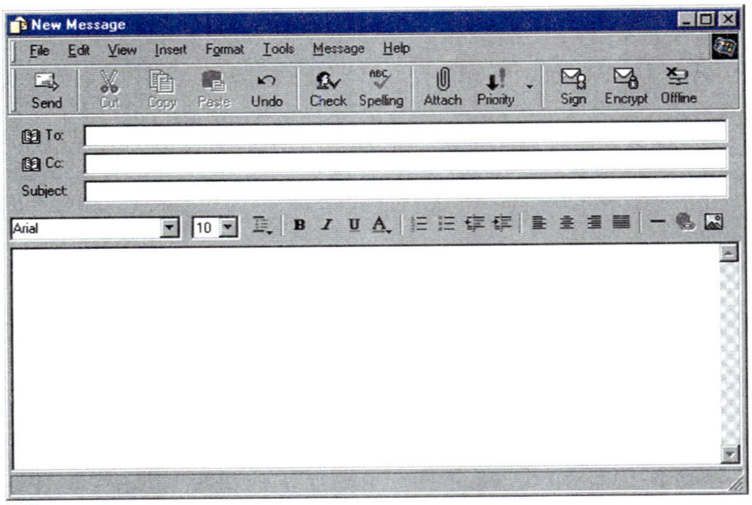

FIGURE 1.62 The New Message window of Outlook Express used for creating an E-mail message.

TABLE 1.7 New Message Button Bar

Button	Button Name	Function
	Send	Sends the message to the E-mail server for routing to the recipient.
	Cut	Removes selected text from the document and copies it to the clipboard.
	Copy	Copies selected information to the clipboard.
	Paste	Places the information from the clipboard at the insertion point.
	Undo	Reverses the last action.
	Check	Checks to see if a name matches an address book entry or is in the correct format for an E-mail name, then it is a valid entry.
	Spelling	Performs a spelling check of your message.
	Attach	Allows you to attach one or more files to an E-mail message. You can, for instance, use this command to send a graphic file to the recipient.
	Priority	Allows you to assign a priority via the pull-down menu.
	Sign	Signs the message with your digital signature (if you have obtained one).
	Encrypt message	Encrypts the message for secure transmission (if you have the encryption feature activated).

Several text boxes appear in the New Message window. The To text box contains the account/address information of the person to receive the message. You must enter this information correctly or the message will be returned to you as part of an invalid address message. The Cc: and Bcc: text boxes contain the account/address information of anyone that you wish to receive a copy of the message. The Subject: text box contains a brief description of the message; you must always enter a subject, according to the dictates of proper E-mail etiquette.

Once you have finished the message, click the Send button. A message now appears in the status line indicating that the message is being sent.

You can also check for mail in your electronic mailbox by clicking the Send and Receive button of the Outlook Express Window.

Including a Signature

A signature is text that you want to have included at the end of any message that you send. When you click the Send button, that text is automatically added to the end of your message. It is not visible to the sender, but is visible to the recipient.

You create the signature by issuing the Tools, Options command and then selecting the Signatures tab of the Options dialog box (Figure 1.63). Click the New button and enter your signature. Indicate whether this signature should be attached to all outgoing messages (Figure 1.64). Click the OK button. The text will now be embedded at the end of every message.

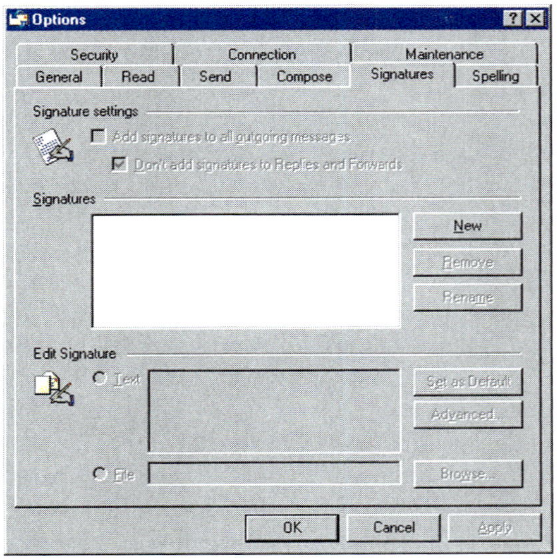

FIGURE 1.63 The Stationery tab of the Options dialog box used to access the Signature feature of Outlook Express.

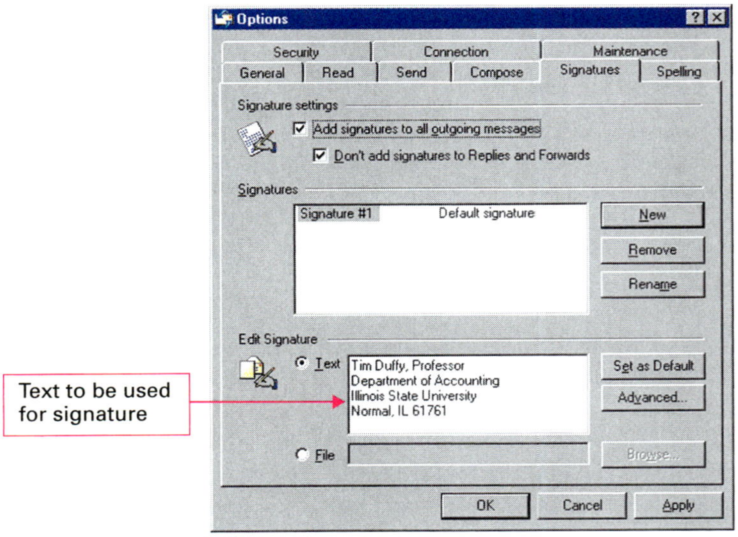

FIGURE 1.64 The Signature dialog box used for creating a text signature that can appear at the end of each outgoing message.

Session Review

A network is a set of hardware and software components that support several people working together using computers. The Internet is a network of networks. The Internet allows you to communicate with any of the millions of Internet users.

The Internet has historically been oriented toward text-based data. The World Wide Web (WWW or Web), a component of the Internet that became popular during the early 1990s, supports text, graphic, and sound data. To use the Web, you need software called a browser.

Accessing the Internet requires a computer, a modem, Internet software, and an Internet provider. Anyone on the Internet who wishes to receive messages has to have an account and address. An address consists of a subdomain and one of six topdomains. An address outside the United States also has a country designator.

Services of the Internet include E-mail, newsgroups, file transfer protocol (FTP), Telnet, Gopher, Internet Relay Chat, Usenet groups, and the World Wide Web. You can access any of these services by using specially designed software or a general-purpose package, like Internet Explorer, that provides many of these services.

Using the Web requires hypermedia. A Web page has hypertext, which uses pointers to link to other pages or other Web sites. To create a Web document, you use Hypertext Markup Language (HTML), which is a fairly easy to understand set of instructions. Hypertext Transfer Protocol (HTTP) provides a version of FTP software that is capable of sending and receiving text, graphics, and sound files.

Internet Explorer is bundled with the Windows operating system and Office 2000. When you start Internet Explorer, the start page associated with your version of Internet Explorer is automatically loaded. By entering the URL (uniform resource locator) of another site, you can access a Web page at another World Wide Web site.

Key Terms and Concepts

Session Quiz

Multiple Choice

1. The process of transferring files from one computer to another is called:

a. Telnet
b. file transfer protocol (FTP)
c. Internet
d. browsing

2. Which of the following items is not associated with a Web site?
   a. start or home page
   b. Hypertext Transfer Protocol (HTTP)
   c. Hypertext Markup Language (HTML)
   d. Veronica
3. An Internet service that allows individuals with interest in a particular topic to share information and ideas is:
   a. a newsgroup
   b. a Web site
   c. an address
   d. an interest group
4. Opening a specific home page requires that you enter the URL for that location. URL stands for:
   a. uniform regional locator
   b. uniform request locator
   c. uniform resource locator
   d. none of the above
5. Which of the following indicates the location of an Internet address?
   a. address/domain
   b. superdomain
   c. city indicator (co)
   d. login

True/False

6. The .sch topdomain is used to designate an educational institution.
7. A password is needed to check the contents of your electronic mail mailbox.
8. Emoticons are used in E-mail to let the reader know how you were feeling when you sent the message.
9. Internet Explorer allows you to subscribe to a newsgroup and read messages for that particular topic.
10. The page that is automatically loaded when you start Internet Explorer is known as the hyper page.

Session Review Exercises

1. Define or describe each of the following:
   a. browser
   b. FTP
   c. emoticons
   d. e-mail
2. The ____________ is a network of networks that can access millions of computers.
3. A ____________ is a device that allows computers to trade information over telephone lines.
4. The ____________ is a person's unique identifier at a location or address.
5. The ____________ topdomain indicates that the location is a commercial or business site.
6. ____________ refers to the ability to send and receive electronic messages using the computer.
7. ____________ refers to sending nasty messages to someone using E-mail.
8. The ____________ in a newsgroup name indicates that this newsgroup deals with a hobby.
9. A ____________ file contains information about a newsgroup as well as the guidelines for using that newsgroup.
10. ____________ refers to the practice of spending a few days or weeks to see how the flow of a newsgroup progresses as well as allowing time to examine personalities of participants.
11. The ____________ system is a text-based precursor to the World Wide Web.
12. ____________ is a service that allows you to have remote access to another computer.
13. The World Wide Web was designed in 1989 by ____________.
14. Web pages are written in a language called ____________ ____________ ____________.
15. A special protocol called the ____________ ____________ ____________ (a version of FTP) transfers files across the Web.

16. The special piece of software used to access a Web site is called a ____________.
17. The Internet Explorer ____________ text box allows you to enter the URL for a Web site you want to access.
18. A Web page entry that transfers you to a different location in the document or to a different document is called a ____________.
19. The ____________ ____________ ____________ is a service that allows you to communicate "live" via typed messages with other individuals using special chat rooms.
20. The ____________ ____________ program is bundled with Internet Explorer to provide E-mail access.

Computer Exercises

Some of the exercises will require you to use the Web document Sample Links page in the Web site for this text, (http://www.prenhall.com/duffy).

1. Use the Web sites in the above document to accomplish the following:
   a. Visit three of the Web sites.
   b. Print the start or home page of each site.
2. Use the search feature of Internet Explorer to find information related to astronomy.
3. Select a topic of your choice and perform a search.
   a. Choose Save As from the File menu to save the text of any Web pages that are of interest to you.
   b. Print any Web pages that you think you may need.
4. Use the Today's Links entry of the Quick Links bar to examine the Web sites that Microsoft currently thinks are interesting. Print the first Web page of three of the sites. (If the Today's Links button does not appear, use the Best of the Web button.)
5. Get a news magazine and record the number of ads that have Web addresses.
6. Send an E-mail message to a friend or a relative.
7. Subscribe to one or more newsgroups that interest you. Examine postings.

Internet Exercises

1. Open a Web site. For each link, open that document in a new window. Open six sites. Examine the taskbar. Are they present?
2. Examine the history of sites on your computer. How many are there? If a site that someone else has visited interests you, double-click it to visit that site.
3. Choose Source from the View menu to display the HTML messages to the NotePad. Choose Print from the File menu to print the HTML commands.
4. Get information about building a Web page of your own.
   a. Open the Web page supported by this text (http://www.prenhall.com/duffy).
   b. Click the Constructing a Home Page link.
   c. Investigate how a home page is constructed.
   d. Print at least one Web page.
5. Find clip art and background files for use in constructing a Web page.
   a. Open the Web page supported by this text (http://www.prenhall.com/duffy).
   b. Click the Sample of World Wide Web link and activate it.
   c. Click the Computers, HTML, and Internet link.
   d. Visit the various links that contain clip art and backgrounds.
   e. Download a piece of clip art and a background.
   f. If you have a color printer, you might want to print the Web document you accessed via the link HTML: Backgrounds and Color Notes.

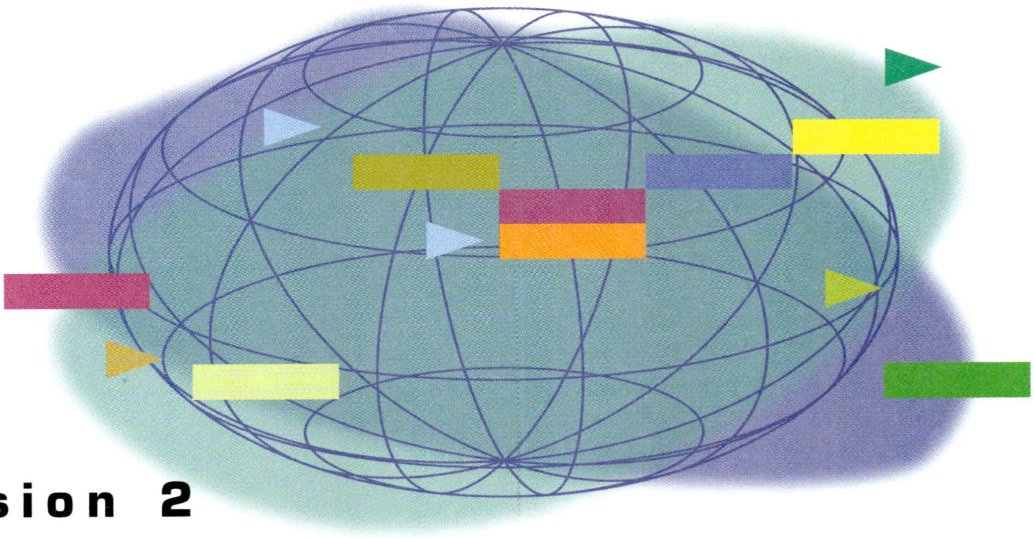

Session 2
OUTLOOK 2000

After completing this session, you should be able to:

- Use the Outlook bar
- Maintain a contact list
- Send and receive E-mail using Outlook
- Manage E-mail messages
- Use the Calendar feature to maintain a schedule
- Keep a Task (To Do) list
- Use the Notes feature
- Print Outlook documents

In this module, you are to assume that you have been assigned to a group project in a CIS 120 class that you are taking. Four other individuals; Jim Dougherty, Anita Benson, Rajiv Sandel, and Deanna Johnson have also been assigned to your group. Your group has been assigned the task of writing a report about Microsoft Corporation. You are supposed to do research using the Internet, Library (journal articles and online articles), and corporate financial statements. You will be using various features of Outlook to keep track of the project tasks and communicate with one another. The group members have selected you as the project leader. As such, you will be responsible for coordinating the various tasks associated with this project using Outlook 2000.

INTRODUCTION TO OUTLOOK 2000

In the previous session you were introduced to the E-mail feature using Outlook Express. Outlook Express is a piece of E-mail software that is automatically provided by Microsoft for anyone who has Internet Explorer. Microsoft provides a much more powerful E-mail package, Outlook 2000, with its Office 2000 software suite. Outlook 2000, however, is much more than just E-mail software. It also functions as a personal information manager (PIM). This type of software allows you to manage your E-mail messages, keep a calendar of your schedule, maintain a list of personal and business contacts as well as information about those contacts, keep track of tasks that have to be performed (to do lists), and create and place notes.

Outlook can be kept open all of the time. When you are not directly using Outlook, it can be reduced to a button on the taskbar. If you need to schedule an appointment, enter an item on a to do list, create new contact information, or perform some other task; you can click the taskbar button and have access to the feature that you need at the moment.

Start Outlook by double-clicking the shortcut icon on the desktop, by accessing Outlook using the Start menu or by invoking Outlook using a toolbar from the taskbar.

Unless Outlook has been reconfigured for your computer, the window shown in Figure 2.1 appears.

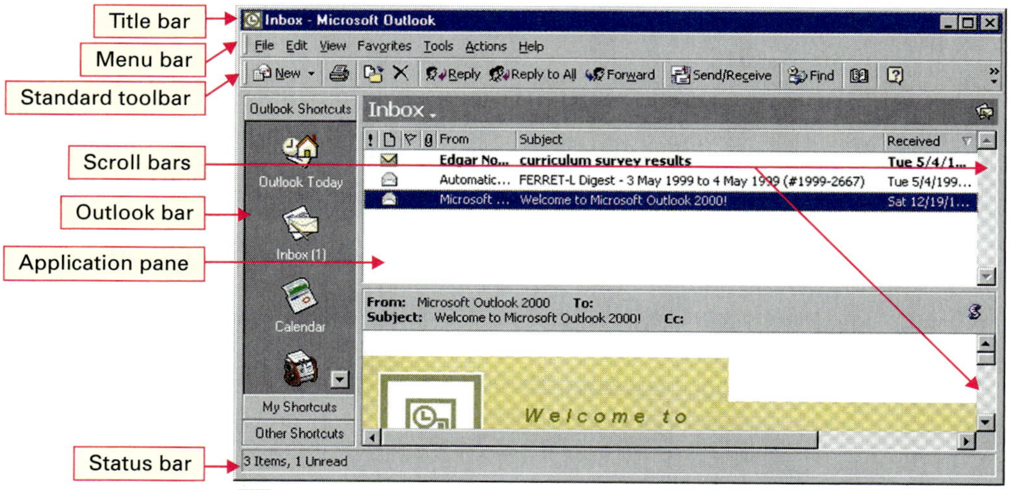

FIGURE 2.1 The various parts of the Outlook window.

PARTS OF OUTLOOK WINDOW

The Outlook window contains two basic parts: the Outlook bar and the application pane. The large vertical bar in the left-hand side of the screen is the **Outlook bar**. It contains a number of shortcut buttons as well as icons that allow you to access various features of Outlook. The application pane appears to the right of the Outlook bar and automatically displays the Inbox containing any messages that you have received. The contents of the application pane change as selections are made in the Outlook bar.

Outlook Bar

The outlook bar shown in Figure 2.1 contains a number of icons and buttons. These icons are used to invoke varioius features of Outlook, look at different mailboxes, or access files at other locations. Table 2.1 shows the icons and the tasks associated with those icons. Unless it has been changed, Outlook has three grouping buttons in the Outlook bar. Clicking the Outlook Shortcuts, My Shortcuts, or Other Shortcuts buttons displays different groupings of icons in the Outlook bar. When an arrow button appears in the Outlook bar it indicates that there are icons that are not visible, and clicking the arrow button will display one or more additional icons.

TABLE 2.1 Outlook Bar Icons

Grouping	Icon Name	Purpose
Outlook Shortcuts		
	Outlook Today	Allows you to preview the activities scheduled for today, any tasks that have to be accomplished, and provides information about any E-mail messages.
	Inbox	The default pane/view that stores messages that you have received. The upper part of the pane stores the message header, while the bottom portion allows you to scroll through the selected message.
	Calendar	Allows you to schedule any appointments and meetings.
	Contacts	Records business and personal contact information in a file for easy access.
	Tasks	Allows you to make "To Do" lists of things that need to be accomplished.
	Notes	Allows you to store short notes about items that might need your attention later. These notes can now act like electronic "sticky notes" and can be attached to various documents as reminders.
	Deleted Items	As long as it has not been emptied, it allows you to retrieve items that have been deleted.
My Shortcuts		
	Drafts	Allows you to access any unfinished messages that you have stored using the File, Save command. Any draft messages can be accessed, finished, and then sent.
	Outbox	This is the location where messages are placed if you want to delay delivery. Click the Options button when you are creating a new message, and then enter the date and time in the Delivery options box. You can indicate the date by clicking the down arrow to display a calendar.
	Sent Items	This contains any messages that you have sent previously. To access one of these messages, double-click it. The message opens in a separate window.
	Journal	A file in which E-mail messages, meeting requests, responses, or cancellations as well as tasks requests and responses can be stored for a contact. It can also automatically track Office documents for associated/indicated contacts.
	Outlook Update	Invokes Internet Explorer and goes to the Microsoft Web site to query if an update for Outlook 2000 is available.

TABLE 2.1 Outlook Bar Icons (continued)

Grouping	Icon Name	Purpose
Other Shortcuts		
	My Computer	Allows you to access any storage facilities available on your computer or accessible over the network.
	My Documents	Provides access to the My Documents folder on your computer.
	Favorites	Provides access to any shortcuts that have been stored in your Favorites folder.

Application Pane

The **application pane**, shown in Figure 2.1, is where you can create, view, and edit an E-mail message, maintain your schedule, enter tasks, and access storage devices as well as numerous other tasks. The contents of this pane vary based on the application/task selected in the Output bar.

Other Parts of the Application Window

Other parts of the application window include the title bar, menu bar, toolbar, and status bar. Some of these items appear slightly different from one Outlook application to another.

Title Bar

The **title bar** (Figure 2.1) is located at the top of an application or document window. It contains the application name (Microsoft Outlook) along with the Minimize, Maximize or Restore, and Close buttons.

Menu Bar

The **menu bar** (Figure 2.1) contains menu options that activate pull-down menus. The menu options and menus displayed follow standard Office 2000 conventions discussed previously in Windows.

FIGURE 2.2 The options of the New menu allow you to create different types of Outlook documents.

Standard Toolbar

The **Standard toolbar** (Figure 2.1), located beneath the menu bar, contains buttons that enable you to execute commands more quickly than you can by going through various menus. The buttons vary from application to application. Table 2.2 shows and describes each button associated with the Standard toolbar of the Inbox.

Scroll Bar

The scroll bar can be used to scroll through large numbers of messages that are contained in the Inbox. When you want to read a message, click it and the text of that message appears at the bottom of the pane.

Status Bar

The status bar (Figure 2.1) is at the bottom of the application window. In the Inbox pane, the left side shows the number of messages and how many are unread.

TABLE 2.2 Standard Toolbar Buttons

Button	Button Name	Purpose
	New	This appearance button changes from application to application. Clicking on the down arrow opens a menu that allows you to create different types of documents (Figure 2.2).
	Print	Prints the active page using the current defaults.
	Move to Folder	Allows you to move a message to a specified folder that you indicate from the various options presented.
	Delete	Deletes any selected messages and places them in the Deleted Items receptacle.
	Reply	Reply to the sender of this document.
	Reply to All	Reply to all recipients as well as the sender.
	Forward	Allows you to forward the message to a different recipient.
	Send/Receive	Check for new messages and send any that have not been sent.
	Find	Activates the Find feature for locating text within a message, sender, or subject of a message.
	Address Book	Activates the Address Book feature for indicating which of the contacts you wish to address the message to.
	Help	Activates the Help feature of Outlook.

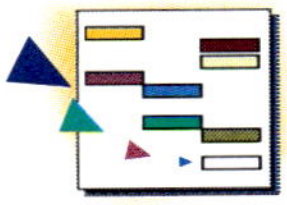

Hands-On Exercise: Interacting with Outlook

The following hands-on exercise introduces you to some rudimentary Outlook features.

1. Start Outlook 2000. If necessary, click the Maximize button to enlarge the Outlook window.

2. Activate the Outlook Shortcut grouping.

Click to activate this grouping.

Click to scroll through the various items in the grouping. As you move from one application to the next, notice how the items in the toolbar differ.

Click to activate the Calendar pane (Figure 2.3).

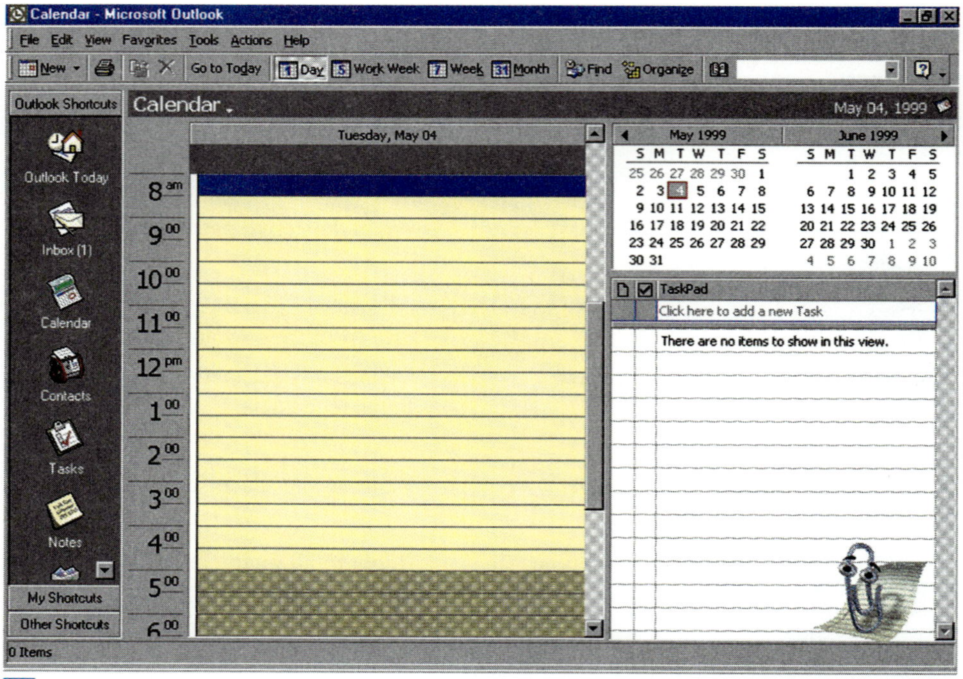

FIGURE 2.3 The Calendar pane permits you to keep track of your schedule.

Click to see if you have anything scheduled for today. Unless someone else has entered something, your pane should be empty.

3. Examine other groupings.

Click to activate this grouping. You should now see entries for Drafts, Outbox, Sent Items, and so forth.

Click to activate this grouping. You should now see entries for My Computer, My Documents, and Favorites.

4. Return to the Outlook Shortcuts grouping and activate the Inbox.

TIMELY TIP

To see more shortcut icons in the Outlook bar, right-click the background of the Outlook bar and then click Small items.

Reinforcing the Exercise

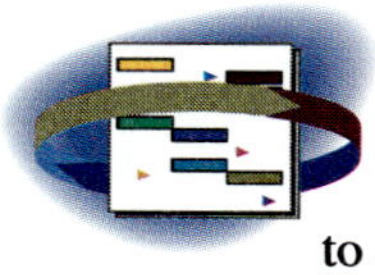

1. The Outlook bar allows you to move from one Outlook application to another.
2. If all icons in a grouping do not appear, you can use the arrow keys to scroll through the options in the Outlook bar.
3. There are at least three groupings as a default in the Outlook bar.
4. The items in the Standard toolbar change as different applications are invoked.

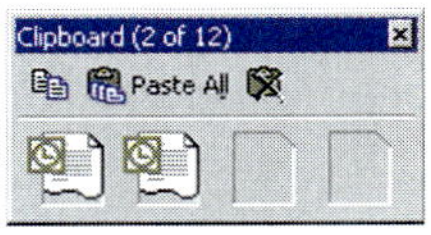

FIGURE 2.4
The Clipboard toolbar appears when multiple Copy commands have been issued. It allows you to select the item to be pasted at the insertion point location.

Copy, Cut and Paste Buttons

The Copy, Cut, and Paste commands all use the Windows clipboard discussed in Session 1 of Module 1: Windows 98. The text included in a selected block is cut or copied from the document to the clipboard. You can then paste it elsewhere in the active document or in another document. In most Windows applications, each time you issue a Cut or Copy command, any previous text or graphics on the clipboard is deleted and replaced with the newly selected text. Office 2000 applications allow you to place up to 12 different items to the clipboard. When you issue a Paste command, a little menu appears prompting you for which Copy that resides on the clipboard is to be pasted to your document (Figure 2.4). This process of having multiple items available for pasting is called **c**ollect and paste.

Copy

Clicking the Copy button leaves the original text in your document and copies it to the clipboard. Up to twelve different items can be copied to the Office clipboard.

Cut

Clicking the Cut button removes the selected text from your document and places it on the clipboard. Up to twelve different items can be copied to the Office clipboard.

Paste

Clicking the Paste button inserts cut or copied text anywhere in the document. First position the insertion point at the exact location to receive the cut or copied text, and then click the Paste button. The text is inserted, beginning at the location of the insertion point. If multiple items have been copied to the Office clipboard, a Paste menu similar to that depicted in Figure 2.4 appears on your screen. The first fifty characters of text appear as a tooltip when the mouse is hovered over text items that have been copied to the Clipboard.

Timely Tip

The following keyboard shortcut commands can be used instead of clicking toolbar buttons:

Copy	CTRL + C
Cut	CTRL + X
Paste	CTRL + V

Using the Contacts Feature

The **Contacts** feature (accessed using the Contacts icon of the Outlook Shortcuts grouping) allows you to store information like names, addresses, phone numbers, E-mail addresses, and so forth about your personal and/or business contacts. You can use information that has been stored in your Contacts to use in letters or databases. Storing information in Contacts entries also allows you to send E-mail messages directly to those people who have E-mail address information stored as part of their data.

In order to communicate easily with individuals in your project group, you are going to want to store information about each of those individuals using the Contacts feature of Outlook. Information about each group member can be found in Table 2.3. You will be including address information that you make up and that is relevant to where you currently live and/or go to school. The first entry will have information about you.

When the Contacts feature is activated, a screen with the existing entries appears on your monitor with the names in alphabetical order. If contact groups are specified, their heading is displayed as a multiple-group icon.

You can also control how Contacts entries are displayed and any other items related to this feature using the context menu. The Contacts screen along with the context menu can be seen in Figure 2.5.

TABLE 2.3 Project Group members

NAME	ADDITIONAL INFORMATION
Your name	Enter your personal information.
Jim Dougherty	Enter information that you make up, but that is relevant to your geographic area.
Anita Benson	Leave the E-mail addresses for each of these four individuals blank.
Rajiv Sandel	
Deanna Johnson	

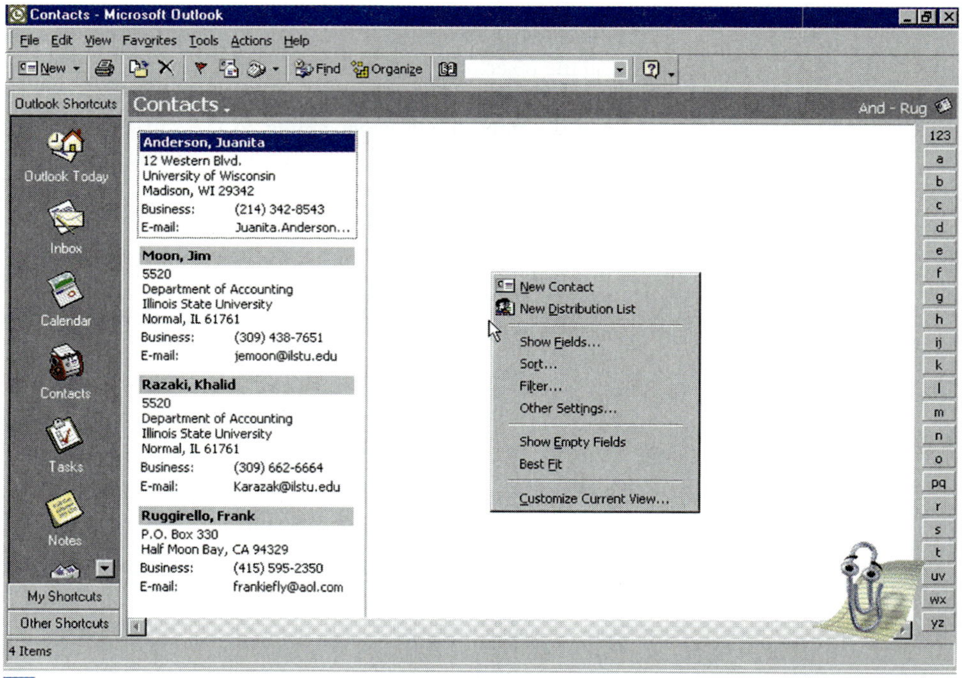

FIGURE 2.5 The Contacts screen contains any contact information that you have entered.

If you want to make changes to an existing entry, double-click it and a window containing that information now appears (Figure 2.6). If you want to enter new contact information, double-click the blank area or invoke the context menu and select the New Contact entry. A blank window like that depicted in Figure 2.6 now appears.

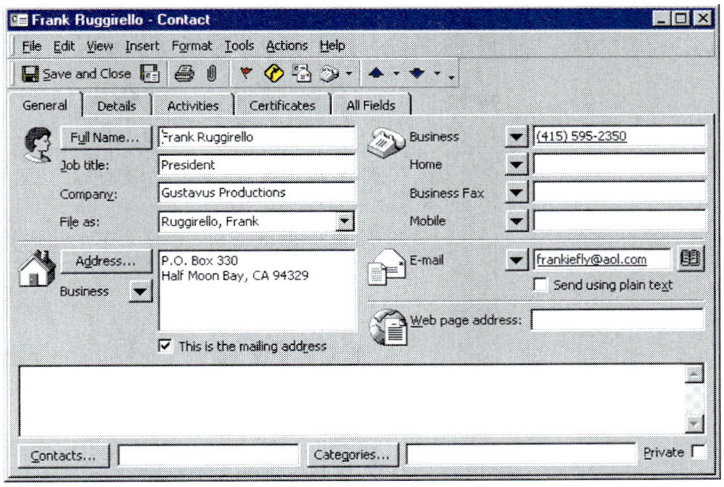

FIGURE 2.6 The Contacts window with information from a previously entered contact.

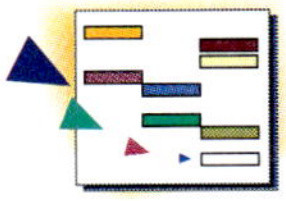

HANDS-ON EXERCISE: CREATING CONTACTS USING OUTOOK

The following hands-on exercise introduces you to entering information using the Outlook Contacts feature.

1. If necessary, start Outlook 2000.

2. Activate the Outlook Shortcut grouping.

Click to activate this grouping.

Click to activate the Contacts pane. Any contacts that have been previously created are now visible. Your screen will probably be blank.

3. Activate the Contacts window.

Double-click Double-click the blank area of the Contacts pane. An untitled Contact window now appears (Figure 2.7). Enter your personal information in this window. Change the Address to *Home* via the drop-down menu. When you have finished, your Contacts window should look like Figure 2.8.

Click the Save & New button to save the current record and display an empty window for the next Contact record. Continue entering the contacts for the remaining four project members. Be sure to leave the E-mail entry blank.

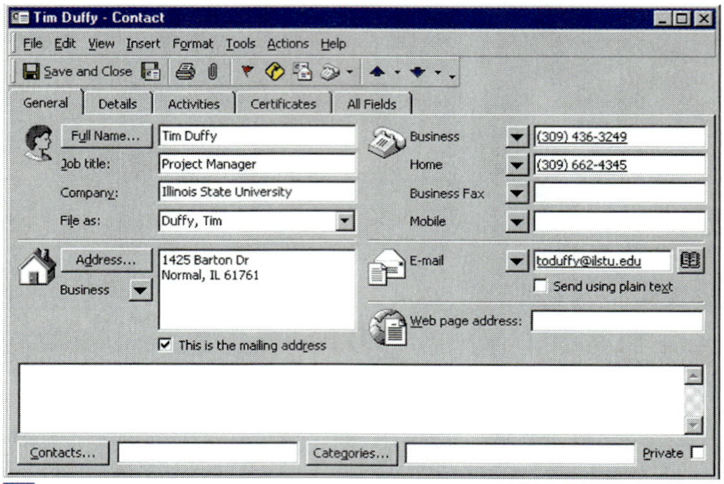

FIGURE 2.7 The blank, untitled Contacts window.

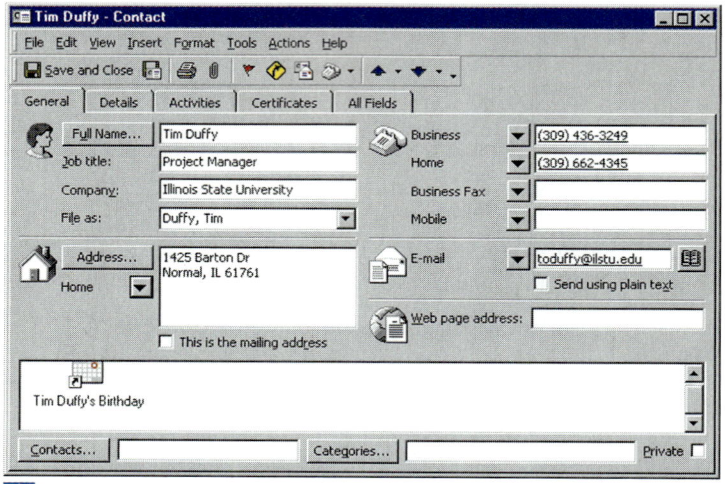

FIGURE 2.8 The completed Contacts window.

TIMELY TIP

If you enter an E-mail address improperly and don't catch it right away, you can't just edit the field. Rather you must invoke the context menu and then select the Properties command. A dialog box now appears with the E-mail address for editing.

4. After the last record is entered, issue the following command.

Save and Close Save the last record and close the Contacts box. You should now see the five names that you entered from Table 2.3 on the Contacts pane.

5. Examine other aspects of the Contacts window.

Double-click Activate your individual record that you created previously. Click the Details tab to examine what other types of information can be stored about a contact. Once you have examined this tab, examine the three remaining tabs.

6. Change and print your individual record.

Double-click	Activate your Contacts listing. Enter a business address. Click the Details tab and enter an office address and your birthday.
Save and Close	Save the changes.
Right-click	Invoke the context menu for your contact record.
	Click to print your contact record.

7. For each of the members of the group project, enter the E-mail address of a classmate. After you enter the first E-mail address, select the text and issue a CTRL + C command to copy the address. For the other group members, issue a CTRL + V to paste the address in the E-mail text box.

Timely Tip

If you inadvertently entered a contact incorrectly, you can delete that contact by right-clicking it to invoke the context menu, and selecting the Delete command.

Reinforcing the Exercise

1. The Outlook Shortcuts grouping of the Outlook bar allows you to access the Contacts feature.
2. The Contacts pane displays any names for which contact information has been entered.
3. You can insert a new Contacts record by either double-clicking a blank area in that pane or by selecting New Contact from the context menu.
4. Each record in the Contacts window has multiple tabs in which information can be entered or specified.

Maintaining Journal Entries for Contacts

Outlook provides the ability to create journal entries that allow you to keep a record of your interaction with individuals in the Contacts feature and activities you perform on Microsoft Office documents. The Journal feature of Outlook provides the ability of developing an "audit trail" of your interaction with individuals about whom information is stored in the Contacts feature. You can include such things as phone conversations, E-mail messages, meetings, task requests, and so forth.

You can manually record a journal entry about a contact by issuing the File, New command sequence and then selecting the Journal Entry option. A Journal Entry window now appears and you can enter information about the activity that you wish to document (Figure 2.9). You can, for instance, click the Contacts button to relate this activity with someone in the Contacts feature. Figure 2.9 shows a completed Journal Entry scheduling a round of golf.

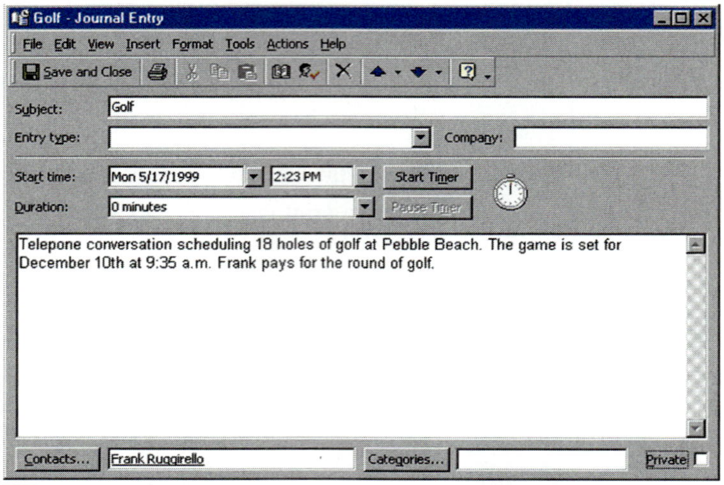

FIGURE 2.9 The Journal Entry dialog box for recording an activity.

Once a Journal entry has been recorded, you can use the Journal option of the My Shortcuts grouping to examine this or any other journal entry. Click the Journal entry of the Outlook bar to activate the Journal pane. Journal entries appear with buttons containing a plus sign (+). Click the plus sign and the topic of the journal appears (Figure 2.10). Double-click the topic and the Journal window depicted in Figure 2.9 appears.

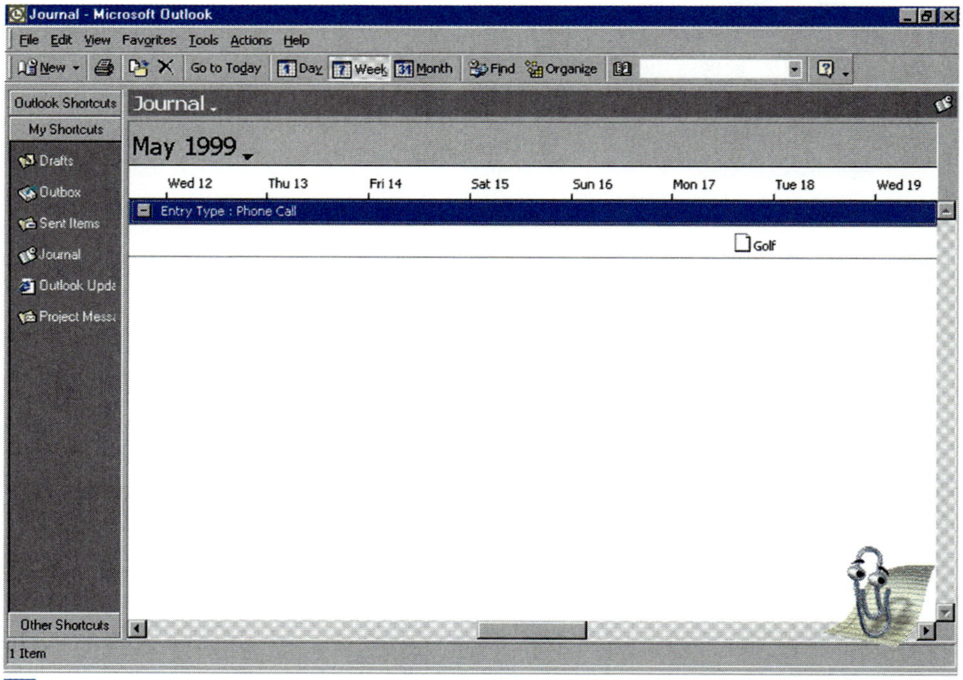

FIGURE 2.10 The Journal Entry for recording a round of golf at Pebble Beach.

OUTLOOK E-MAIL

The **E-mail** feature of Outlook 2000 works much like that of Outlook Express covered in the previous session. Outlook allows you to send E-mail over a network/intranet or to a different address on the Internet. Depending upon your situation, you may have to go through a logon procedure before you can send messages.

The Inbox contains messages that you have received from others. The Outbox, found in the My Shortcuts grouping, contains any messages that have been created while you are working offline. When you logon again, the Outbox messages will be sent.

To customize the menu and taskbars issue the Tools, Customize commands. You can now make changes to the toolbar and/or taskbar.

TIMELY TIP

Below are two tips about using Outlook in an environment that requires the use of modems instead of a direct network link. Modem connections are most frequently found in a residence, while network links are usually found in school computer labs.

Before you can use Outlook to access mail, you may have to establish a connection to your school or Internet service provider (ISP). Once you have logged on to your school computer or ISP, you can invoke Outlook and send and receive E-mail.

If you are using Outlook at home and have only one phone line, you can keep the phone free by using Outlook in offline mode. Once you have downloaded any E-mail messages, Offline mode allows you to read messages, respond to messages, or create new messages and stores any messages in an output queue or waiting area. Once you are ready to send these messages, you reconnect to your ISP and send the messages in the queue by clicking the Send and Receive button. In the interim, your telephone line is free to send and receive calls.

CREATING, SENDING, AND RECEIVING E-MAIL

You send and receive messages using the Inbox. Outlook requires that you have the Inbox activated before you can send or receive E-mail messages. Outlook typically defaults to the Inbox when you start it. When you are creating an E-mail message, you can send a plain E-mail document or specify that your message be formatted using a template.

You can also tell Outlook to include a signature like that specified in the prior session using Outlook Express. Such a signature contains information about you that you want to transmit at the end of a message like your name, contact information, and possibly any telephone numbers at which you can be reached.

To create an E-mail message, click the New button of the Inbox pane. You will probably activate a plain text message window like that shown in Figure 2.11. Instead of sending just a plain text message, you can also specify a template that can be used to control fonts and background effects that will be used in constructing your message. Use the Actions, New Mail Message Using, More Stationery command sequence to accomplish this. These commands invoke the Select a Stationery dialog box. Figure 2.12 shows the Select a Stationery dialog box with the Story Book template selected, while Figure 2.13 shows that template applied to a new message window.

You can use the Filter feature to view only those items or files that meet conditions you have specified. For example, you can filter items so that you do not see any items from a particular person. Those messages are still in the Inbox and can be seen again by removing the filter. A "filter applied" message is present in the status bar when a filter is active.

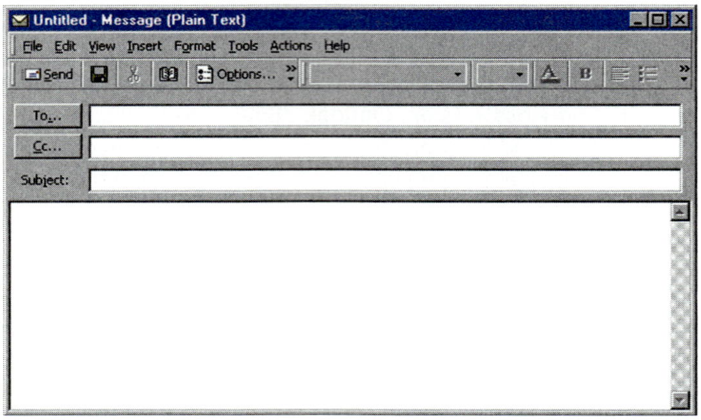

FIGURE 2.11 **The Message window for plain text.**

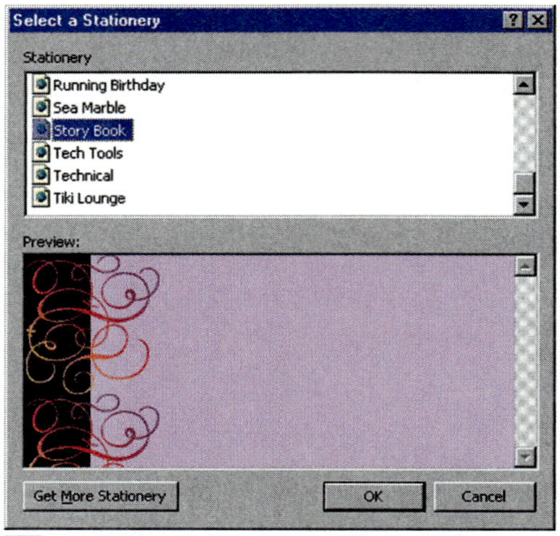

FIGURE 2.12 **The Story Book template selected in the Select a Stationery dialog box.**

Timely Tip

When you want to check to see if new E-mail features that you have invoked are working properly, send an E-mail addressed to yourself with the feature(s) invoked. Then click the Send and Receive button to retrieve any new messages. You can now open the message that you just sent and check to see if the feature(s) are present. Using this method can save the embarrassment of sending an improper message if you have not properly applied the new feature (a new signature, for example) or have inadvertently included spelling errors.

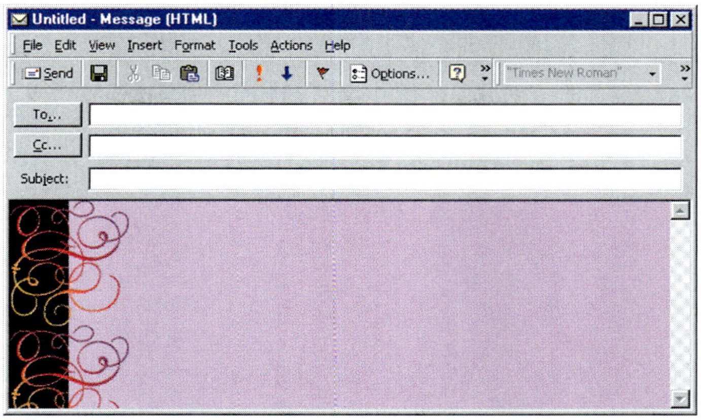

FIGURE 2.13 **The Story Book template applied to the new message window.**

Hands-On Exercise: Creating and Sending an E-mail Message

The following hands-on exercise steps you through the process of creating sending an E-mail message using a template and a signature.

1. If necessary, start Outlook 2000.

2. Activate the Outlook Shortcut grouping.

Outlook Shortcuts	Click to activate this grouping.
	Click to activate the Inbox pane.

3. Create a text-based signature.

Tools	Click to open the Tools menu.
Options . . .	Invoke the Options dialog box.
Mail Format	Invoke the Mail Format tab of the Options dialog box.
Signature Picker...	Click to invoke the Signature Picker dialog box (Figure 2.14).
New...	Click to invoke the Create New Signature dialog box.

Type: ***Your Name*** Enter the name of the signature to be created. Your Create New Signature dialog box should now look like Figure 2.15.

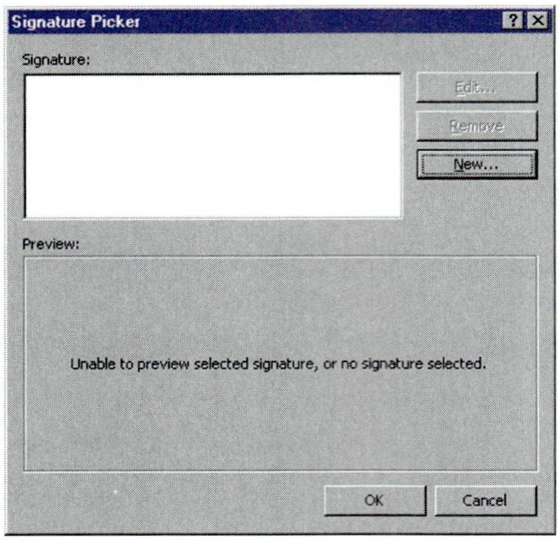

FIGURE 2.14 The Signature Picker dialog box.

FIGURE 2.15 The completed Create New Signature dialog box.

Next > Click to proceed to the edit Signature dialog box.

4. Enter your name and any information that you want to include at the end of E-mail messages. See Figure 2.16 for an example.

Finish Click to return to the Signature Picker.

OK Click to save the signature and return to the Options dialog box.

OK Click to specify this signature as the default and return to the Inbox.

5. Apply a template for a new message window.

Actions Click to open the Actions menu.

New Mail Message Using Click to open this menu. If Ivy appears at the top of this menu select it and proceed to step 6, otherwise, issue the next command.

More Stationery . . . Invoke the More Stationery dialog box depicted previously in Figure 2.12.

Ivy Click to select this stationery.

OK Click to activate this stationery. Your signature should appear on the stationery.

6. Specify yourself as the recipient.

To... Click to activate the Select Names dialog box with the Contacts list (Figure 2.17). If you have more than one recipient, hold down (CTRL) and click all of the other recipients. (Use (SHIFT) if the names are in adjacent positions.) You could also click the button to access the Select Names dialog box.

Double-click Select your name.

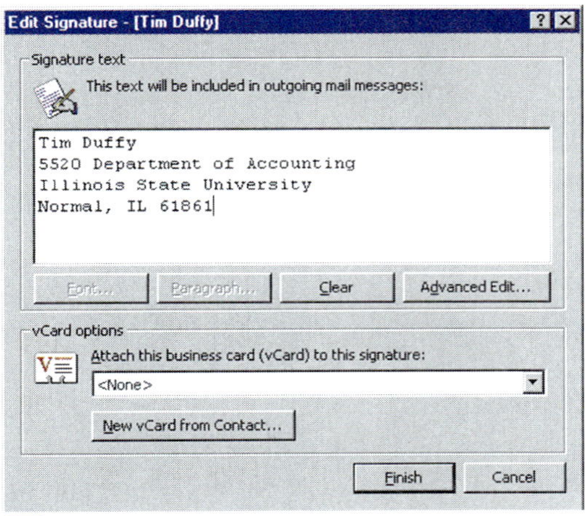

FIGURE 2.16 **A sample signature.**

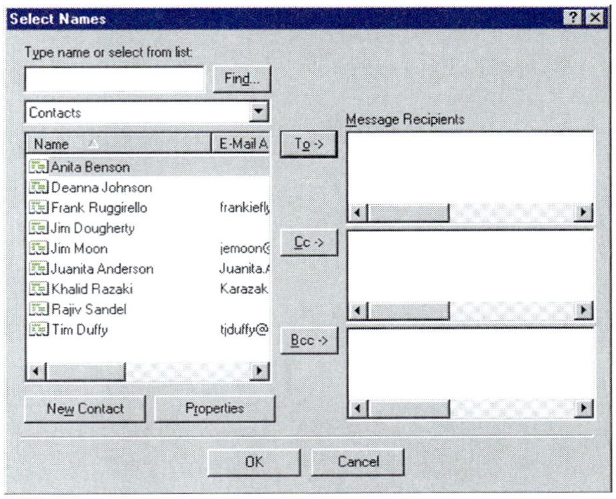

FIGURE 2.17 **The Select Names dialog box with the Contacts list for selecting the recipient.**

Click to specify the recipient. Notice that your underlined name instead of your E-mail address appears. Outlook has automatically substituted the name specified originally in the Contacts list. When the message is sent, the exact E-mail account/address data specified in the E-mail text box will be used.

Click Click the Subject text box to place the insertion point at that location.

Type: `Test` Enter this text in the Subject box.

TAB Position to the message text box.

Type: `This is the first E-mail message sent for the Outlook session of this module.`

Type this message text. Your message window should now appear like that depicted in Figure 2.18.

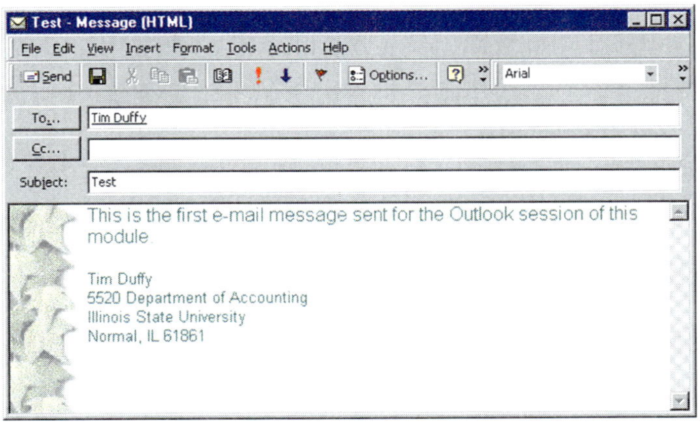

FIGURE 2.18 **The completed message using the Ivy template.**

7. Send the message.

Click to send the message and return to the Inbox.

8. Check your mail.

Click to get your mail.

9. Look at the message in its own window.

Double-click Double-click your message to open it in a separate window.

Click to print your E-mail message.

10. Examine other messages using the navigation buttons.

Click to go to the previous item. Examine several of the messages that reside above this message in the list.

Click to go to the next item. Use this button to go down the list of messages. Click the down arrow of one of the buttons and examine the options. For example select the next unread message.

Click to close the message window.

11. Find a record with specified text.

Click Position at the beginning of your E-mail messages in the Inbox.

Click to invoke the find text box.

Type: ***Your Name*** Enter your name exactly as you entered it for the signature.

Click to find the text. Your message heading should now highlighted in the Inbox.

Click the Close button in the Find Pane to close it.

12. Click the New button to send a plain message. Your signature in plain text should appear. Use step 6 to again create the text of the document. Instead of using the Select Names dialog box, enter the E-mail address of a fellow student manually in the To: box and send him or her the E-mail message.

TIMELY TIP

You can have more than one signature specified in Outlook. You can, however, have only one active for any single message. If you want to invoke a different signature for a message, issue the Tools, Options, commands; invoke the Mail Format tab, and then select the desired signature from the pull-down menu.

Reinforcing the Exercise

1. A signature containing text data can be created and made to appear at the end of every message.
2. A plain message or one created using a template can be used to send an E-mail message.
3. You can use the Select Names dialog box to specify one or more names in the To: box of an E-mail message.
4. Instead of using the Select Names dialog box, you can manually enter the E-mail address in the To: box.
5. When you are using new features, you can make certain that you have specified them correctly by sending yourself an E-mail with those features invoked.
6. You can change the signature being used via the Mail Format tab of the Options dialog box.
7. The Previous Item and Next Item buttons can be used to move from message to message in the Inbox.

On Your Own

Besides allowing you to specify your signature, the Options dialog box allows you to customize Outlook to your exact preferences. You might want to spend some time examining the various tabs contained in this dialog box and examine what types of changes you can make to Outlook and its applications.

Timely Tip

Many instructors require that their students supply them with phone numbers and E-mail address information so that if a class has to be canceled, or a student has to be contacted for help these tasks can be done efficiently. To most easily provide this information, get to Contacts, right-click your Contact record, and then select Forward as vCard. A new message window opens with a rolodex card icon containing your Contact information. Enter the E-mail address of the recipient, insert any additional text, and click the Send button to send this information.

Using the Address Book Feature for Addressing Mail

Besides using the To: button to access the Contacts feature for obtaining an address(es) for routing an E-mail message, Outlook provides the Address Book feature that also allows you to address an E-mail message. Once a message window is displayed, you can invoke the Address Book feature by clicking the button on the toolbar to invoke the Select Names dialog box depicted in Figure 2.19.

As you can see in Figure 2.19, the Contacts entries reside in the left-hand box. You can select a single recipient and then click the To, CC, or Bcc button to place that name in the desired box. You can also use the Shift key to select adjacent names or the CTRL key to select multiple nonadjacent names. If you want to include those selected names as the recipient of the E-mail message, click the To button. The selected name(s) are not included in the To box. When you have finished selecting names, click the OK button to return to the original message window for your E-mail message (Figure 2.20).

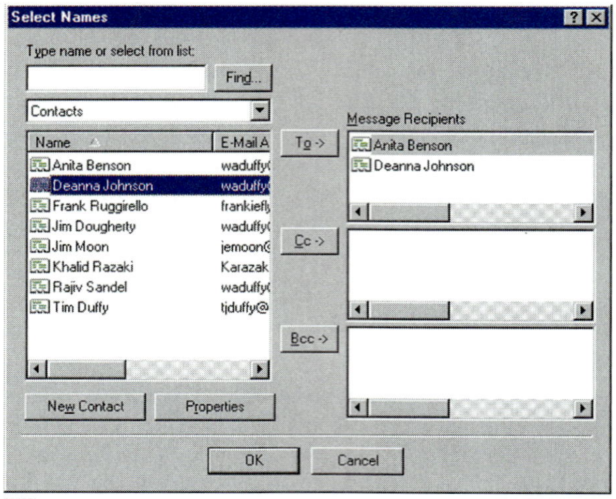

FIGURE 2.19 The Select Names dialog box with two names selected as recipients for an E-mail message.

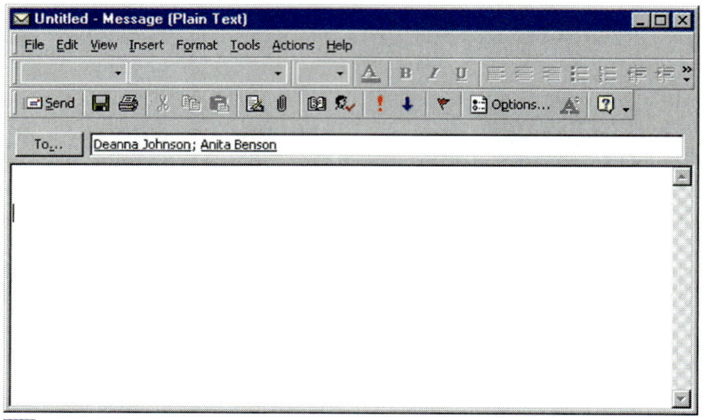

FIGURE 2.20 The message window with the names previously specified using the Address Book feature of Outlook.

If you find yourself frequently sending messages to the same group of people, you can create a Personal Distribution list that will make this process easier. You may, for instance, want to send a message to each student in a group project about a change in that project and want to make certain that you do not omit anyone. To create a recipient group, issue the commands Tools, Address Book. The Address Book window now appears (Figure 2.21).

Once Address Book window appears, use that menu to issue the File, New Group commands to invoke the Properties dialog box. You enter the name of the group and then click the Select Members button. The Select Group Members dialog box appears and allows you to select the names from your Contacts list for this group (Figure 2.22). Once you click the OK button, you are returned to the completed CIS 120 Project Properties dialog box (Figure 2.23).

Once you have created a grouping, that grouping appears as part of your contact list anytime that the Address Book feature is invoked for addressing an E-mail message (Figure 2.24).

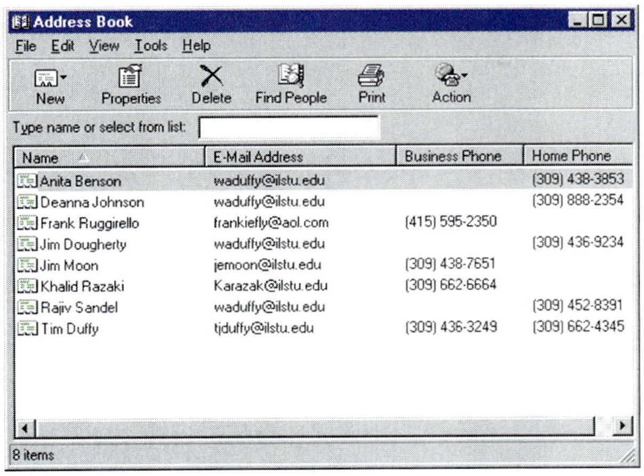

FIGURE 2.21 The Address Book window of Outlook.

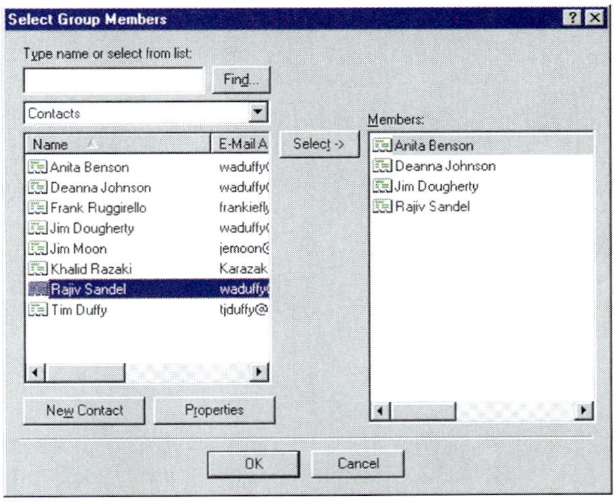

FIGURE 2.22 The Select Group Members dialog box with the selected names for the new grouping.

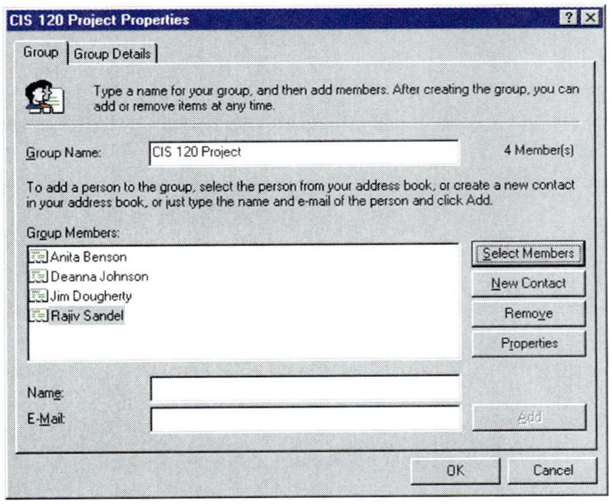

FIGURE 2.23 The Select Group Members dialog box with the selected names for the new grouping.

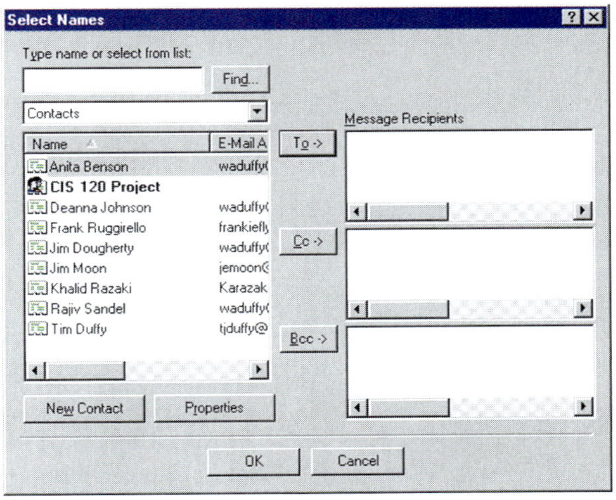

FIGURE 2.24 The Select Group Members dialog box with the selected names for the new grouping.

Customizing Mail Appearance

Outlook allows you to control the appearance of messages via the Options dialog box (Figure 2.25) that is accessed from the Tools menu. Once the Options dialog box is present, click the E-mail Options button to access the E-mail Options dialog box (Figure 2.26). You can, for example, activate the item at the bottom of the dialog box that automatically includes anyone that you send a reply in your Contacts component of Outlook. If you have a permanent communication link via a network connection, you can indicate to Outlook that a notification message (or play a sound) appears on your screen any time that a new E-mail message arrives.

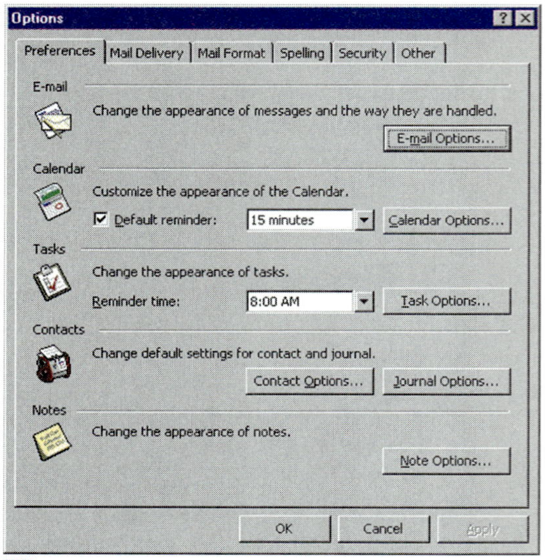

FIGURE 2.25 The Options dialog box provides access to various components of Outlook that can be further customized.

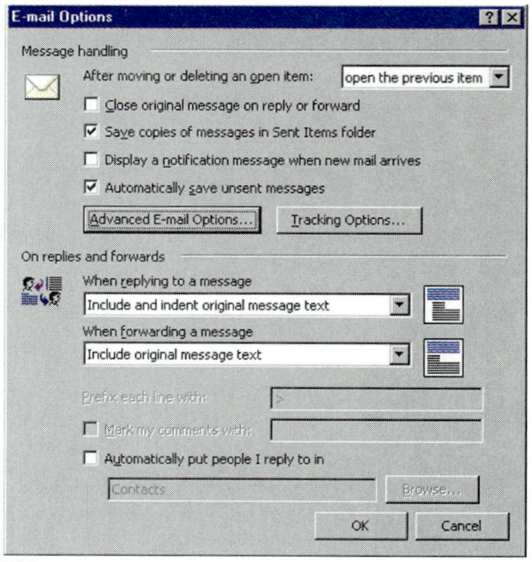

FIGURE 2.26 The E-mail Options dialog box provides the ability to customize various E-mail features.

The Advanced E-mail Options dialog box (Figure 2.27), allows you to control how messages are saved as well as what actions Outlook takes when messages arrive. It also controls what actions are to be taken when an E-mail message is sent. You can, for instance, set the sensitivity of all messages to Private.

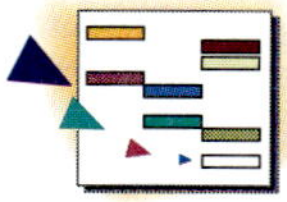

Hands-On Exercise: Using the Address Book and Printing Options

The following hands-on exercise steps you through the process of using the Address Book feature and using print options.

1. If necessary, start Outlook 2000 and invoke the Inbox.

2. Address an E-mail message using the Address Book.

Click to invoke the Message window.

Click to invoke the Select Names dialog box depicted previously in Figure 2.19.

Anita Benson Double-click this name (or the name of a classmate). The name should now appear in the To box for Message recipients.

Deanna Johnson Double-click this name (or the name of a classmate). The name should now appear in the To box for Message recipients. Your Select Names dialog box should now appear like that depicted previously in Figure 2.19.

Click to return to the message window. Your addresses should now be specified (see the previous Figure 2.20).

3. Add a brief message to the message window. If you do not want to send the message, click the Close button and then respond No when prompted about saving changes.

Click to send the message.

4. Examine Print Table option for E-mail. This option prints the header information for messages.

File Click to invoke the File menu.

Print . . . Click to invoke the Print dialog box.

Table Style Click this style (Figure 2.28). Notice that this dialog box also shows that all rows will be printed. If you want to limit the header records to be printed, make your selection before issuing the Print command.

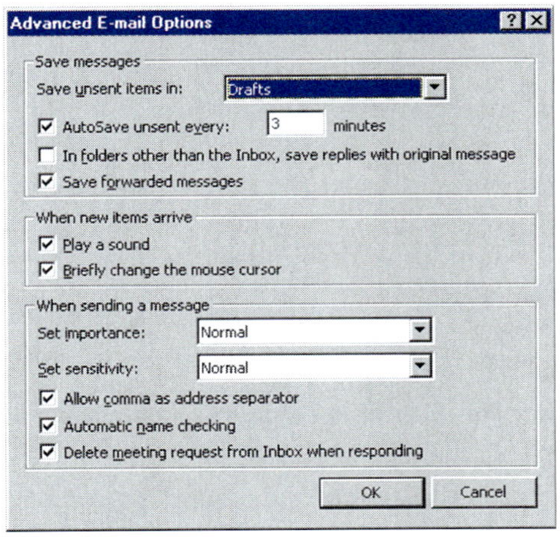

FIGURE 2.27 The E-mail Options dialog box provides the ability to customize various E-mail features.

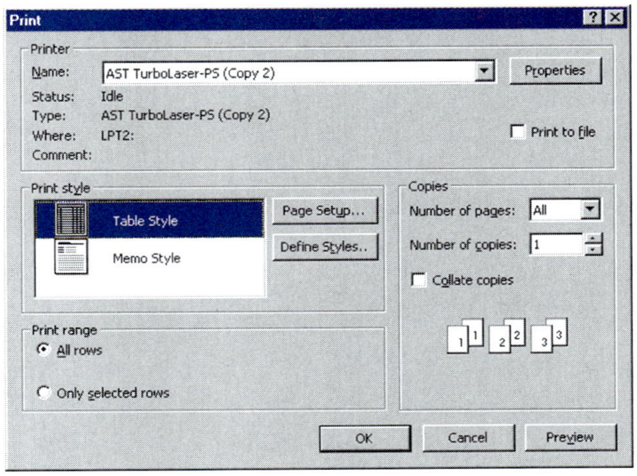

FIGURE 2.28 The Print dialog box for printing multiple E-mail message headers.

Click to see how the report will be generated (Figure 2.29).

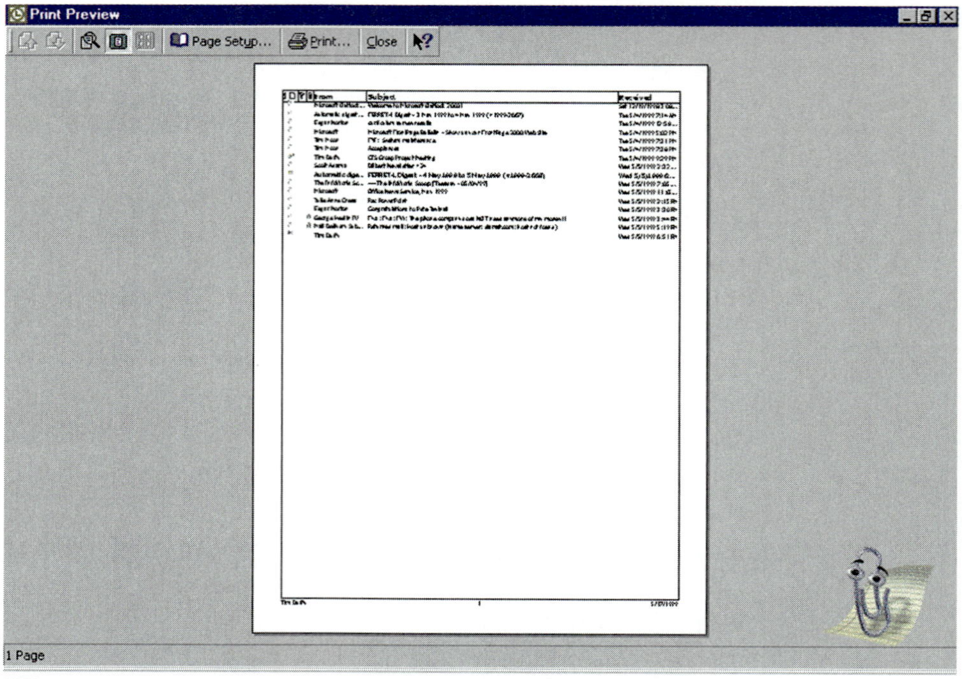

FIGURE 2.29 The Print Preview window for examining how the message headers will print.

Click to return to Outlook.

5. Examine Print Memo option for E-mail messages. This option allows you to print multiple messages.

Click — Click a message header in the Inbox at the top of your screen.

SHIFT + Click — Hold down the Shift key and click a message about five messages below the first message clicked. Several messages should now be selected.

File — Click to invoke the File menu.

Print . . . — Click to invoke the Print dialog box. The Memo style is selected. This dialog box also allows you to start each message at the top of a separate page as well as include attached files in the printed message.

Click to see how the report will be generated (Figure 2.30).

Click to return to Outlook.

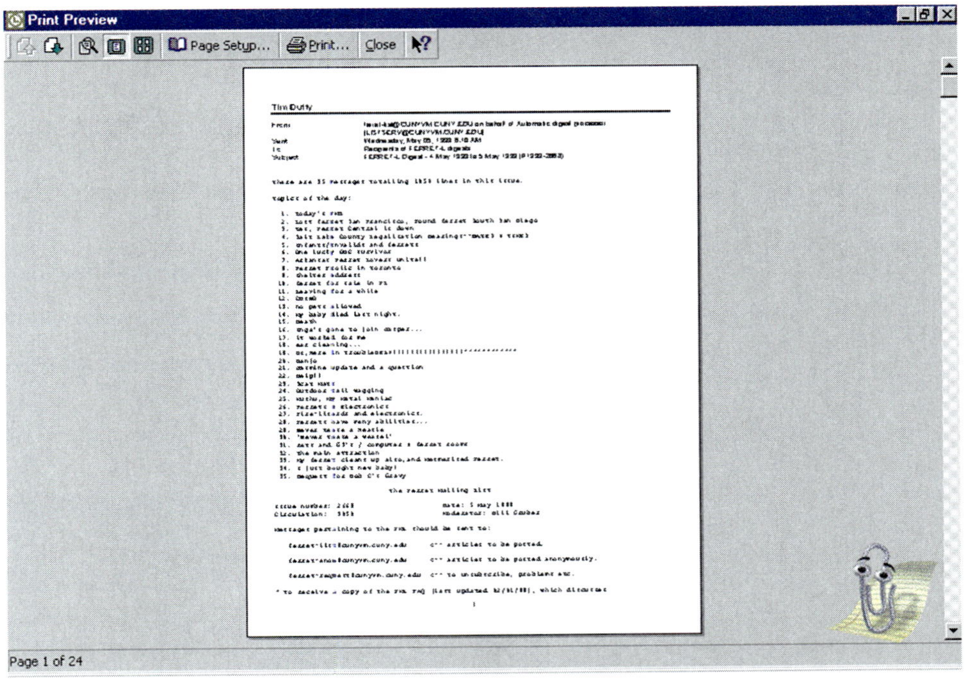

FIGURE 2.30 The Print Preview window for examining how the complete selected messages will print.

Reinforcing the Exercise

1. The Address Book feature can be used for addressing an E-mail message.
2. The Print dialog box of the E-mail feature is used to print one or more message headers from the Inbox.
3. The Print dialog box of the E-mail feature is used to print several messages from the Inbox at one time.

Replying To and Forwarding E-mail Messages

Many times when you receive an E-mail message the sender wants you to answer a question that has been posed in the message just received. In such a situation, you have the option of replying only to the original sender or to the sender and all other recipients. When a reply has been specified, the text of the original message is included and a RE appears in the title bar and becomes part of the subject text.

You may also find that you have received a message that you think might be interesting to a person who was not originally specified as a recipient. In this case, you can use the Forward button to send a copy of the E-mail to the new recipient.

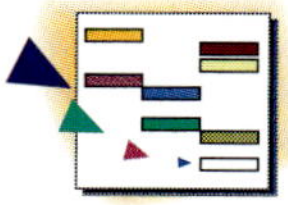

Hands-On Exercise: Replying to and Forwarding Messages

The following hands-on exercise steps you through the process of replying or forwarding an E-mail message.

1. If necessary, start Outlook 2000 and invoke the Inbox.

2. Reply to the message that you just sent yourself.

3. Select the message that you just sent yourself.

Click to open the message window for a reply (Figure 2.31). You can now enter any text, respond to questions, and so forth.

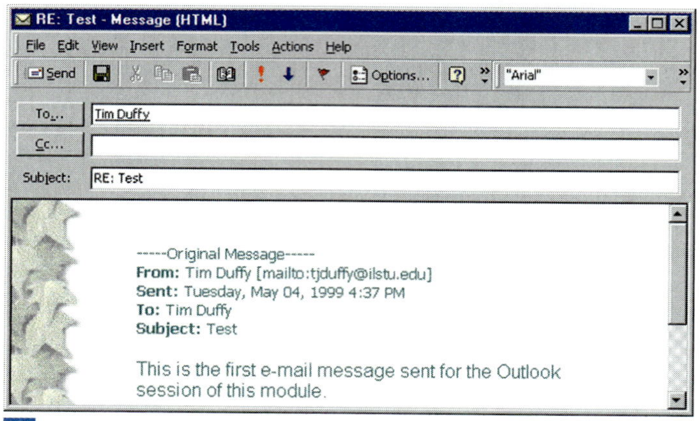

FIGURE 2.31 The message window for replying to a message.

Type: `Thanks for the information.`

Send the reply. You are now returned to the Inbox. Notice that a purple arrow indicating that a reply has been sent now appears on the opened envelope icon for this message.

4. If there are multiple recipients (cc: entries) that you want to respond to, click the 

button. Make certain, however, that you are replying to the correct individuals. You don't want to be embarrassed by sending your reply to the wrong audience. When you have verified the recipients, click the Send button.

5. Forward the message.

Click Click your original message.

Click to invoke the Forward message window. An FW now appears in the title bar as well as the subject text, and the To: box is blank. Enter the E-mail address of a fellow student in the To: box and forward the message to him or her.

Click Position the insertion point in the text box of the message window.

Type: `I thought you might be interested in this.`

Send the forwarded message. You are now returned to the Inbox. Notice that a blue arrow indicating a forwarded message now appears by the original message.

Reinforcing the Exercise

1. A reply command sends a response to the original sender.
2. A Reply to All command sends a response to the original sender as well as any other recipients.
3. The Forward command can send a message to someone who was not an original recipient of the message.
4. Once any changes have been made to any of the above, click the Send button.
5. A reply is indicated by the appearance of a purple left-hand arrow on the message icon.
6. A forward is indicated by the appearance of a blue right-hand arrow on the original message icon.

On Your Own

You may wish to be able to have a message available for a given amount of time and then recall that message if there has been no reply. This can be used for time-sensitive applications that need a fast response. In such a situation, you click the Options entry of the message toolbar, and then use the calendar that is activated by clicking the date and then entering the time. After the specified date and time, the message is no longer available.

E-MAIL ATTACHMENTS

You may have occasion to include a picture of the baby, workbook, word processing, or output file generated by some type of application software package with an E-mail message. The problem with these types of files is that they are not stored in a regular ASCII file format. If these types of files are to be attached to an E-mail message they must be encoded using the Bin Hex feature so that the binary representation of the file can be transmitted with the message.

To attach a file issue the Insert, File command sequence from the new message window to invoke the Insert File dialog box (Figure 2.32). If necessary change the drive and directory, select the file to be attached, and then click the Insert button to include the file with the message. When you now click the Send button, the message along with the attached file will be sent. In this example, the Excel workbook file *4Ch3 Exercise 1* is being attached to a message.

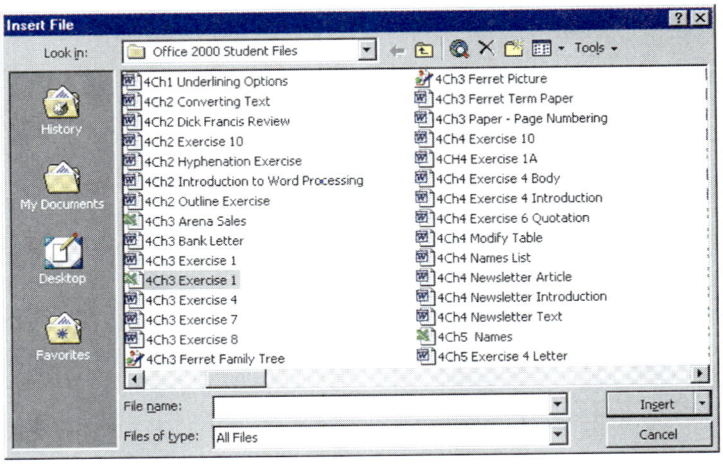

FIGURE 2.32 The Insert File window for attaching a file to a message.

HANDS-ON EXERCISE: ATTACHING A FILE

The following hands-on exercise steps you through the process of attaching a file to an E-mail message.

1. If necessary, start Outlook 2000 and invoke the Inbox.

2. Create a new message. Address it to yourself.

3. Specify *Excel Workbook* as the subject.

4. Type the following text for the body of the message.

```
Jim,

Attached is the Excel workbook that we discussed on the phone
yesterday.
```

5. Attach the file.

Insert	Click to open the Insert menu.
File . . .	Invoke the Insert File dialog box shown previously in Figure 2.32.
4Ch3 Exercise 1	Select this Excel file.
Insert	Click to insert the file as an attachment. The completed message with the attachment now looks like that depicted in Figure 2.33.

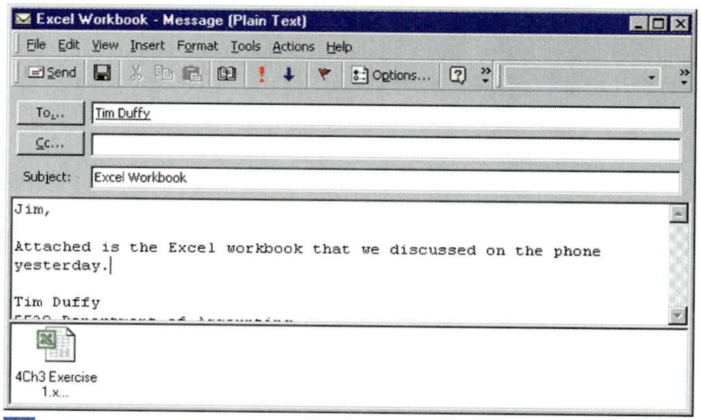

FIGURE 2.33 The message window with the indicated attachment.

Send	Send the message. You are now returned to the Inbox.

6. Get your mail using the Send/Receive button.

7. Double-click to open the message with the attachment in a message window. Notice that the message contains a paperclip indicating that an attachment is present.

8. The attachment appears as a link at the end of the message. To open the workbook, double-click the Excel workbook icon.

9. Close Excel and return to Outlook.

10. Close the message window and return to the Inbox.

On Your Own

If necessary, activate the Office Assistant using the Help, Show the Office Assistant command sequence. Click the Office Assistant to activate its query mode. Type the word *flag*. Examine the various links that explain how to use the flag feature and Journal. Print the first page for each topic.

- Flag
  - About Flags
  - Flag a message or contact as completed
  - Flag a message or contact for follow up
  - Change the due date on a flag
- Journal
  - Record an activity in a journal

Reinforcing the Exercise

1. Files that contain other than text data can be attached to an E-mail message.
2. The Insert, File sequence is used to attach a file.
3. A message with an attachment has a paperclip icon in the Inbox.
4. When a message has an attachment, that file can be opened by double-clicking the file icon of the attachment.

Hands-On Exercise: Sending Contact Information Via E-mail

The following hands-on exercise steps you through the process of sending contact information using the E-mail feature of Outlook

1. If necessary, start Outlook 2000 and invoke Contacts.

2. Select your contact record. The header with your name should now be blue and your record should have a blue border around it.

3. Send the information.

Right-click Right-click your Contacts entry to invoke the context menu.

Forward as vCard Select this option from the context menu. A message window like that depicted in Figure 2.34 appears. The Contact card appears as an attachment to the message.

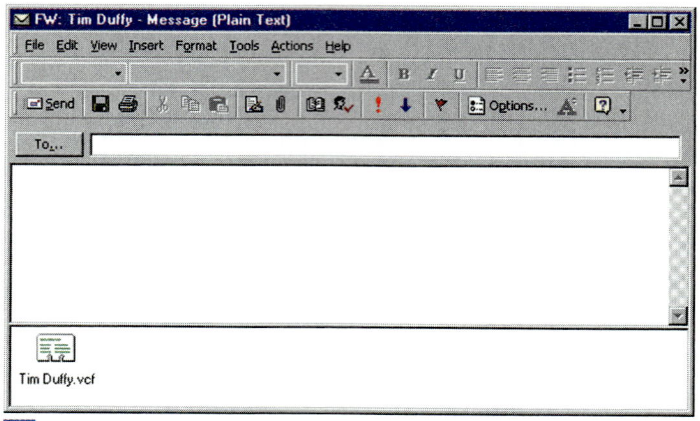

FIGURE 2.34 The message window for sending Contact card information. Notice that the card appears as a attachment to the message.

Type: ***E-mail address*** Enter the E-mail address of a class-mate.

Click to send the Contacts information.

Reinforcing the Exercise

1. Contacts information can be sent via E-mail.
2. Select Send as vCard from the context menu.
3. Enter the To information in the message window and click the Send button.

CUSTOMIZING OUTLOOK MENUS AND TOOLBARS

You may find that as you use an Outlook application there are many features that are of little or no use to you, while other features are used on an everyday basis. Every application in Outlook provides you with the ability to configure menus and toolbars to your specific needs. This means that you can determine what options appear in menus and which buttons appear on the Standard toolbar within the various Outlook applications.

Outlook, like other Office applications, automatically customizes menus and toolbars based on how often you use those commands. When you first start using Outlook only the most basic commands appear in the menus. If you open a menu and do not find the desired command in the menu, you will notice an option at the bottom of the menu with two down arrows. Click that menu option to see all of the hidden options for that menu. If you now position to other menus using the mouse or keyboard arrow keys, all menu options are displayed for each new menu invoked.

Outlook also defaults to specific options on the Standard toolbar displayed for each application. You can use the command sequence View, Toolbars, Customize to invoke the Customize dialog box to change which buttons are displayed on the desired toolbar. You can also use the grab handle (vertical line) of a toolbar to drag it to a new position on the screen using the mouse. If you have multiple toolbars appearing on the screen, you can even drag them to occupy the same horizontal position on the screen.

The down arrow next to the Help button on the Standard toolbar also allows you to add or remove buttons from the standard toolbar of the current application (Figure 2.35). Currently used buttons contain a check mark. Click any current button to inhibit its display. You can also click the Customize option to add some other button to the toolbar.

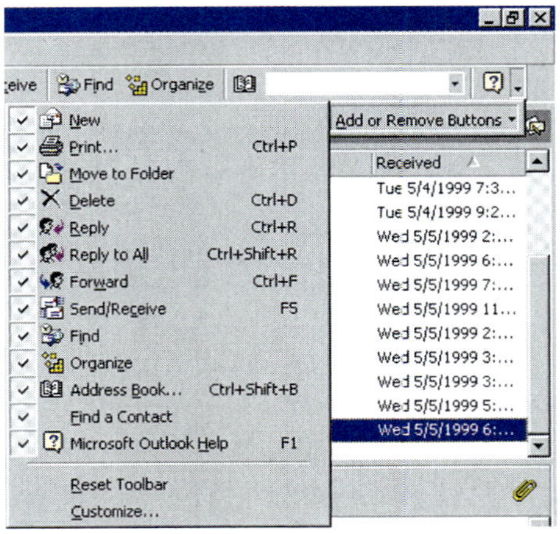

FIGURE 2.35 The Add or Remove Buttons pull-down menu provides control over which buttons appear on the Standard toolbar of an Outlook application.

USING THE CALENDAR

The **Calendar** feature of Outlook can be used to keep track of appointments or assignments. The Calendar feature makes use of a calendar motif like that used on the yearly calendar that most people have hanging on a wall. Appointments can be entered directly on the schedule that appears when the calendar feature is invoked (Figure 2.36) or on the calendar dialog box invoked by double-clicking the time on the appointment sheet (Figure 2.37).

If you examine the Calendar pane of Outlook you can see that today's date is marked in red on the monthly calendar on the left as well as appearing on the Calendar bar. The date at the top of the hourly schedule changes as you click/change the date on the calendar. If you click the bar of a calendar, a menu of surrounding months appears from which you specify a new calendar. You can also progress forward or backward a month at a time by clicking the arrows on the calendar. The TaskPad contains any tasks that you have entered that have to be accomplished. You can enter appointments directly on the yellow schedule.

TIMELY TIP

Double-click any time entry on the schedule of the calendar to invoke the Appointment window. Double-click the title bar at the top of the schedule to invoke the Event window.

On Your Own

Outlook provides a number of ways you can use to customize the Calendar features' appearance.

- You can change the appearance of the calendar by positioning the mouse on any of the borders and dragging in the desired direction.
- You can also customize its features using the Tools, Options, Preferences Calendar Options to invoke the Calendar Options dialog box.

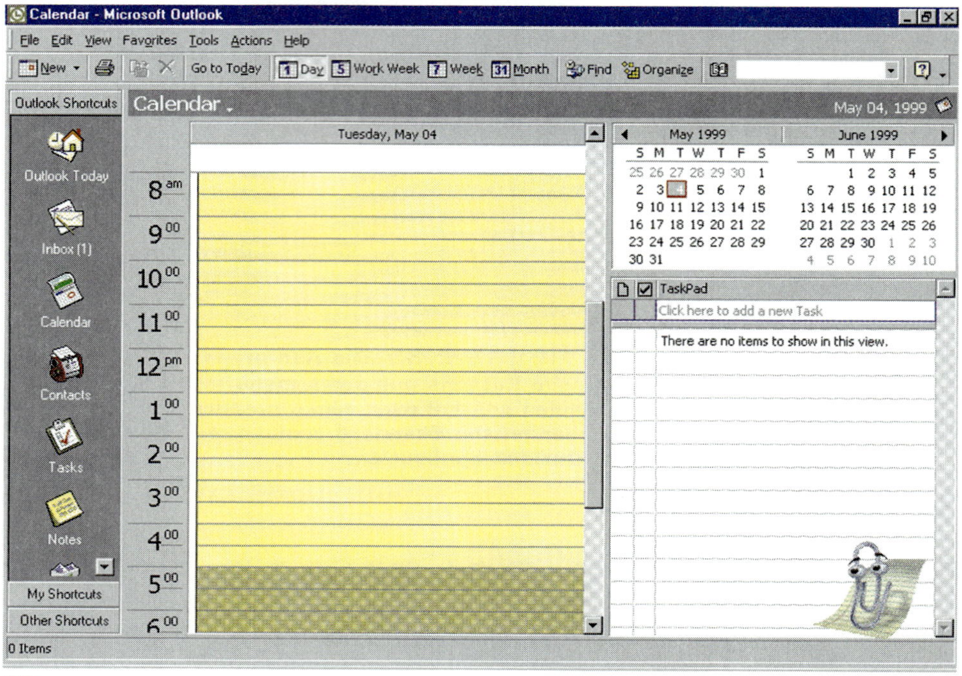

FIGURE 2.36 The Calendar pane of Outlook.

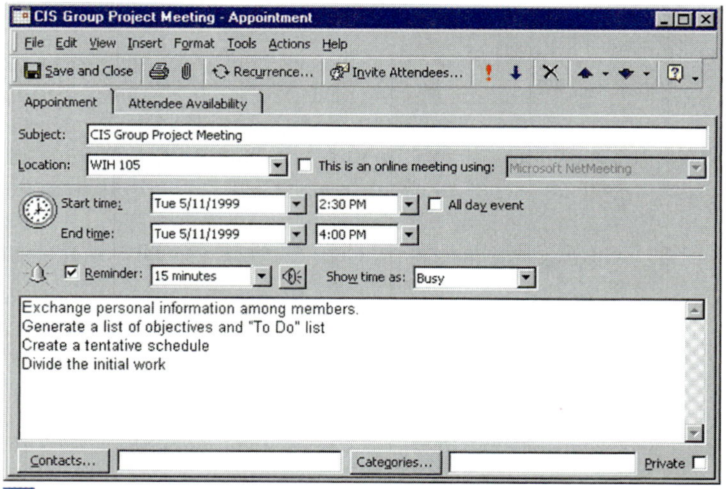

FIGURE 2.37 The Calendar dialog box activated by double-clicking the time of the appointment list.

The Appointment dialog box provides an alternative, more detailed method of entering appointments. The Calendar pane is ordered at hourly intervals, while the exact beginning and ending time can be entered in the dialog box. If a multi-day meeting is to be recorded, click the down arrow and indicate the ending day on the calendar. This dialog box not only allows you to enter subject data, but also include notes at the bottom of the dialog box. To receive a reminder, Outlook must be running. The exact location of the meeting can be indicated. If the meeting is to be online, this along with the software to be used can be indicated.

If more than one attendee is to be included, the Attendee Availability tab (Figure 2.38) can be used to not only check on the availability, but also to schedule in their appearance for a meeting. A notice of the meeting can also be sent to participants.

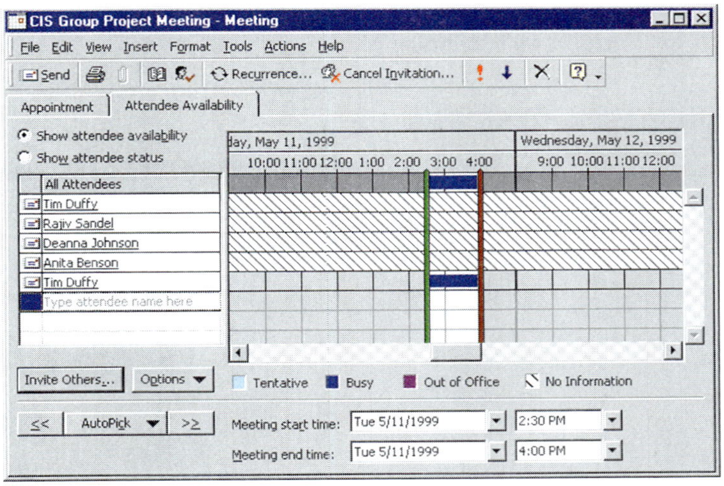

FIGURE 2.38 The Calendar dialog box's Attendee Availability tab provides for arranging a meeting for multiple individuals.

FIGURE 2.39 The reminder displayed when the indicated time for a task has passed.

Once a reminder has been recorded, Outlook keeps track of it. If the date due passes without the task being marked as completed, Outlook displays a message like that depicted in Figure 2.39. You can select any of the bulleted choices or indicate that Outlook is to remind in so many minutes (5 unless you indicate otherwise).

You may find that you have scheduled someone by mistake as an attendee for a meeting and want to remove that individual as an attendee. In such a situation, double-click the meeting on your schedule to activate the meeting window. Click the Attendee Availability tab to show the individuals invited to the meeting. Select the individual erroneously invited by clicking that entry. Issue the Actions, Add or Remove Attendees command sequence to invoke the Select attendees and Resources dialog box. Right-click the individual erroneously invited and select Remove from the context menu. Click the OK button and close any remaining open windows. The indicated individual is not longer an invitee to the meeting.

Customizing Calendar Options

The Calendar feature allows you to configure display as well as print options for this feature of Outlook.

Display Options

Outlook allows you to control the appearance of your schedule via the Options dialog box that is accessed from the Tools menu. Once the Options dialog box is present, click the

Calendar Options button to access the Calendar Options dialog box (Figure 2.40). You can, for example, indicate which days of the week to include in the workweek on your schedule. You can also indicate the time zone, holidays as well as other options using this dialog box.

Print Options

The Print dialog box of the Calendar feature provides control over how the calendar is to be printed. This dialog box (Figure 2.41) is reached via the File, Print command sequence. Once you have activated the Print dialog box, you can see that you have several options from which you can choose in the Print Style selection box. Table 2.4 contains a summary of each of the styles. Notice that the Print dialog box also provides you with options for determining the print rage via the starting and ending dates. You also have the option of hiding private appointments. Use the Preview button to see how the selected style will appear on the printed page.

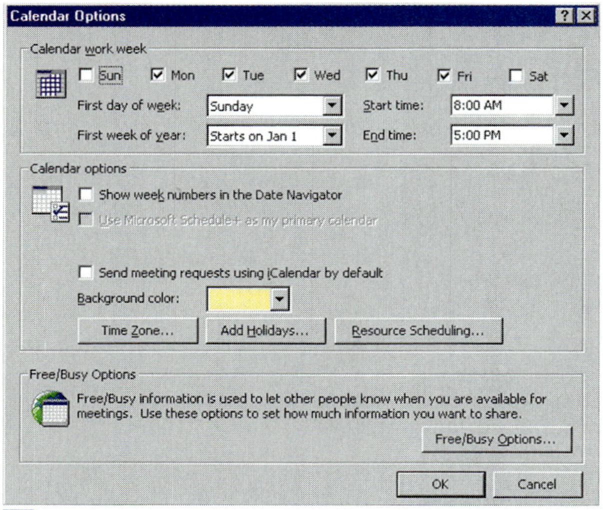

FIGURE 2.40 The Calendar Options dialog allows you to change various defaults used in keeping track of your schedule and workweek.

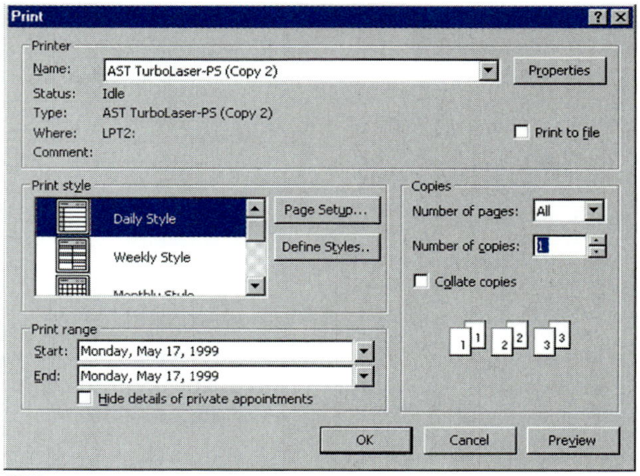

FIGURE 2.41 The Calendar Print dialog allows you to determine the type of report that will be printed.

TABLE 2.4 Print Styles for the Calendar Feature

Style	Report Generated
Daily	Each page printed contains one day's activities
Weekly	Each page contains one week's activities without tasks and notes areas
Monthly	Each page contains one month's activities without tasks and notes areas
Tri-fold	Each page contains one day, one month, and the taskpad as sections on a page for folding evenly into three parts
Calendar Details	Calendar items including the body text for the item

Integration with Other Outlook Applications

The Calendar feature provides tight integration with other Outlook applications. E-mail can automatically be sent when other individuals are invited as attendees to a meeting. Tasks can be entered in the Calendar and then again accessed or modified using the Tasks pane of Outlook. Attendees for a meeting can be invited via the Contacts feature or by accessing the Address Book feature of Outlook. Tasks that are created using the Tasks feature appear in the Calendar pane. Finally, any calendar view can be converted to an HTML file for placement on the World Wide Web.

Hands-On Exercise: Scheduling an Appointment

1. If necessary, start Outlook 2000 and invoke the Calendar.

2. On the calendar, click the calendar day for a week from this Friday. Notice that the date at the top of the schedule has changed.

3. Click the bar at the top of the left-most calendar. Select the month two months from now. Notice how the calendar has changed. If you have two calendars, both have advanced to months.

4. Set the calendars back to their original settings. Make certain that today's date has been selected.

5. Invoke the appointment dialog box by double-clicking a time in the schedule. (*Note*: if you are already on the desired date of the schedule, you can also double-click the time to invoke the Calendar dialog box.)

6. Using Figure 2.37 as a guideline, enter the information for this meeting. The meeting should be scheduled for Tuesday of next week. All other entries should stay the same.

7. Invite the other group project members by doing the following: click the Attendee Availability tab; click the Invite Others button; hold down (CTRL) and click each of the other project members; click the Required button; click the OK button. Your Attendee Availability tab should now look like that depicted in Figure 2.42. Click the Send button to send out notices of the meeting. If you add the wrong person, select Delete form the context menu.

8. Save and close.

Save and Close	Click to close the dialog box. You are returned to the Calendar feature.

9. Verify that the meeting is scheduled.

Click	Click on Tuesday of next week on the calendar. The appointment should appear with a blue bar to its left (Figure 2.42). The bell indicates that a reminder has been scheduled, while the heads indicate that others have been invited.

10. Use the Calendar feature to schedule a seminar for Wednesday, Thursday, and Friday of next week.

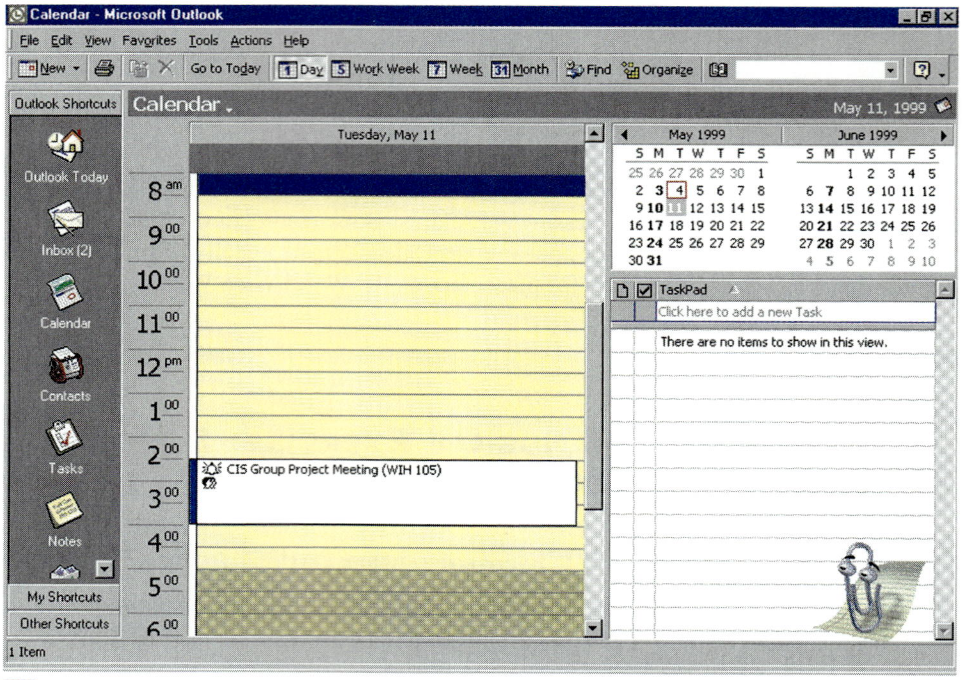

FIGURE 2.42 **The CIS 120 Group Meeting appears on the calendar.**

11. Schedule the CIS 120 class for 4:00 to 7:00 p.m. each Monday evening using the following criteria: begin with this Monday; double-click 4:00 p.m. on the schedule; set the ending time for 7:00 p.m.; click the Recurrence button on the toolbar; make certain that the dialog box will properly schedule the class for each Monday; specify the last week of the semester for End by; click the OK button. Issue the Save and Close command.

12. Check several Monday schedules to verify that the time is reserved.

13. Activate the Inbox pane and get any E-mail messages. You should have an announcement of the group project meeting like that depicted in Figure 2.43.

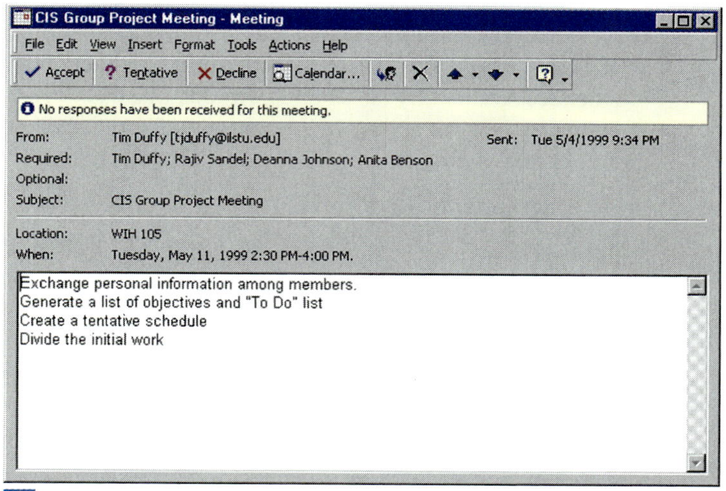

FIGURE 2.43 **The E-mail message sent to CIS 120 Group members about the meeting.**

14. Go back to the Calendar feature.

15. Print the calendar. Click the Print button. Specify the Monthly calendar. Click the OK button.

16. Generate a Web page for the following week using the following steps: click the Work Week button of the toolbar; issue the File, Save as Web Page command sequence; use the Browse button to change the directory to that used for storing your student files; type *M2Next_Wee*k for the filename, and click the Select button. The finished dialog box should look like Figure 2.44. Click the Save button to create the Web page.

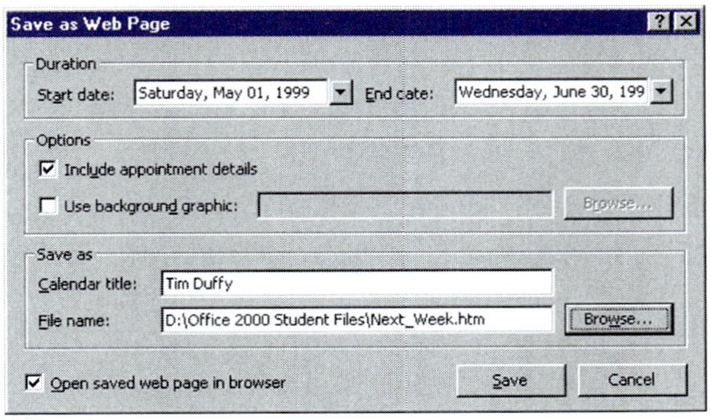

FIGURE 2.44 The completed Save as Web Page dialog box.

17. Click the Save button to create the Web page. The finished Web page appears like Figure 2.45.

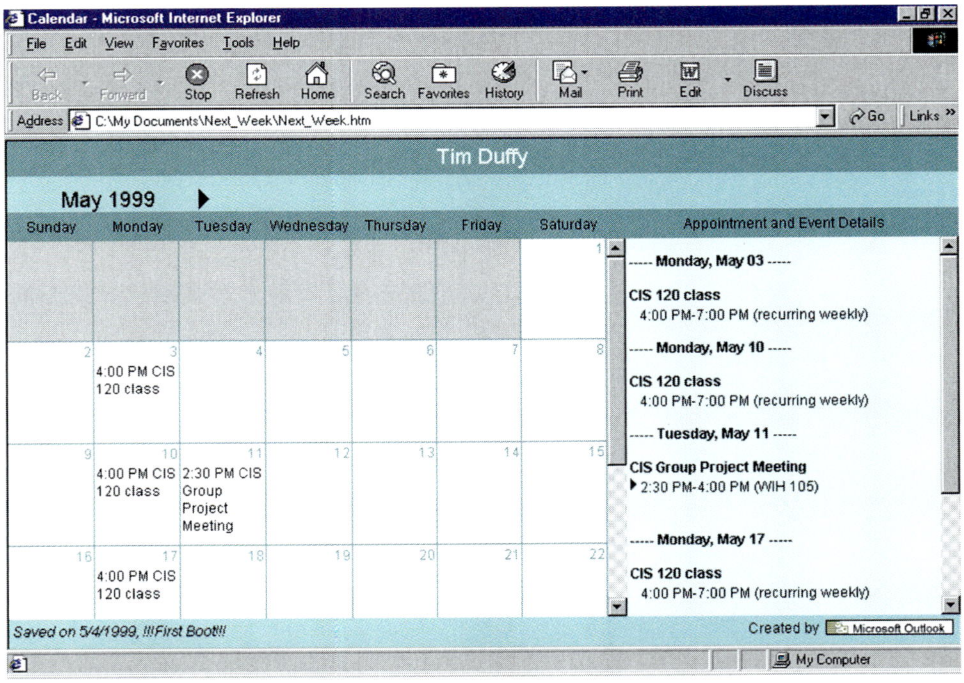

FIGURE 2.45 The Next_Week Web Page displayed by Internet Explorer.

TIMELY TIP

If it is available and supported by your installation, you can use the meeting scheduler to reserve such things as a conference room, audiovisual materials, and so forth. A resource must have been configured to have its own mailbox on your server. A designated individual in an organization is responsible for administering the mailbox. Once it is set up, the resource is self-sufficient, accepting and rejecting reservations/invitations automatically. To schedule a resource, simply invite it to the meeting (it will appear as a contact). If the resource is available, your invitation is accepted.

Reinforcing the Exercise

1. Appointments can be entered using the Calendar feature.
2. Appointments can also be entered directly on the schedule or by using the Calendar dialog box activated by double-clicking a time on the schedule.
3. A number of actions can be associated with an appointment.
4. An appointment can be a single event, occur over multiple days, or reoccur at the same time each week.
5. Multiple individuals can be scheduled and invited to a meeting. E-mail messages can be sent to the attendees.
6. A schedule can be published as a Web document.

USING THE TASKPAD OR TASKS FEATURE

The **TaskPad** appears as part of the Calendar, and allows you to create tasks that you or someone else is to perform. Once a task has been assigned, it can be tracked to see if it has been accomplished. Tasks are entered in the text box at the top of the TaskPad. If desired, you can double-click on the text box to open a Tasks dialog box (Figure 2.46). You can also invoke the Tasks feature to enter tasks. The Tasks pane (Figure 2.47) takes up the entire screen.

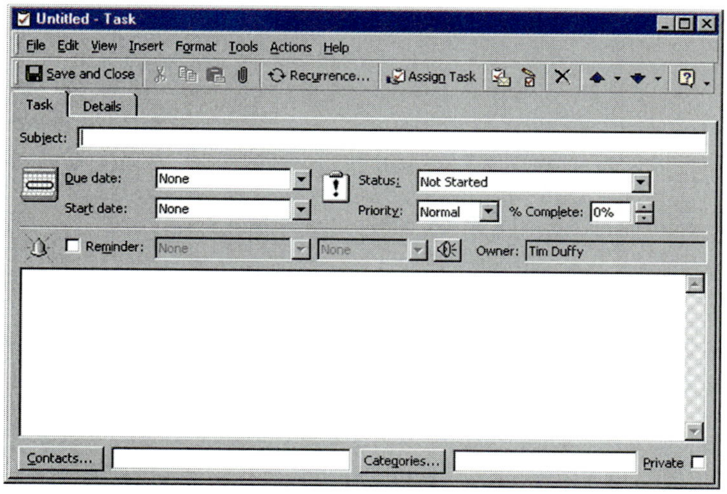

FIGURE 2.46 The Tasks dialog box allows you to indicate which tasks are to be assigned as well as to whom it is assigned and any relevant due dates.

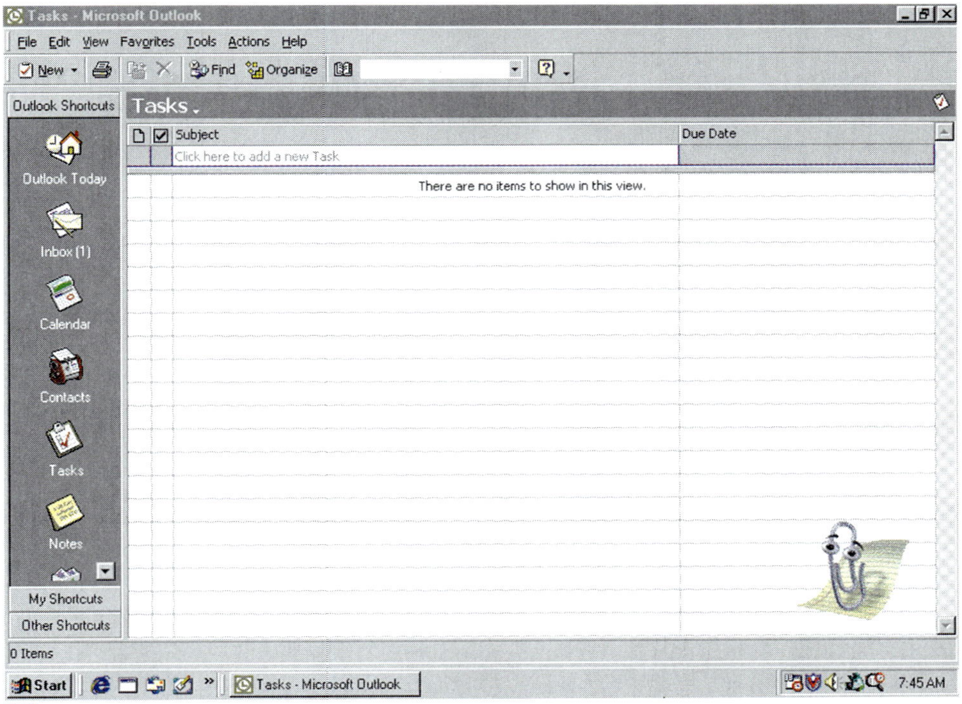

FIGURE 2.47 The Tasks pane can also be used for entering a to do item.

Once a task has been created it appears as part of your task pad in the Calendar. As you finish a task you can click the check box to indicate that the task is completed. A checkmark now appears in the completed box. Outlook also draws a line through the task text indicating that the task has been completed.

In the following hands-on exercise, you will be assigning tasks based on those shown in Table 2.5 for your group project. All assignments are due one week from today.

TABLE 2.5 Tasks Assigned to Project Group members

Name	Task Assigned
Your name	Review Microsoft financial statements.
Jim Dougherty	Research library for paper-based journal/magazine articles.
Anita Benson	Research library for on-line articles.
Rajiv Sandel	Search the Web for references.
Deanna Johnson	Research library for paper-based journal/magazine articles.

Assigned Tasks

An assigned task generates an E-mail message to the individual to whom the task was assigned. When the individual assigned a task receives their task-generated E-mail message they can accept the task, decline the task, or assign the task to someone else. If they accept the task, they become the new owner of that task and become the only individual who can edit that task. If they decline the task, it is sent back to the person who originally sent the task. If that person assigns the task to someone else, they can keep a copy of the task and receive status reports, but the actual ownership of the task is transferred to the individual who receives and accepts the assignment.

Hands-On Exercise: Assigning/Recording Tasks

1. If necessary, start Outlook 2000.

2. Invoke the TaskPad

Other Shortcuts — Click to invoke the Outlook Shortcuts grouping.

Click to start the Tasks feature. The Tasks pane now appears (Figure 2.47).

3. Enter the first general task.

Click — Click the task box at the top of the screen.

Type: `Call the organizational meeting`

(ENTER) — Complete the entry.

4. Indicate that you have completed this task.

Click — Click the blank check box to place a check there. A line now appears through the task text indicating that the task is completed

5. Assign the first task from Table 2.4. Remember that you are assigned this task.

Double-click — Double-click the text box to invoke the Tasks dialog box (see Figure 2.46).

Type: `Review Microsoft financial statements` If necessary, select any existing text and replace it with this text.

6. Change the due date to a week from today using the drop-down calendar. Change the start date to today. Your completed Tasks dialog box is now shown in Figure 2.48.

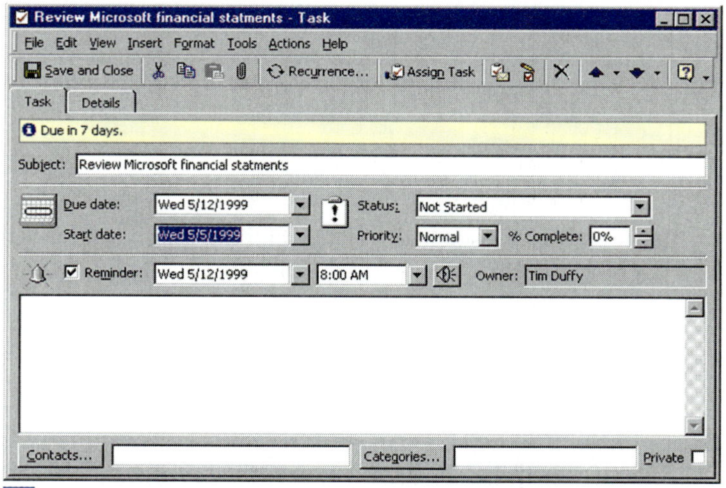

FIGURE 2.48 The completed Tasks window dialog box for the first assigned group project task.

Save and Close — Save the task.

7. Assign the remaining tasks to the other group members. First, activate the Tasks dialog box.

Activate the To: text box.

Click to activate the contact list.

Jim Dougherty Double-click this group project member to move to the Message Recipient box.

Return to the Tasks dialog box. Use Table 2.4 and the above steps to complete the Tasks dialog box. Notice that an E-mail message will be sent to this individual. Save the task. (If you forgot to include a classmate's E-mail, you will receive an error message. In that case, click OK when informed that this record does not have an E-mail account.) Continue to enter the remaining tasks.

8. Use the View, Current View to examine the types of views that are available. When finished specify the second option.

Timely Tip

When a task is assigned to another person, he or she receives an E-mail that allows him or her to accept or reject the assignment. You can also indicate reasons for your decision. Your response is returned to the sender.

9. Your completed Tasks list should look like Figure 2.49.

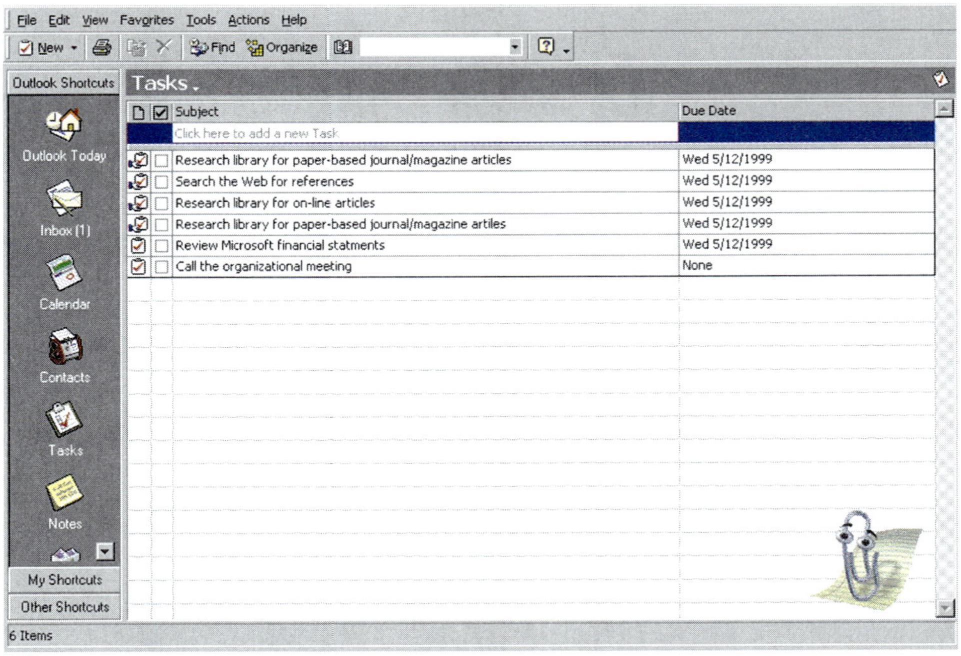

FIGURE 2.49 The completed Tasks window dialog box for the assigned group project tasks.

10. You can review a task by double-clicking the icon in the first column. A task window now appears summarizing that task. To actually edit the task, double-click the text entry for the desired task.

Timely Tip

When a task is overdue, the color of the task text changes to red.

11. Sort by subject. This involves clicking the title bar at the top of the screen. The position of the arrow indicates ascending or descending alphabetical order. You can also sort by Due Date.

On Your Own

Outlook provides the ability to link tasks entered via the TaskPad to a selected contact record listed in Contacts. Open the contact and enter the commands Actions, Link, Items. Next select the folder (Tasks, for instance) containing the information you want to link. Click OK. You can now invoke the contact window and open the Activities tab to see a list of items that have included this contact form, in this case, the Tasks folder.

Reinforcing the Exercise

1. Specifying tasks can be accomplished using either the Calendar or the Tasks feature.
2. The Tasks dialog box is invoked any time a task entry is double-clicked.
3. A task assigned to another individual generates an E-mail message to that individual.
4. The recipient has the option of clicking a button to accept or reject the task.
5. Overdue tasks appear in red.

MANAGING OUTLOOK APPLICATIONS

Features incorporated in Outlook provide the ability to manage how information is presented in its various applications. Outlook, as just demonstrated, provides the ability to rearrange how information is stored in lists by clicking the title bar to sort the data in ascending or descending order. It also provides the ability to create categories and store information entered via Outlook (tasks, contacts, and messages) using these categories.

Inbox

You can manage your E-mail messages by creating folders in which messages for various topics can be stored. As messages arrive in your **Inbox**, you are required to drag them to the appropriate folder. When a folder reaches the maximum number of messages that you have defined, you can archive messages and/or remove messages from the folder.

An **archive** is a storage area that can be used to store older messages to which you no longer have to have direct access. You can perform this manually by issuing the File, Archive commands to invoke the Archive dialog box. You can enter the date before which messages are to be saved. If you are at the Inbox, that folder is automatically selected in the dialog box. To set the archive date for other applications, select that folder and then specify the archive date at the bottom of the dialog box and it defaults to C:\WINDOWS\Profiles\user\Local Settings\Application Data\Microsoft\Outlook\archive.pst.

If you click the *Archive all folders according to their AutoArchive settings* button, the AutoArchive feature will automatically run whenever you start Outlook. The AutoArchive properties of each folder are checked by date, and old items are moved to your archive file. Items in the Deleted items folder are deleted.

Hands-On Exercise: Create Folders, Sort E-Mail and Archive Files

1. If necessary, start Outlook 2000.

2. If necessary, get to the Inbox.

3. Invoke the My Shortcuts grouping.

File Open the File menu.

Folder Click to invoke the Folder menu.

New Folder . . . Click to activate the New Folder dialog box. The Inbox folder should be selected.

Type: `Project Messages` Enter the name of the folder in the Name text box. Make certain that the Inbox is selected. Your finished dialog box should look like that depicted in Figure 2.50.

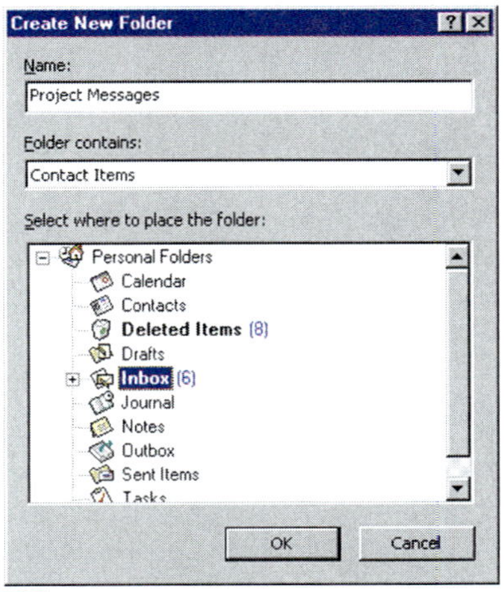

FIGURE 2.50 The completed Create New Folder dialog box for creating a Project Messages folder.

Click to create the folder. A prompt is now displayed asking if you want to create a shortcut and add it to the Outlook Bar.

Add the folder to the Outlook Bar.

4. Drag the project messages and any project messages that you have sent yourself to this folder.

Timely Tip

Once you have created the folder, you can drag messages from the Inbox to this folder. You can also use the CTRL and SHIFT keys to select multiple messages before dragging them to the new location.

5. Sort the messages. If necessary, get back to the Inbox.

Subject Click the Subject bar. Depending upon the original setting, the messages are now sorted in ascending or descending order by subject. If an up arrow is present, descending order was selected.

From Click the From bar. Depending upon the original setting, the messages are now sorted in ascending or descending order by sender. Again, the arrow position indicates the order.

6. If you click the paperclip button the messages with attachments appear at the top. Clicking the Received bar sorts the messages in order by date sent. Note that many Outlook applications can be sorted in this fashion.

7. If you have lots of messages in a folder and just want to view the last week's messages, select your folder in the My Shortcuts grouping and issue the following commands: View, Current View, Last Seven Days. Only the past week's messages are displayed.

8. If you receive messages that require you to do something, you can flag that message using the message using the commands Actions, Flag for Follow Up to invoke that dialog box. Click the OK button and the message is now marked with a red flag to serve as a reminder. Once you have completed the task, clear the flag using the same dialog box.

9. Archive messages using the command sequence File, Archive. If necessary, select your newly created folder and specify a date two days ago. Click the title bar of the calendar and then click this month to set the month. Click the OK button to set the archival date.

Reinforcing the Exercise

1. Outlook provides the ability to create folders in which specific types of E-mail messages can be stored.
2. Single or multiple messages can be selected. Selecting multiple messages requires using the CTRL or SHIFT keys.
3. Outlook application text residing under a bar can usually be sorted by clicking on the bar. The direction of the arrow indicates ascending or descending order.
4. Messages can be placed in storage areas called an archive and a date entered before which messages are archived.
5. Outlook checks to see if messages need to be archived each time it is started.
6. Messages needing additional attention can be flagged for later action.

OUTLOOK MASTER CATEGORIES

Categories in Outlook provide you with a powerful method of organizing information in the various applications that make up this software package. You can use the Edit, Categories command sequence to see listing of the built-in categories that Outlooks uses for classifying information according to some built-in method or organization (Figure 2.51). If you want to modify the Master Category list, click that button to invoke the Master Category List dialog box (Figure 2.52). From this dialog box, you can add, delete, or reset the categories. If you select the Reset button, any categories that you have added manually are lost and the original list of categories is used. Once you have finished with the following hands-on exercise, you will also have the CIS 120 category.

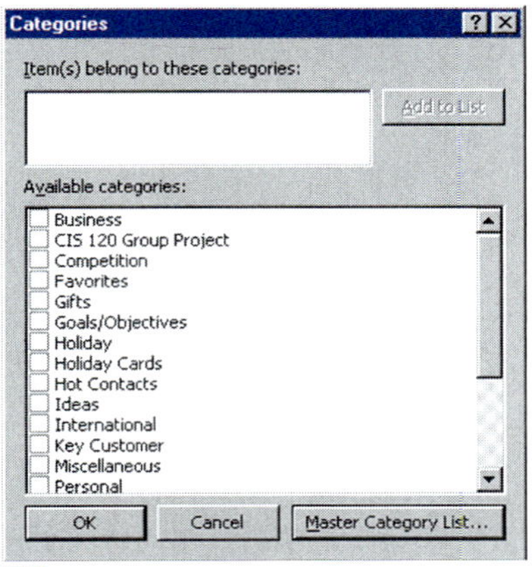

FIGURE 2.51 The Categories dialog box allows you to assign Outlook entities to a specific category.

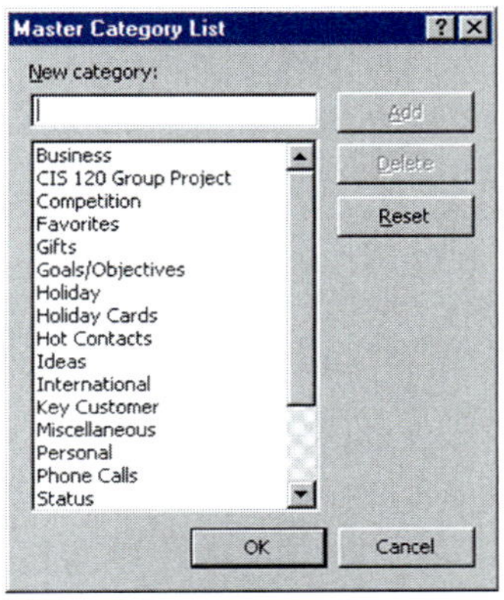

FIGURE 2.52 The Master Categories List dialog box allows you to create, delete or reset Outlook categories.

ASSIGNING TASKS TO CATEGORIES

Once you have created a category, you can assign tasks to that category (or any other category for that matter). Once tasks have been assigned to a category, you can use the Tasks feature to present the tasks organized by category. For instance, you can assign tasks related to the class project you are working on to the CIS 120 Group Project category. This allows you, via the Tasks pane, to easily keep track of tasks related to this particular endeavor.

Once the Task window has been activated, click the Categories button at the bottom of the window. This invokes the Categories dialog box. Click the desired category (Figure 2.53). When you click the OK button that category is now placed in the Tasks window. You can now finish entering the specifics of this particular task.

FIGURE 2.53 The Categories dialog box for assigning a task to a specific category.

After tasks have been assigned to a specific category, you can invoke the Tasks pane and display the tasks by category. If a category appears with a plus sign button, click the button to display the tasks in that category.

Managing Contacts Using Categories

Outlook allows you to create special categories for storing contacts, tasks, appointments, messages, and so forth when the existing categories that are used by Outlook are not sufficient. For example, you might want to place all of the contacts related to your group project in a special folder.

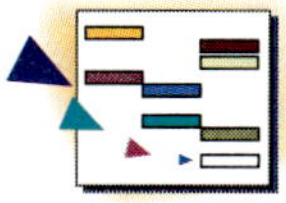

Hands-On Exercise: Creating and Managing a Category

1. If necessary, start Outlook 2000.

2. Get to the Outlook Shortcuts grouping and activate the Contacts application.

Click to invoke the Organize Contacts pane.

Click Activate the Create a new category called text box.

Type: `CIS 120 Group Project` Your completed pane should now look like Figure 2.54.

Click to create the category.

3. Turn off the Organize Contacts pane.

Click to turn off the Organize Contacts pane.

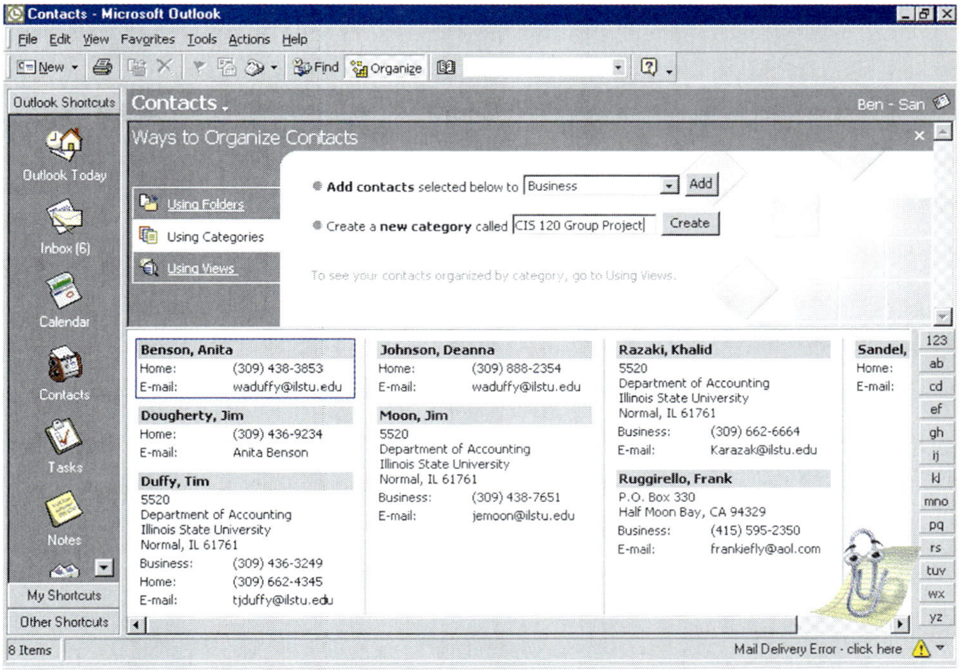

FIGURE 2.54 **The completed Organize Contacts pane with the appropriate records selected.**

4. Issue the Edit, Categories commands to verify that the new category has been added. You should see the just created category in the list. Click the Cancel button to close.

5. Add Contacts to the new category.

Double-click Select the first record (Anita Benson) and open the Contacts window for this record.

Categories... Click to invoke the Categories dialog box.

CIS 120 Group Project Click this entry. The completed dialog box now appears like Figure 2.55.

FIGURE 2.55 **The completed Categories dialog box for the first group project member.**

OK	Click to effect the change.
Save and Close	Save the change.

6. Update the remaining group members.

7. View the just created category.

View	Open the View menu.
Current View	Click to open the Current View menu.
By Category	Select this option. The Contacts are now arranged by category. You should see two categories. One of them should be the CIS 120 Group Project.
Click	Click the plus sign (+) to open the CIS 120 Group Project category (Figure 2.56).

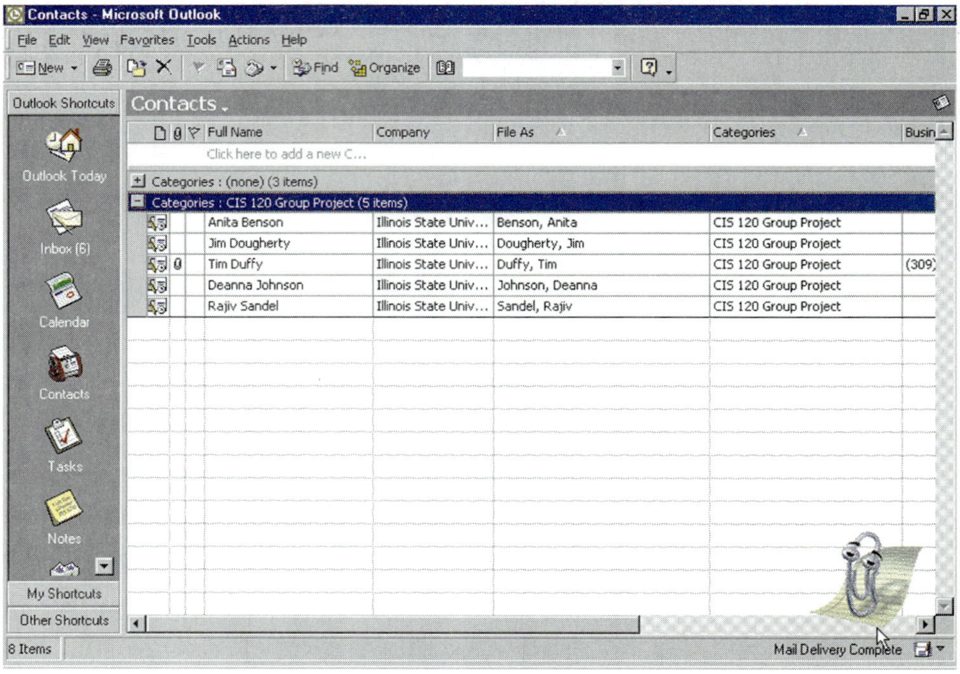

FIGURE 2.56 The category pane for the first group project.

8. Open the other category of records.

9. Sort the records by the Full name, Company, and then File As columns. If a column cannot be sorted, you will receive a message to that effect.

10. Issue the View, Current View, Address Cards to return the Contacts pane back to its original state.

11. Invoke the Calendar feature of Outlook.

12. Double-click a task entry on the Task Pad of the Calendar. The Task window appears.

Categories...	Click this button to invoke the Categories dialog box.

CIS 120 Group Project Click this option to select it.

OK Return to the Task window.

Subject: Click this text box of the Tasks window.

Type: **`Write first draft`** Enter the task topic.

Save and Close Click to save the task.

13. Enter the second task. Double-click a task entry on the Task Pad of the Calendar. The Task window appears.

Categories... Click this button to invoke the Categories dialog box.

CIS 120 Group Project Click this option to select it.

OK Return to the Task window.

Subject: Click this text box of the Tasks window.

Type: **`Review and edit first draft`** Enter the task topic.

Save and Close Click to save the task.

14. Examine the tasks by category. Invoke the Tasks pane.

Click Click any plus sign buttons to open the tasks in the categories. You should now see a pane like that depicted in Figure 2.57. The task items in red are past due in this example.

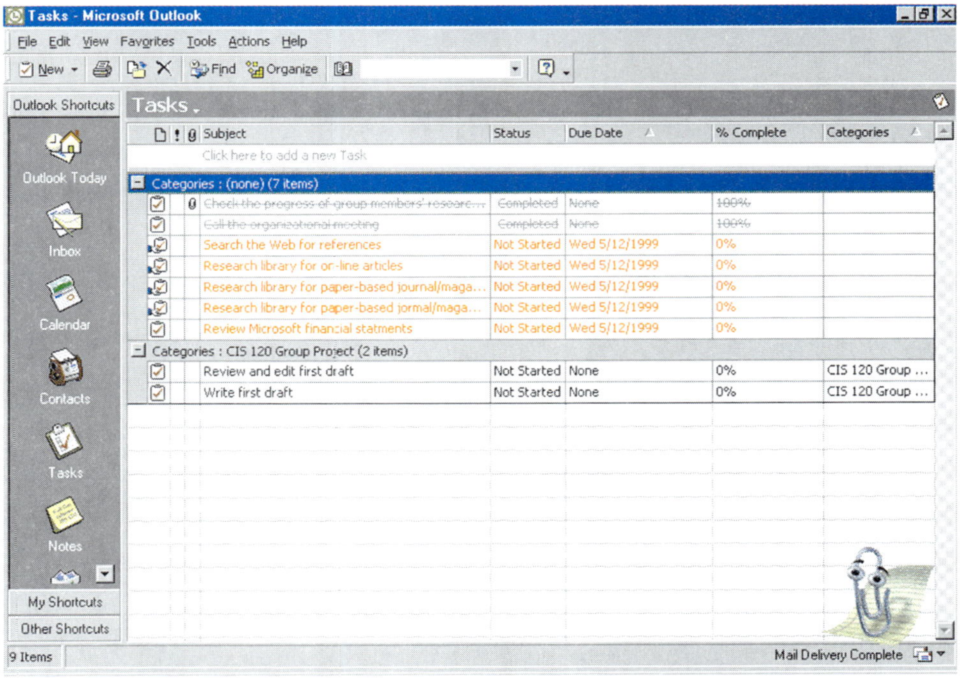

FIGURE 2.57 **Task window.**

Reinforcing the Exercise

1. Outlook provides the ability to store contacts in a special category.
2. Click the Organize button to invoke the Organize pane.
3. Once a category is created, contacts can be added using the Categories button of the Contacts dialog box.
4. Use the View, Current View, by Category to see a listing of the records in a specific category.
5. Once any categories are opened, information can be sorted by clicking on the title bars of columns that can be sorted.

USING THE NOTES FEATURE

The Outlook **Notes** feature creates notes that are the equivalent of sticky notes. You can use notes to write down questions, ideas, reminders or anything else that you would write down on a piece of note paper. Notes can also be used to store information you may need later, directions to Saturday night's party, for instance.

Notes can be left open on the screen while you work, or they can be saved for later use. When you make changes to a note, the changes are automatically saved. You can edit notes just like you would any other message or document file.

Hands-On Exercise: Creating and Managing Notes

1. If necessary, start Outlook 2000.

2. Get to the Outlook Shortcuts grouping.

Click to activate the Notes application.

Right-click Invoke the context menu by right-clicking in the Notes pane.

New Note Click to create a blank note (Figure 2.58). Notice that the note looks like a standard sticky note, but also has a title bar and a Close button. The date and time are also recorded at the bottom of the note.

Type: `Check the status of group members' research for the CIS 120 project on Thursday.` Enter the text of the note.

Click to close the note. The note is now placed on the Notes pane. A note icon appears above the note text.

3. Edit the note.

Double-click Open the note by double-clicking anywhere on the note.

status Double-click this word to select it.

Type: `progress` Enter the new word.

Click to close the note.

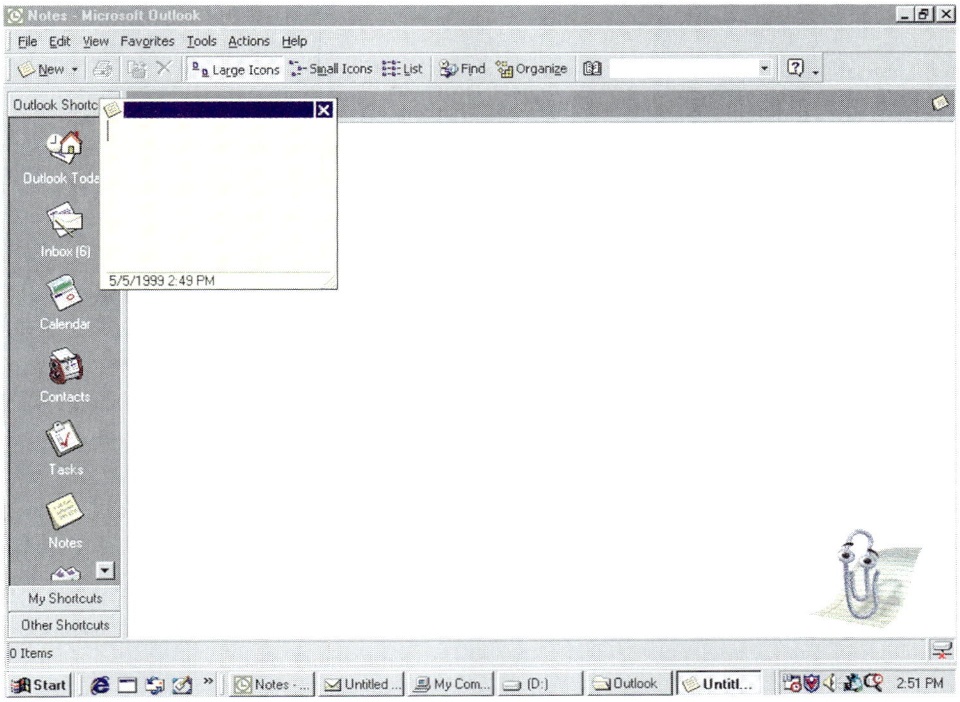

FIGURE 2.58 **A note created in the Notes pane.**

4. Move the Note to the Tasks pane.

Click to invoke the Organize pane for the Notes application.

Click to invoke the drop-down menu.

Other folder . . . Click to invoke the Select Folder dialog box.

Tasks Select the Tasks folder.

Click to indicate where the note is to reside.

Click to move the note. A new Tasks window appears with the note in the comment section.

5. Save the change.

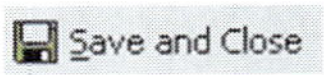

Save the change and close the window.

6. Verify that the note has been moved.

You should now see the note as part of the TaskPad. Double-click the task to open the Tasks window. Double-click the note icon to read the note.

On Your Own

Outlook also allows you to control exactly how you want your notes to appear. Issue the Tools, Options commands. Get to the Preferences tab and click the Note Options button to invoke that dialog box. You can now change the color of the note, size of the note, and the font used to create the note.

Reinforcing the Exercise

1. Outlook provides the ability to create sticky like notes.
2. Notes are initially stored on the Notes pane.
3. A note can be moved using the Organize button of the Notes pane.
4. Outlook also permits you to customize your notes.

PRINTING

Outlook provides you with great flexibility in printing a document that resides in an Outlook application. You typically have the choice of printing an item or a view. Previously we printed your record from the contacts list as well as an E-mail message. These are examples of items. You may also have the option of printing an item when you invoke the Print dialog box. Items are usually listed in a selection box. You select the item/style that you want to print and then click the OK button to print that entity.

You may have a specific view activated (the Work Week on the Calendar feature, for example) and want to print it. When you click the Print icon, that style comes up as the default, click the OK button to proceed.

To control how the actual output is generated, the paper used, the headers/footers that appear on each page, and so forth, click the Page Setup button to invoke that dialog box. Once your changes are made, click the OK button and return to the Print dialog box. Once any other changes are made, click the OK button to start printing. Figure 2.59 depicts the print dialog box for the Contacts feature. Click the Preview button to see a Print Preview window showing exactly how the document will print.

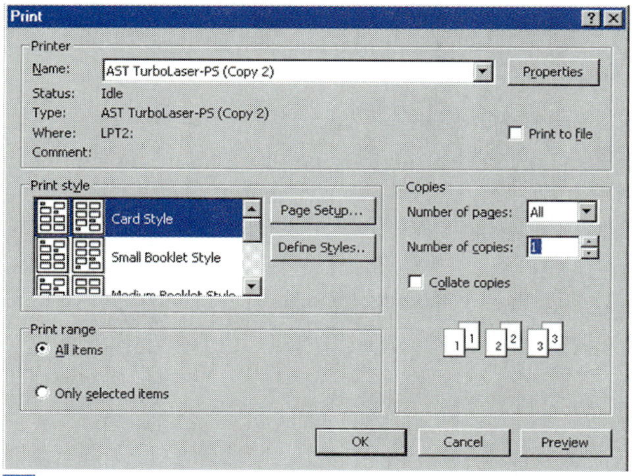

FIGURE 2.59 A Print dialog box for the Contacts feature of Outlook.

Hands-On Exercise: Printing

1. If necessary, start Outlook 2000.

2. Get to the Outlook Shortcuts grouping and start the Contacts application.

Invoke the Contacts Print dialog box (Figure 2.59).

Click to see how the document will print. The Print Preview window now appears. When you have finished examining the preview, click the Close button.

Reinvoke the Print dialog box.

Print the document.

3. Activate the Calendar application. Click the Month button in the toolbar to place the calendar in month mode.

Timely Tip

Many times you can print just one entity by invoking the context menu and selecting the Print option. You did this when you printed out your Contacts record.

4. Print the monthly schedule.

Invoke the Calendar Print dialog box. Verify that the Monthly Style is selected. Verify that only this month will be printed using the Start and End boxes.

Print the document.

Reinforcing the Exercise

1. Outlook provides versatility in printing documents.
2. Clicking the Print icon of the toolbar usually invokes the Print dialog box.
3. Use the Preview button of the Print dialog box to see exactly how a document will print.
4. Use the Print command from the context menu to print a single item.

On Your Own

Invoke the Outlook Today feature from the Outlook Shortcuts grouping.

What has been the effect of the changes that you made this session?

Session Review

Outlook provides you with the ability of a personal information manager (PIM) to track contacts, send and receive E-mail, track appointments, maintain to do lists, and keep notes about anything that you desire. Outlook can be open all the time and reduced to a button on the taskbar. When it is needed, it can be invoked by clicking the taskbar button.

The Outlook bar provides access to several groupings of icons. The Outlook Shortcuts grouping provides access to the various Outlook applications. The My Shortcuts grouping provides access to several other storage entities associated with Outlook. The Other Shortcuts grouping provides access to storage areas associated with your computer.

You can use Outlook to store information in the Contacts feature about people that you interact with in a business or personal environment. Contact/address information as well as some personal information can be saved using this feature.

Outlook contains an E-mail facility, which allows you to send, reply, and forward messages, and it contains features found in most popular E-mail software packages.

Appointments can be created and warnings about important meetings can be issued. A meeting for a specific time, several days, or one which reoccurs at the same time over a specific time period can be scheduled. Invitations can be sent to other people.

Key Terms and Concepts

application pane 52
archive 90
Calendar 79
Contacts 55
E-mail 61
Inbox 90
menu bar 52
Notes 98
Outlook bar 50
Standard toolbar 52
TaskPad 86
title bar 52

Session Quiz

Multiple Choice

1. Which of the following is not a valid Outlook application?
   - **a.** Inbox/E-mail
   - **b.** Calendar
   - **c.** Post-it
   - **d.** Contacts
2. Which of the following groupings is NOT present in the Contacts bar?
   - **a.** Outlook Shortcuts
   - **b.** Project Shortcuts
   - **c.** My Shortcuts
   - **d.** Other Shortcuts
3. Which of the following is NOT a valid E-mail operation?
   - **a.** Send a message.
   - **b.** Forward a message.
   - **c.** Reply to a message.
   - **d.** All of the above are valid E-mail operations.
4. Which of the following statements about the Calendar feature are false?
   - **a.** Appointments can be directly entered on the date of the monthly calendar.
   - **b.** Appointments can be entered directly in the time spot of the schedule.
   - **c.** No multi-day appointments can be entered.
   - **d.** Double-clicking a schedule time invokes the Appointment window.
5. Which of the following statements about Printing is false?
   - **a.** You cannot invoke a print operation via the context menu.
   - **b.** Clicking the Print toolbar button usually invokes the Print dialog box.
   - **c.** Click the Preview button on the Print dialog box to see exactly how a document will print.
   - **d.** All of the above statements are true.

True/False

6. No folders can be added to the Outlook bar.
7. Because it takes up so many computer resources, one limitation of Outlook is that it cannot be constantly running.
8. Any type of information can be included in an Outlook note.
9. Contacts records can be grouped to form different categories.
10. A reminder about a meeting can be sent even when Outlook is closed.

Session Review Exercises

1. Define or describe each of the following:
   a. Outlook 2000
   b. Outlook bar
   c. My Shortcuts bar
2. The personal information manager provided with Office is called ______________ ______________.
3. The ______________ ______________ along the left-hand side of the window allows you to activate different applications or access different storage resources.
4. The ______________ entry of the My Shortcuts bar is used to store unfinished E-mail messages.
5. The ______________ feature must be activated to send or receive E-mail messages.
6. The ______________ feature is used to record appointments.
7. The ______________ ______________ at the top of each application pane changes to reflect the needs of that application.
8. The ______________ feature allows you to record information about business associates or friends.
9. The ______________ button at the top of the message window allows you to send a reply to the sender of the original message.
10. The ______________ button at the top of the message window allows you to send a copy of a message to anyone you wish.
11. The information entered in the ______________ application can be used to address an E-mail message.
12. A message ______________ can be used to include a file like a picture with an E-mail message.
13. When you double-click a time on the schedule of the calendar, you invoke the ______________ dialog box.
14. You can use the Outlook command ______________ ______________ from the File menu to create or edit messages without tying up a phone line.
15. When a task is assigned to another person, they receive an ______________ message.
16. Out-of-date messages are transferred to the ______________
17. The ______________ feature of Contacts allows you to group like contacts together.
18. The ______________ feature allows you to create sticky notes that can be placed in an application.
19. When you want to print a document, you usually interact with the ______________ dialog box.
20. Click the ______________ button of the Print dialog box to see exactly how the document will print.

Computer Exercises

1. Enter your class schedule using the Calendar feature.
   a. Be sure to open the appointment window.
   b. Make certain that you use the Recurrence button to indicate how long the class will last.
   c. Refer to the example in the session for information on how to accomplish this task.
2. Enter the following appointments for the CIS 120 Group Project. Each of them should be scheduled for one hour of time. If you enter a task incorrectly, right-click that task and then select Delete from the context menu.
   a. Two weeks from now—Review the research results
   b. Three weeks from now—Generate an outline of the paper

c. Four weeks from now—Divide the sections of the paper for the initial draft (assign each part to an individual as a task). Make certain that each individual receives an E-mail message about his or her assigned task. You decide who accomplishes which task. Make certain that your classmate responds so that the tasks will be accepted.
   - History of Microsoft
   - Operating Systems
   - Programming Languages
   - Application Software
   - Financial Position of the Corporation

d. Review and revise the drafts 5 weeks from now.

3. Once you have finished the tasks in step 2, create a Web document of your Calendar using the File, Save as Web Page command sequence. (This assumes that this feature has been installed at your installation.)
4. In this exercise, you will take text from an E-mail message and use that text to create a Word document.
   a. Use a copy command to copy the contents of one of your E-mail messages (select the text and use a CTRL + C command).
   b. Issue the File, New, Office Document command sequence to invoke the New Office Document dialog box.
   c. Double-click the Microsoft Word Document icon. You now get a prompt concerning where you want to post the document. Select the *Post document in this folder* option, and click OK.
   d. A blank Word document now appears on the screen.
   e. Issue the CTRL + V command.
   f. Click the Post toolbar button to save the file to the folder that was open when you started this exercise (the Inbox).
5. Have one of your classmates assign a task to you. Make certain that the appropriate task E-mail is generated by your fellow student and sent to you.
   a. Double-click the message in your Inbox that contains the task request.
   b. Accept, decline, or reassign the task by selecting the appropriate option.
   c. Add any comments by clicking the Edit the Response Before Sending option and type your comment, if any, in the text box.
   d. Click the Send button.

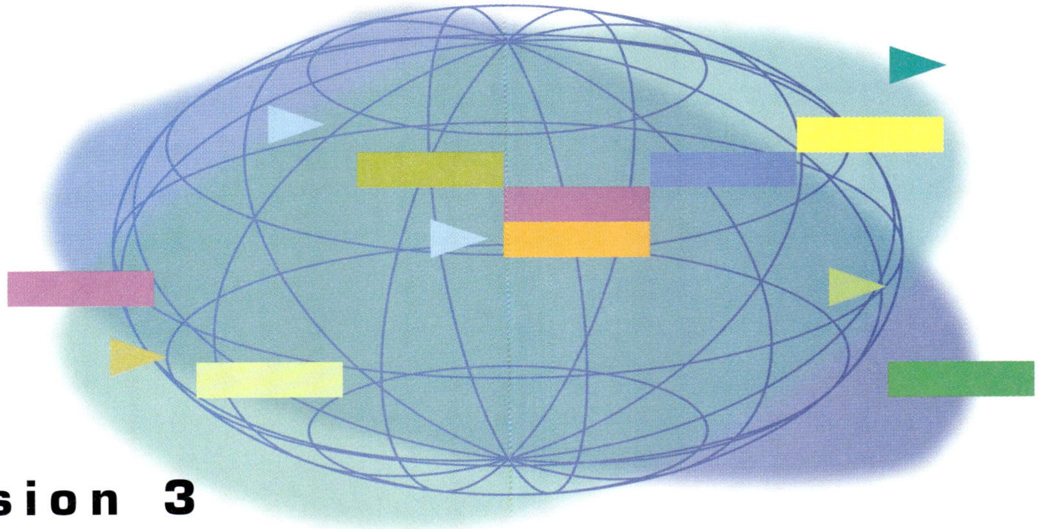

Session 3
Building a Web Page

After completing this session, you should be able to:

- Build an elementary Web page
- Use elementary HTML commands
- Use FrontPage Editor to build an elementary Web page
- Link to files and other sites
- Insert image files and text files in a Web page
- Control text display in a Web page
- Add a theme to a Web page
- Make changes to HTML commands created by FrontPage Editor

Your instructor may elect to wait until you have completed the Word portion of this text before starting this chapter on building a Web page.

INTRODUCTION TO WEB PAGE DEVELOPMENT

As you no doubt learned in the first session, the documents that you see on the Word Wide Web (Web) are called Web pages. Web pages are built using an easy to understand language called HTML (Hypertext Markup Language). This language controls the appearance of the Web page. Any computer that is running a Web browser program can read these Web pages and their HTML commands. This Web browser software translates the HTML commands and creates text, images, and plays sounds based on these commands.

When a Web page appears on your screen displayed via a Web browser, it appears to be a document with text and images (Figure 3.1). Actually, Web pages are simply text documents with embedded, special HTML commands or tags that tell the Web browser how to display the text and image files referenced by the Web page (Figure 3.2). These HTML tags are not visible in the browser, however, the text and images referenced by the Web page are visible. Any sounds, graphic images, or animations that you see appearing in a Web page are really separate files that are combined and displayed by the browser. The filenames, location of the files, as well as instructions on where to place the files are provided by HTML tags. An **HTML tag** is text contained between less than (<) and greater than (>) characters. When the browser encounters an HTML tag, it performs the instructions contained in that tag.

As a result of the various Web page components being referenced in HTML tags, different parts of a Web page appear faster than other components of the Web page. Typically, the page text appears first followed by any images or sounds associated with the Web page. The amount of time it takes a Web page to appear on your screen is dependent upon the speed of your modem as well as the amount of traffic on the Internet. The more graphics and sound files contained in a Web page the longer it takes that Web page to load.

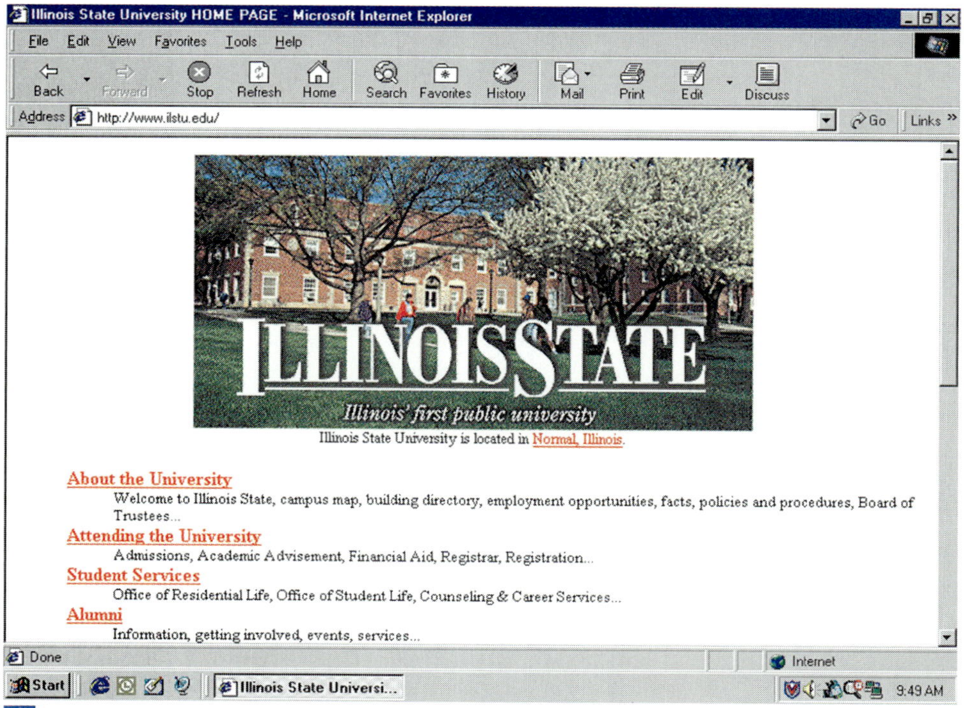

FIGURE 3.1 **A Web page displayed in a browser.**

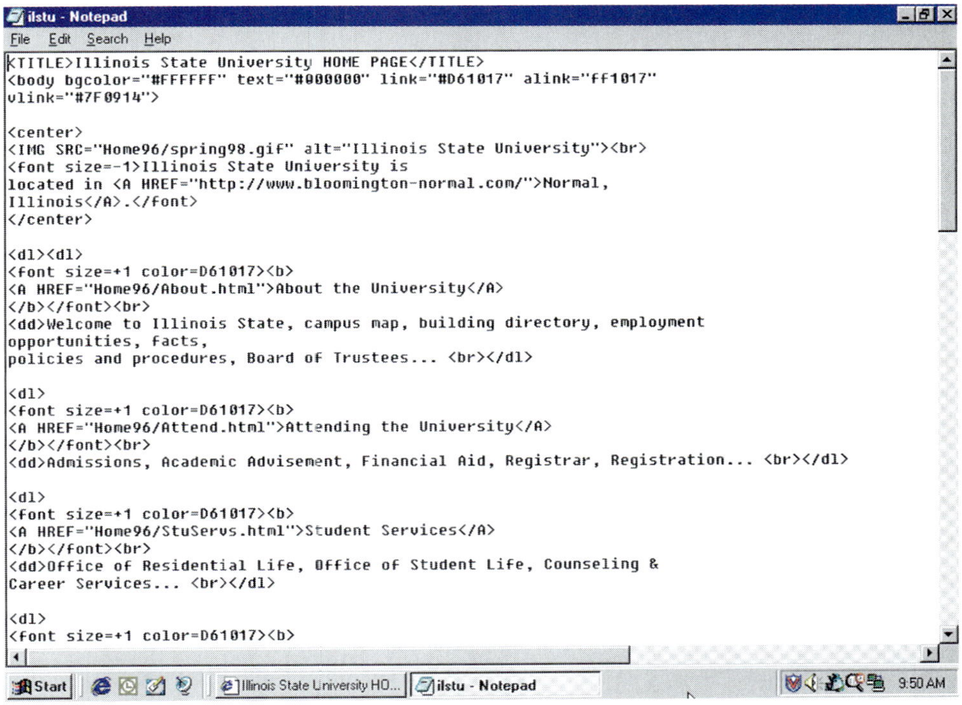


```
<TITLE>Illinois State University HOME PAGE</TITLE>
<body bgcolor="#FFFFFF" text="#000000" link="#D61017" alink="ff1017"
vlink="#7F0914">

<center>
<IMG SRC="Home96/spring98.gif" alt="Illinois State University"><br>
<font size=-1>Illinois State University is
located in <A HREF="http://www.bloomington-normal.com/">Normal,
Illinois</A>.</font>
</center>

<dl><dl>
<font size=+1 color=D61017><b>
<A HREF="Home96/About.html">About the University</A>
</b></font><br>
<dd>Welcome to Illinois State, campus map, building directory, employment
opportunities, facts,
policies and procedures, Board of Trustees... <br></dl>

<dl>
<font size=+1 color=D61017><b>
<A HREF="Home96/Attend.html">Attending the University</A>
</b></font><br>
<dd>Admissions, Academic Advisement, Financial Aid, Registrar, Registration... <br></dl>

<dl>
<font size=+1 color=D61017><b>
<A HREF="Home96/StuServs.html">Student Services</A>
</b></font><br>
<dd>Office of Residential Life, Office of Student Life, Counseling &
Career Services... <br></dl>

<dl>
<font size=+1 color=D61017><b>
```

FIGURE 3.2 The HTML command used to build the Web page.

Web Sites vs. Web Pages

A group of Web pages for an organization or some other entity is known as a Web site. Your university, for example, probably has a Web site associated with it. The Web site for Illinois State University is www.ilstu.edu. A Web site can be viewed as a catalog or magazine with a number of pages.

The goal of this chapter is to provide you with the skills necessary to build an elementary Web page that contains some personal information about you. This will emphasize interacting with a small number of files rather than the large number of files that are supported by a large Web site.

Planning Your Web Page

Before you start the actual construction of a Web page, you should have some idea of what you want that page to look like. You might want to generate an outline of the content of the Web page and manually sketch out where you want various images to appear in the document. If you are going to be including links to other Web sites, you can save time by having those sites to be addressed copied to a NotePad document like that depicted in Figure 3.3. Having Web URLs copied to a temporary file can save connect time waiting for a Web page to be displayed.

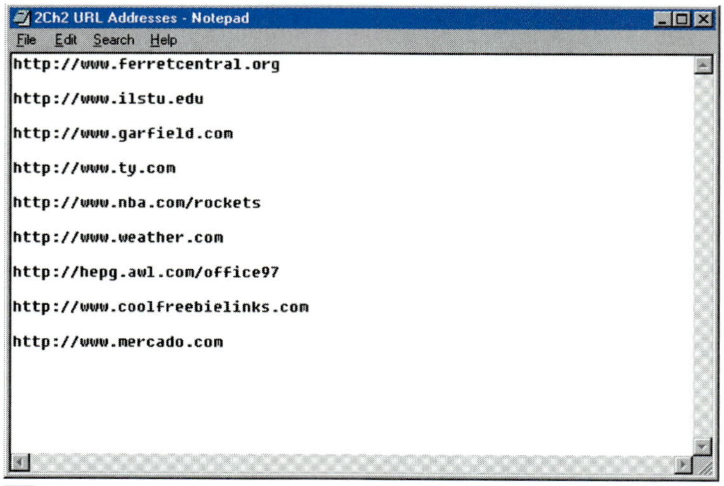

FIGURE 3.3 A NotePad file containing URLs that will be included in a Web page.

If you will be using prepared text files for insertion in the Web document, those text files should be ready and in the same location as any of your other files that you will be including with the Web document.

It is also a good idea to have all of the image files that you will want to include in the Web page in a central location. Typically these image files are usually either .GIF or .JPG files. If you use Office 2000 clip art images (.WMF files) in your Web page, those images can be displayed using Internet Explorer but will not be displayed using other browsers.

Timely Tip

The difference between browsers mentioned above (inability of other browsers to display Office clip art images) is only one of several documented incompatibilities among browsers. It is usually a good idea to use both Netscape and Internet Explorer to test any Web pages that you build. This allows you to see if any special affects or features that work using one of these popular browsers also works with the other piece of browser software.

HTML Commands

Historically, if you wanted to build a Web page, you were required to have an in-depth knowledge of the HTML language. Recently, however, Web editors, using the what-you-see-is-what-you-get (WYSIWYG) philosophy, provide a much easier method of building Web pages. A passing acquaintance with HTML is still desirable. If something goes wrong with your Web page's display or you simply want to make a minor change in the appearance of the Web page, or if you don't have access to the Web page editor, it is sometimes easier to make the change directly to the HTML code.

Hypertext Markup Language (HTML) commands are translated by the Web browser and the information is displayed according to the commands used. HTML commands are contained between less than (<) and greater than (>) symbols. Many HTML commands are used in pairs. The first command turns a feature on. The second command contains a slash (/) to denote the end of that command's influence and to turn the feature off. HTML commands can appear in either upper or lower case characters. Table 3.1 contains HTML commands that appear in every Web document.

TABLE 3.1 Basic HTML Commands for a Web Document

HTML Tag	Purpose
<html>	Beginning of HTML commands
<head>	Marks the beginning of the introductory portion of an HTML document
<title> The Name of the Home Page </title>	Name to appear in title bar
</head>	Marks the ending of the introductory portion of the HTML document
<body>	Beginning of the document body
The text of the Web document now appears.	Document text
</body>	End of the document body
</html>	End of HTML commands

Table 3.2 contains a number of HTML text attribute commands that cover such features as boldfacing, underlining, and italicizing text in a Web document. Notice that most of these commands are used in pairs. The first tag marks the beginning of the command, while the second tag marks the closing part of the command.

TABLE 3.2 HTML Text Attributes Commands

HTML Tag	Purpose
<b>...</b>	Boldface
<u>...</u>	Underline
<I>...</I>	Italics
<em>...</em>	Show text with emphasis
<strong>...</strong>	Boldface
<!---- comment -->	Comment to help document a command, ignored by the HTML processor

Table 3.3 contains a number of HTML formatting and alignment commands that are frequently found in a Web document. Notice that many of these commands do not require a closing tag.

Table 3.4 contains the various HTML commands that are used for creating bulleted lists, numbered lists, and description lists in a Web page.

TABLE 3.3 HTML Formatting and Alignment Commands

HTML Tag	Purpose
<p>...</p>	Paragraph (the </p> is not required)
<p align=type>...</p>	Paragraph with *left*, *center*, or *right* alignment
 	Insert a blank line
<hr>	Insert a horizontal rule line
<hr attributes>	Create a horizontal line with attributes of: align=type left, center, or right size=n height of *n* pixels width=n width of *n* pixels
<hn>...</hn>	Heading size where n can be a value from 1 through 6
<hn align=type>...</hn>	Heading with alignment of left, center or right
<address>...</address>	Specify the author's address information in italics
<BODY BGCOLOR="#FFFFFF" VLINK="#FF0000" ALINK="#800080">	Specify the various colors, using hexadecimal numbers, for the background color, color of visited links, and color of active links

TABLE 3.4 HTML Commands for Creating Lists

HTML Tag	Result
Bulleted List	**Appears as**
<ul>	
<li> Lotus 1-2-3	• Lotus 1-2-3
<li> Excel 2000	• Excel 7.0
<li> Quattro Pro	• Quattro Pro
</ul>	
Ordered List	**Appears as**
<ol>	
<li> Breakfast	1. Breakfast
<li> Lunch	2. Lunch
<li> Dinner	3. Dinner
</ol>	
Description List	**Appears as**
<dl>	
<dt> CBS <dd> Television Network	CBS Television Network
<dt> NPR <dd> National Public Radio	NPR National Public Radio
<dt> DSS <dd> Direct Satellite System	DSS Direct Satellite System
</dl>	

Table 3.5 contains HTML commands that are used to create hyperlinks. These hyperlinks can be used to insert a graphic image, jump to a different location in the same document, jump to a different document at the same location, jump to a document at a different location, or to specify a link for sending E-mail.

TABLE 3.5 HTML Commands for Creating Hypertext Links

HTML Tag	Purpose
<a>...</a>	Indicates that a hypertext link is being defined
<img src = file.gif alt ="Department of Accounting Faculty Home Page at Illinois State University">	Insert a graphic image. If graphic display is off, display the text following the alt parameter.
<a href="http://www.acc.ilstu.edu/ portfol/tjduffy/ welcome.htm">Tim Duffy's Home Page</a> Click to proceed to this location.	Specify a Web document at a different URL location
<a href="samplnks.htm">Visit a sample of World Wide Web sites </a>	Specify a Web document at the same location
<A HREF="#JOKES">Cartoons and Jokes</A>	Specify a location in same document
<A HREF="mailto:tjduffy@rs6000.cmp. ilstu.edu" > email</A>	Specify an E-mail location

INTRODUCTION TO MICROSOFT FRONTPAGE

As indicated previously, the **FrontPage** software program is capable of developing large, complex Web sites. Since we are concerned with concentrating on building a Web page, we will not be examining a number of features of this program. Start FrontPage by double-clicking the shortcut icon on the desktop or by accessing FrontPage using the Start menu.

Unless FrontPage has been reconfigured for your computer, when FrontPage is loaded, the window shown in Figure 3.4 appears.

The FrontPage window contains two basic parts: the FrontPage application window and the Web document window. The vertical line in the upper-left corner of the empty screen is the insertion point, or cursor. Its position shows where you will enter text or where a command will take effect.

Application Window

The **application window** shown in Figure 3.4 contains the title bar, application control buttons, menu bar, Standard toolbar, Formatting toolbar, status bar, scroll bars, workspace tabs, Views bar, and a blank Web document window. In the application window you can have multiple Web document windows open at the same time.

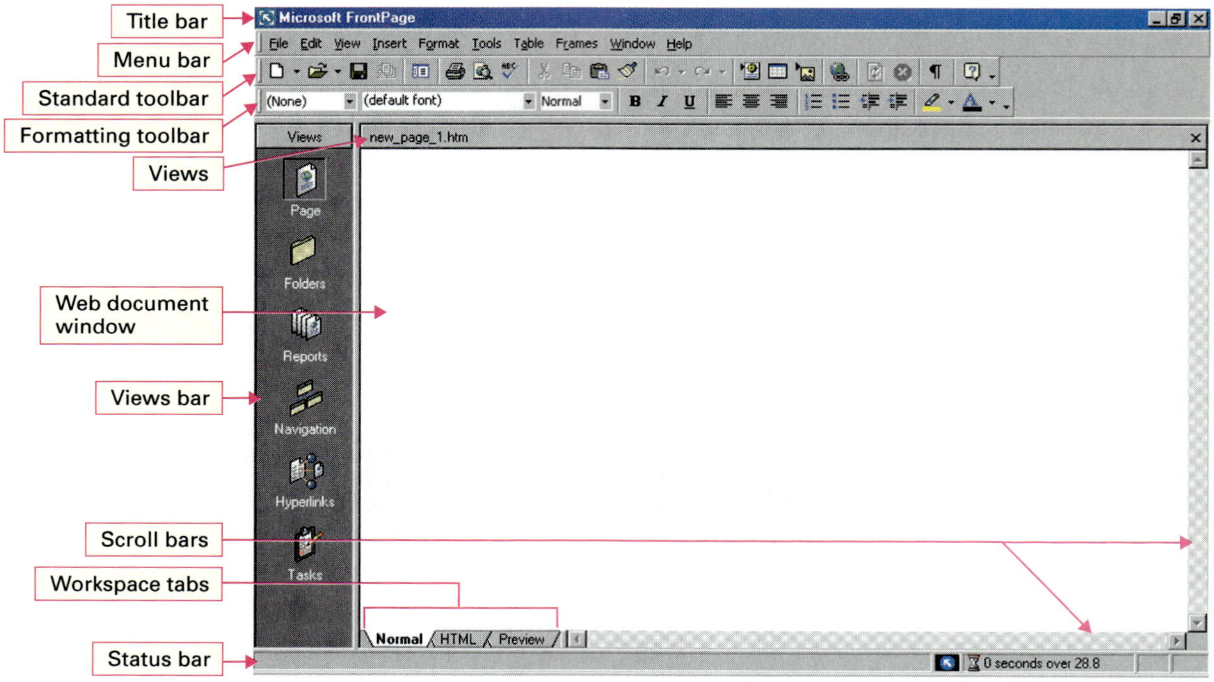

FIGURE 3.4 **The various parts of the FrontPage window.**

Web Document Window

The **web document window**, shown in Figure 3.4, is where you create, view, and edit a document. The name of the Web document is found in the bar at the top of the Web document window.

Views Bar

The **Views bar** (Figure 3.4) allows you to select the desired view by clicking on one of its icons. We will be concentrating on the Page view when building the Web page.

Title Bar

The **title bar** (Figure 3.4) is located at the top of an application or document window. It contains the application name (Microsoft FrontPage) along with the Minimize, Maximize or Restore, and Close buttons.

Menu Bar

The **menu bar** (Figure 3.4) contains menu options that activate pull-down menus. The menu options and menus displayed follow standard Office 2000 conventions discussed in Module 3.

Standard Toolbar

The **Standard toolbar** (Figure 3.4), located beneath the menu bar, contains buttons that enable you to execute commands more quickly than you can by going through various menus. Table 3.6 shows and describes each button.

TABLE 3.6 Standard Toolbar Buttons

Button	Button Name	Purpose
	New Page	Clicking on the down arrow allows you to creates a new page, Web, Folder, or task
	Open	Clicking on the down arrow allows you to open an HTML file or Web
	Save	Saves the active page or Web
	Publish Web	Send files to the Web server
	Folder List	Turn on/off the Folder List pane which displays the list of pages in your Web in folders
	Print	Prints the active page using the current defaults
	Preview in Browser	Activates the default Web browser and loads the page/Web in the browser
	Spelling	Checks the spelling in the active page
	Cut	Cuts the selection and puts it on the clipboard
	Copy	Copies the selection and puts it on the clipboard
	Paste	Inserts the clipboard contents at the insertion point
	Format Painter	Copies the formatting of the selection to a specified location
	Undo	Reverses the last action
	Redo	Undoes the latest Undo
	Insert a Component	Displays a menu of various types of objects that can be added to the page/Web
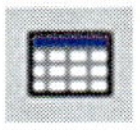	Insert Table	Displays a table icon that allows you to specify the number of rows and columns to be contained in the table
	Insert Picture from File	Activates a dialog box for inserting a picture or piece of clip art in the Web page
	Insert Hyperlink	Inserts or edits the hyperlink you specify
	Refresh	Used to effect some types of changes that do not appear immediately on the screen
	Stop	Stop loading a file
	Show All	Shows or hides nonprinting characters
	Help	Activates the Help feature of FrontPage

Formatting Toolbar

The **Formatting toolbar** (Figure 3.4) enables you to format characters and paragraphs. Using this toolbar, you can select formatting styles, such as the typeface and point size, or apply predefined styles to text. Table 3.7 shows and describes each button.

TABLE 3.7 Formatting Toolbar Buttons

Button	Button Name	Purpose
	Style	Applies an HTML style
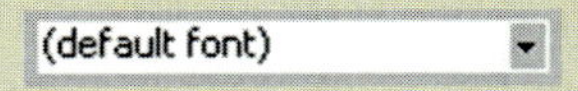	Font	Changes the font of the selection
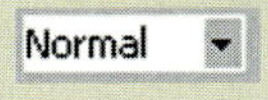	Font Size	Changes the font size of the selection
	Bold	Makes the selection bold (toggle)
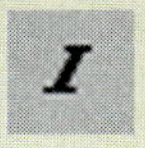	Italic	Makes the selection italic (toggle)
	Underline	Formats the selection with a continuous underline (toggle)
	Align Left	Aligns the left edges of all lines of text
	Center	Aligns the centers of all lines of text
	Align Right	Aligns the right edge of all lines of text
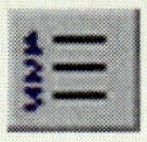	Numbering	Creates a numbered list based on the current default settings
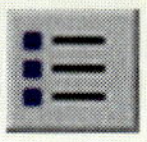	Bullets	Adds or removes the default bullet from the selected paragraph(s)
	Decrease Indent	Decreases the indent or promotes the selection one level
	Increase Indent	Increases the indent or demotes the selection one level
	Highlight	Marks text so that it stands out from surrounding text; the down arrow displays the colors
	Font Color	Changes text color; the down arrow displays the colors

Status Bar

The **status bar** (Figure 3.4) is at the bottom of the application window. The right side shows how long it will take to load the current page at the indicated modem speed. You can right-click this entry and change the speed/mode of access for the Web page. The required download time will then be recomputed. The status bar also shows the toggle keys status.

Scroll Bars

For most documents, only a small portion of the text can be displayed on the screen at a time. The scroll bars provide a way to move through the document in the Web document window. A horizontal scroll bar is located just above the status bar, and a vertical scroll bar is located along the right side of the document window.

Workspace Tabs

At the left end of the horizontal scroll bar are three **workspace tabs** (Figure 3.4), which control how the document is displayed on the screen. Table 3.8 shows and describes each tab.

TABLE 3.8 Workspace Tab Icons

Tab	Name	Function
Normal	Normal	This is the most frequently used tab because it is this tab in which you edit your Web page in WYSIWYG mode.
HTML	HTML	The HTML tab is used when you want to make changes directly to the HTML commands used in your Web page.
Preview	Preview	Displays the page as it will be displayed when accessed by a Web browser. You will see any animated images moving as well as hear any sounds that have been included in your Web page.

PREPARING FOR THE HANDS-ON EXERCISE

Before you can participate in the hands-on exercise for this chapter, you should have a number of files residing on a diskette that will be used to build your Web page. These can be downloaded from the Web site that accompanies this text. The files required for this Exercise are as follows:

Text Files

1. 2Ch3 Background Info	Word RTF file
2. 2Ch3 URL Addresses	NotePad file with Web URL addresses

HTML Web Files

1. 2Ch3_Term_Paper	Web document of a small research paper dealing with ferrets
2. 2Ch3_Ferret_Web_Flyer	Web document announcing Ferret Frolic
3. 2Ch3_Term_Paper_Presentation	PowerPoint presentation concerning ferrets
4. 2Ch3_Term_Paper_Presentation_Files	Disk directory with supporting presentation files

Image Files

1. 2Ch3_Yourpic	GIF image that can be replaced with a digitized picture of you
2. 2Ch3_Ferret_1	JPEG image
3. 2Ch3_Ferret_2	JPEG image
4. 2Ch3_logo	GIF image
5. 2Ch3_book1	GIF image
6. 2Ch3_Reggie	GIF image

Once you have copied the files to a diskette, you are ready to start the hands-on exercise that follows. You will need approximately 267KB of disk space for the above files. You are now ready to create the personal Web page shown in Figure 3.5. If you have a digitized self-portrait, include that file on this diskette.

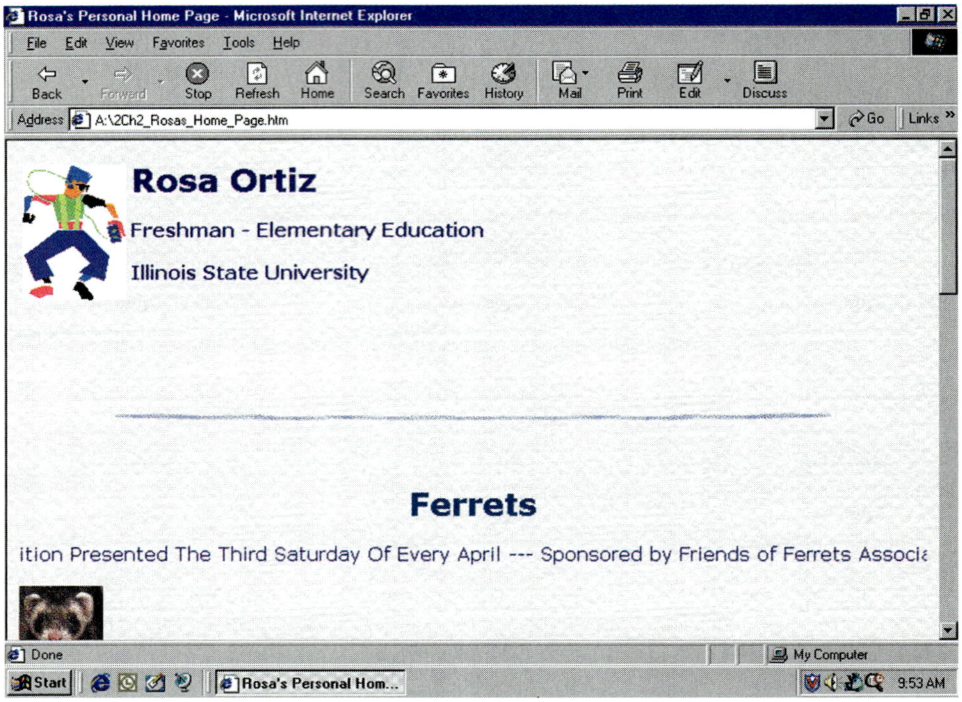

FIGURE 3.5 The first screen of the personal Web page to be created using the downloaded files.

Timely Tip

You have probably noticed the use of underscore characters in the above filenames instead of spaces. While Windows does not care if spaces are embedded in filenames, if such a file is used in a UNIX environment, it will not display to the screen in the browser. Since many Web servers are UNIX-based computers, it is a good idea to replace spaces with the underscore or some other character when you are creating or renaming files that will be used in a Web page.

Hands-On Exercise: Building a Web Page

The following hands-on exercise introduces you to some rudimentary FrontPage features.

1. Start FrontPage. If necessary, click the Maximize button to enlarge the FrontPage window (Figure 3.6). Those tasks which will not be capable of being seen using a browser other than Internet Explorer have an asterisk (*) in front of the numbered step.

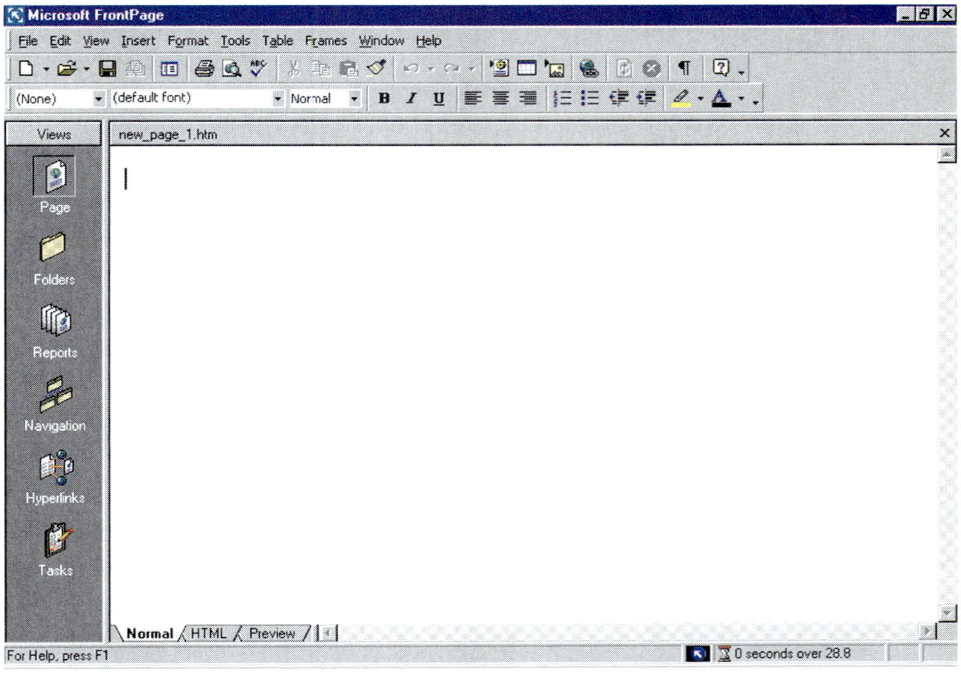

FIGURE 3.6 **The Front Page window.**

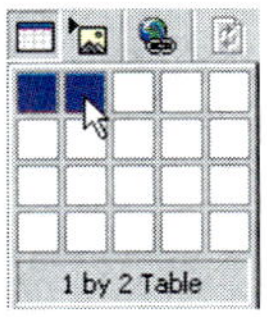

FIGURE 3.7 **The 1 x 2 Table specified in the Table object menu.**

2. Create a two-cell table to hold a picture and text.

Click to invoke the Table object menu.

1 x 2 Table Click this option (Figure 3.7) to specify a one-row table with two cells. Notice that the table is faintly visible.

Click the Show All button to make the paragraph marks visible (Figure 3.8).

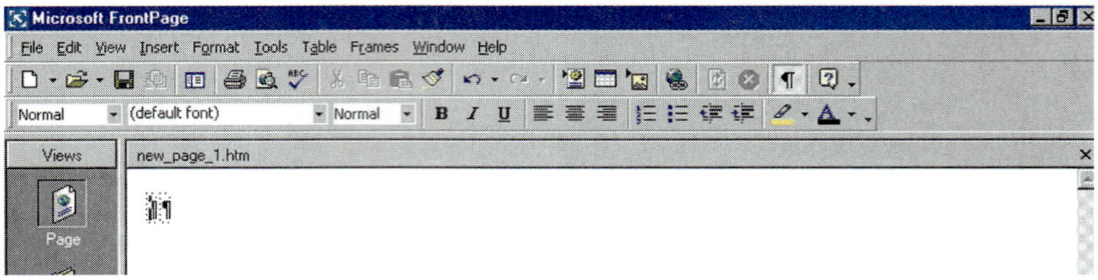

FIGURE 3.8 The created 1 x 2 Table made visible after clicking the Show All toolbar button.

3. Insert a graphic image in the first cell of the table. If you have a digitized image of yourself, you can insert it here.

Click the Insert Picture from File button to open the Picture dialog box. Use the Look in selection box to go to the disk/directory holding the Web files. This example uses drive A for creating the Web page. Your dialog box should now look like that depicted in Figure 3.9.

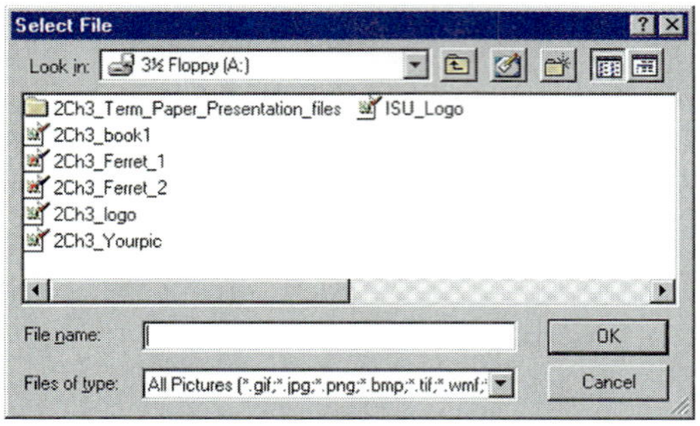

FIGURE 3.9 The Picture dialog box used for inserting a graphic image in a Web page.

2Ch3_Yourpic Double-click this file to insert it in the first cell of the table (Figure 3.10).

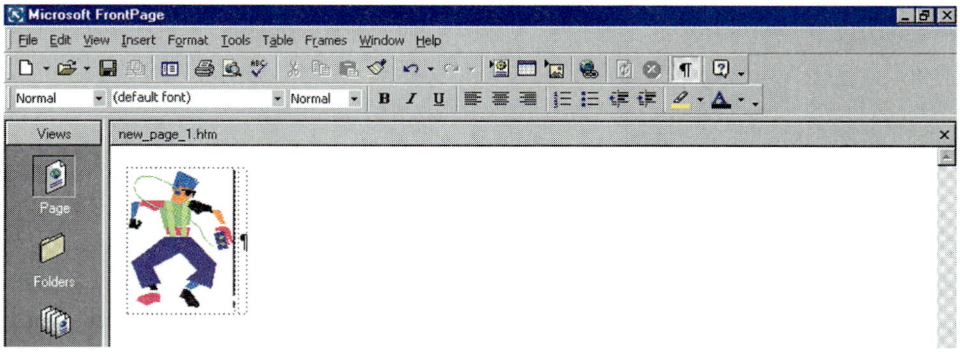

FIGURE 3.10 The image inserted in the first cell of the table.

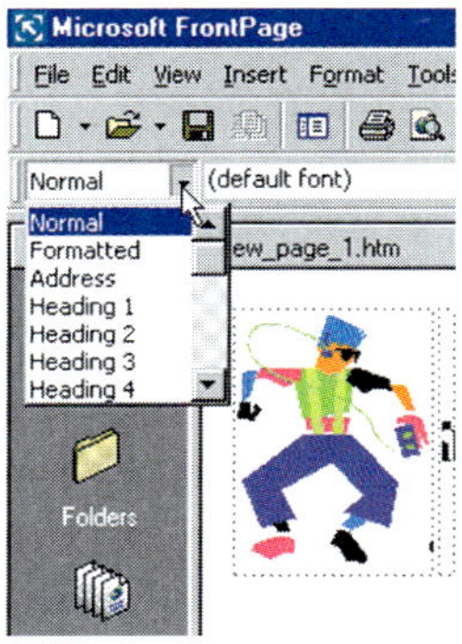

FIGURE 3.11 **The style menu controls the font size.**

4. Insert text in the second cell of the table.

(TAB)	Position to the second cell.
Normal ▾	Click the Style button to invoke the Style menu (Figure 3.11).
Heading 1	Click this style.
Type: `Your Name`	Enter your name in the Web page.
(ENTER)	Press to go to the next line.
Normal ▾	Click the Style button to invoke the Style menu.
Heading 3	Click this style.
Type: `Freshman–Elementary Education`	Enter this text.
(ENTER)	Press to go to the next line.
Normal ▾	Click the Style button to invoke the Style menu.
Heading 3	Click this style.
Type: `Illinois State University`	Enter this text. Your Web page should now look like that depicted in Figure 3.12.

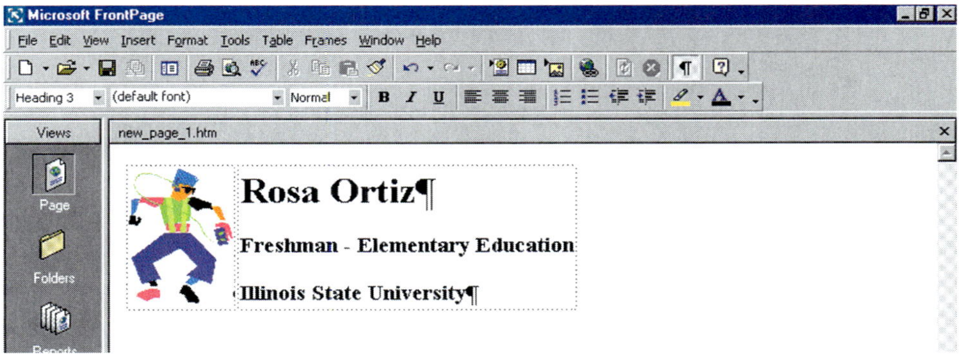

FIGURE 3.12 **The table with an image and text entered.**

5. Place a horizontal line in the Web page.

Click	Move the cursor outside the table to the line below.
(ENTER)	Press to insert a blank line.
Insert	Click to open the Insert menu.
Horizontal Line	Click to insert a horizontal line in the Web page (Figure 3.13).

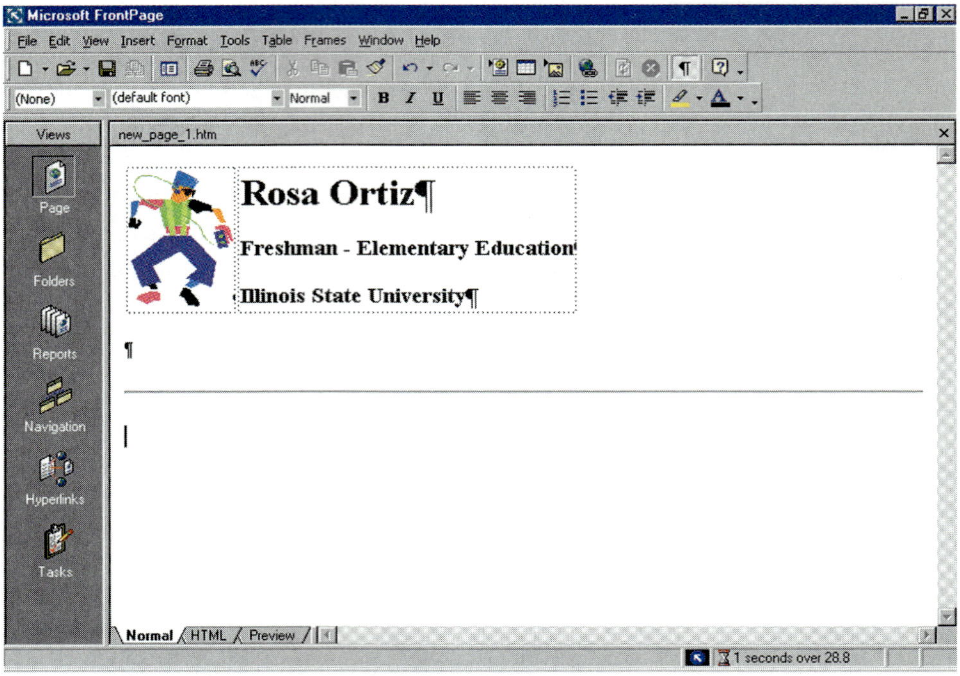

FIGURE 3.13 **The Web page with an inserted horizontal line.**

6. Create and center heading text.

(ENTER) Press to insert a blank line.

Click to center the text.

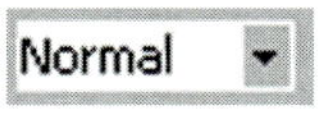

Click the Style button to invoke the Style menu.

Heading 1 Click this style.

Type: `Ferrets` Enter this text in the Web page.

(ENTER) Position to the next line.

Click to left justify text (Figure 3.14).

*7. Create a Marquee of moving text.

Insert Click to open the Insert menu.

Component Click to open the Component menu.

Marquee . . . Click to open the Marquee dialog box (Figure 3.15).

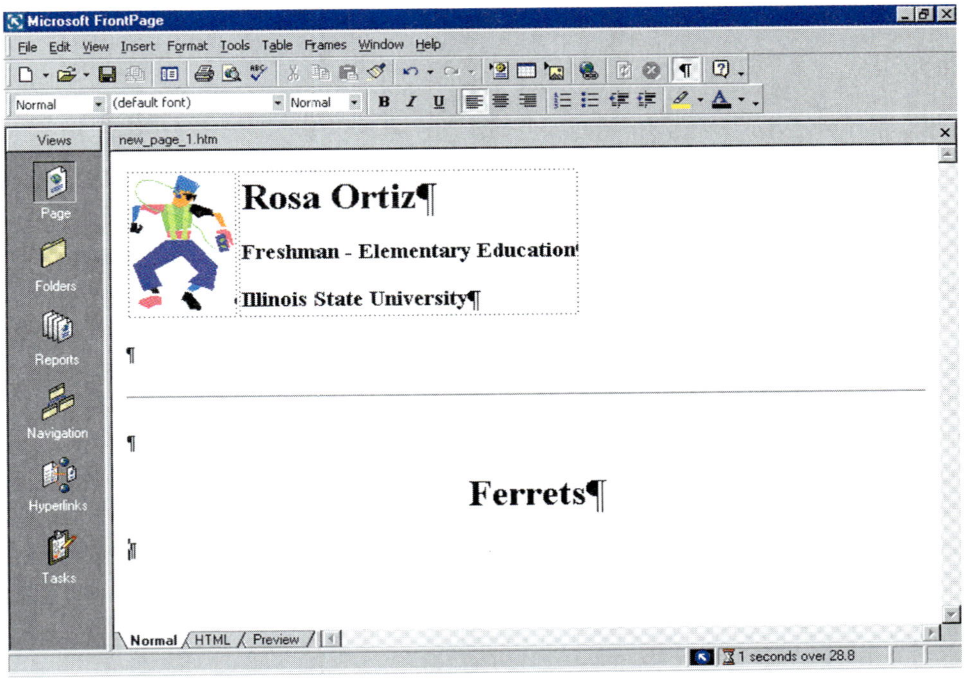

FIGURE 3.14 **The Web page with the centered heading.**

Type: **`Attend the Super Ferrets Exposition Presented the Third Saturday of Each April—Sponsored by Friends of Ferrets Association—Bring Your Ferret!`**

Enter the text for the marquee.

Click to create the marquee. Your Web page should now look like Figure 3.16.

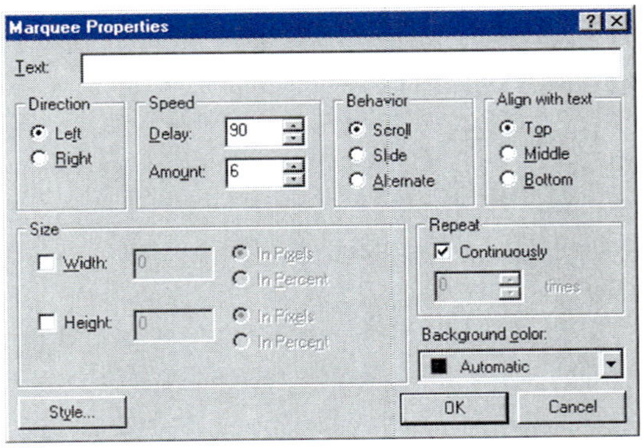

FIGURE 3.15 **The Marquee dialog box.**

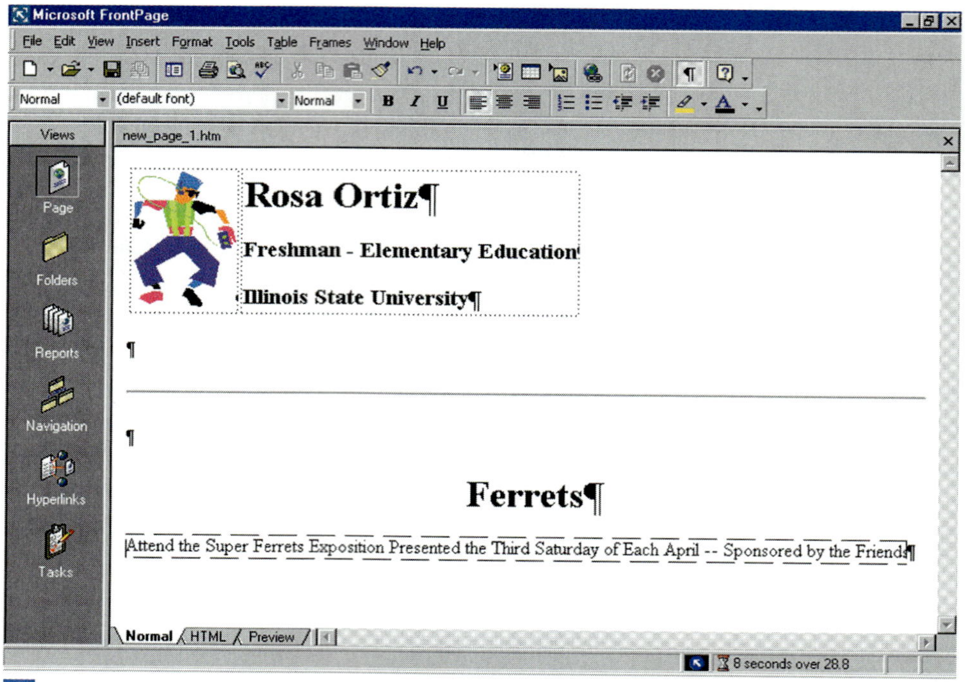

FIGURE 3.16 **The created Marquee text in the Web page.**

***8. Test the marquee.**

Click the Preview tab to see how the marquee works. You should now see the text you entered previously scrolling across the screen.

Click to return to the Normal tab of the FrontPage Web document window.

(ENTER) Press to go to the next line in the Web document.

9. Insert a graphic image and link that image to a document on disk. Once the link is created enter explanatory text.

Click the Insert Picture from File button to open the Picture dialog box. Use the Look in selection box to go to the disk/directory holding the Web files.

2Ch3_Ferret_1 Double-click this file to insert it in the Web page. A large image now appears.

Click Click the image to select it. Click the lower right-hand resize button and size the image so that it appears like that depicted in Figure 3.17.

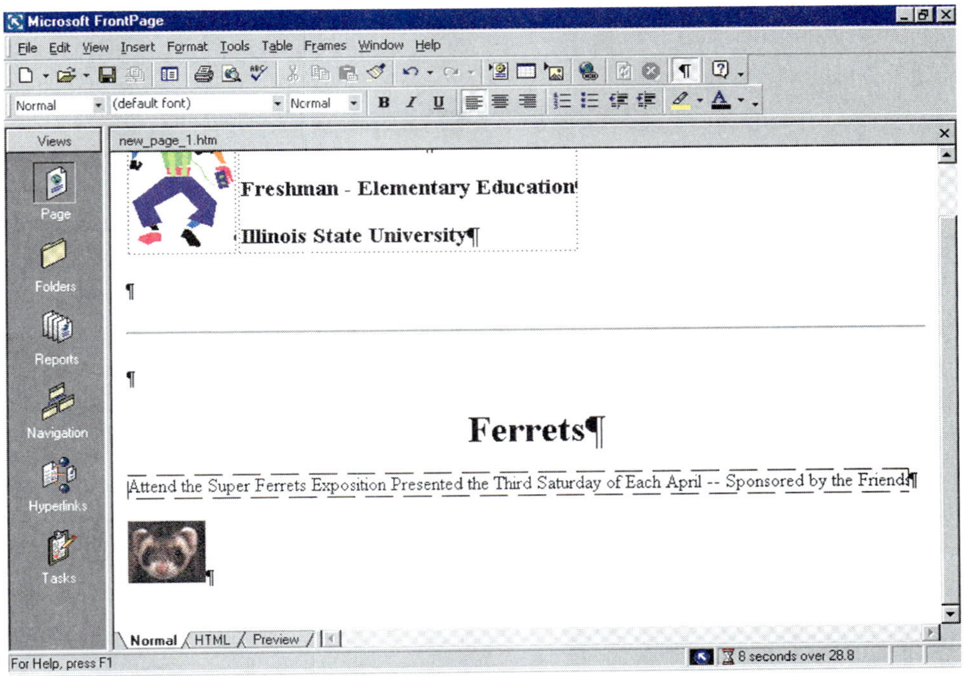

FIGURE 3.17 **The resized ferret image inserted in the Web page.**

*10. Link this image to a PowerPoint presentation.

Click Click the ferret image so that the selection handles appear around the image.

Click the Insert Hyperlink button on the Standard toolbar to invoke the Create Hyperlink dialog box (Figure 3.18).

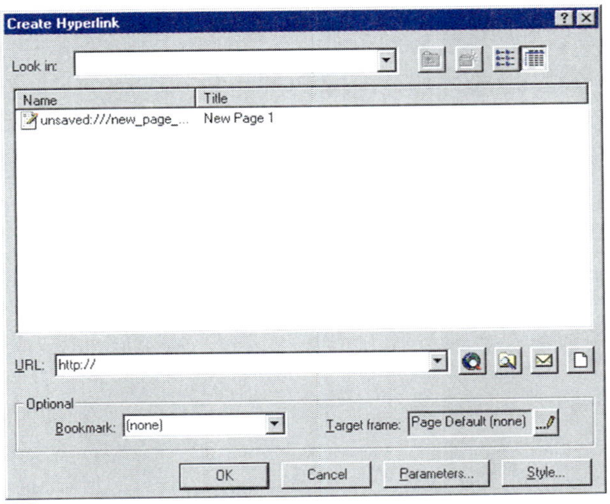

FIGURE 3.18 **The Create Hyperlink dialog box.**

Click the Make a hyperlink to a file on your computer button. This invokes the Select File dialog box shown in Figure 3.19.

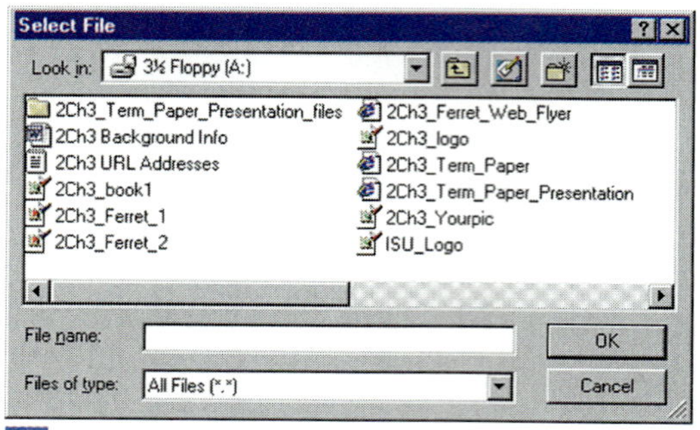

FIGURE 3.19 The Select File dialog box.

2Ch3_Term_Paper_Presentation Double-click this HTML filename to link the image to this file. You are returned to the Web page.

(→) Press to de-select the graphic image.

(SPACE) Press to insert a space after the image.

Type: `Click the image to see a PowerPoint presentation with an introduction to these friendly mammals.`

Enter this explanatory text.

(ENTER) Press to position to the next line. Your Web page should now look like that depicted in Figure 3.20.

TIMELY TIP

If you have an active Internet link and you also have Internet Explorer running, you can go to the desired Web site using Internet Explorer and then invoke the Create Hyperlink dialog box. The link of the Web site is automatically included.

11. Save the Web page.

File Click to invoke the File menu.

Save As . . . Click to invoke the Save As dialog box.

Look in: Use the Look in selection box to switch to the location where you want your Web file to be saved. This example uses drive A.

Type: `2Ch3_Rosas_Home_Page` Enter the name of the file. Your completed Save As dialog box should look like Figure 3.21.

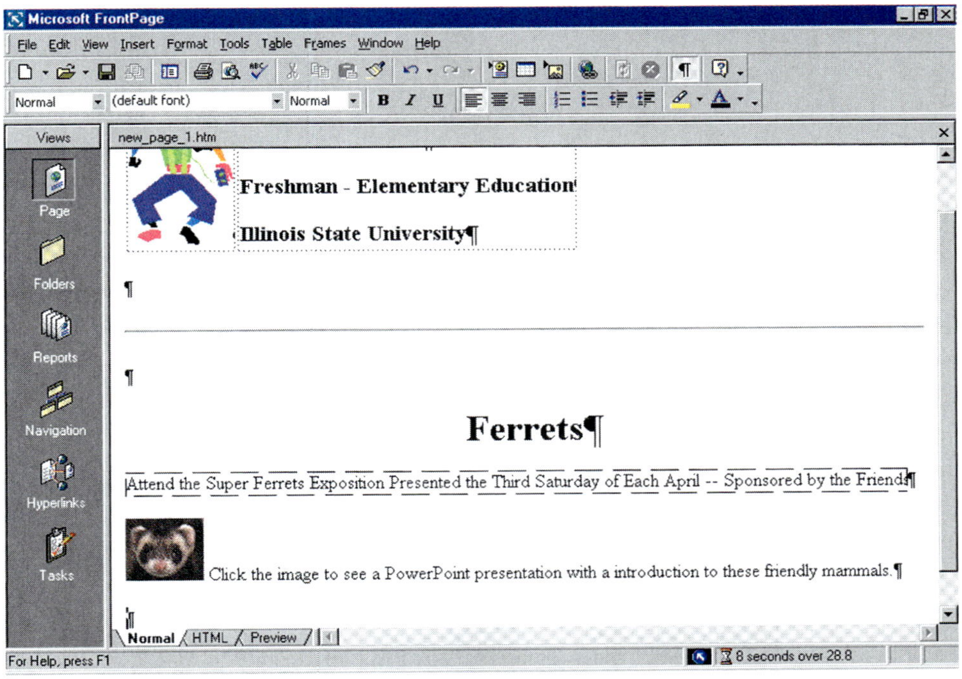

FIGURE 3.20 **The Web page with the inserted PowerPoint image link and text.**

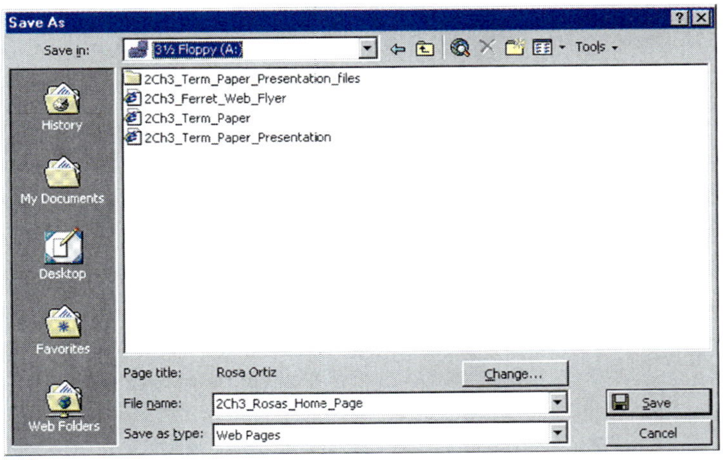

FIGURE 3.21 **The completed Save As dialog box.**

Click to save the Web document. Now when you start FrontPage you can access your Web page using the command sequence File, Open command sequence (Do not use the File, Open Web commands). If necessary, click OK button.

12. Test the link.

Click the Preview in Browser button to see how the Web page will appear. Internet Explorer starts and loads the Web page. You should see the moving marquee.

Click Click the ferret image. You should now see a PowerPoint presentation appear (Figure 3.22). Use the arrow buttons at the bottom or the slide titles in the left-hand frame to move from slide to slide.

Click the Back button until your Web page reappears.

Click to return to the Normal tab of the FrontPage Web document window. In the future, if you want to test your Web page; click the Save button, click the Internet Explorer taskbar button, and then click the Refresh button of Internet Explorer to load the saved changes.

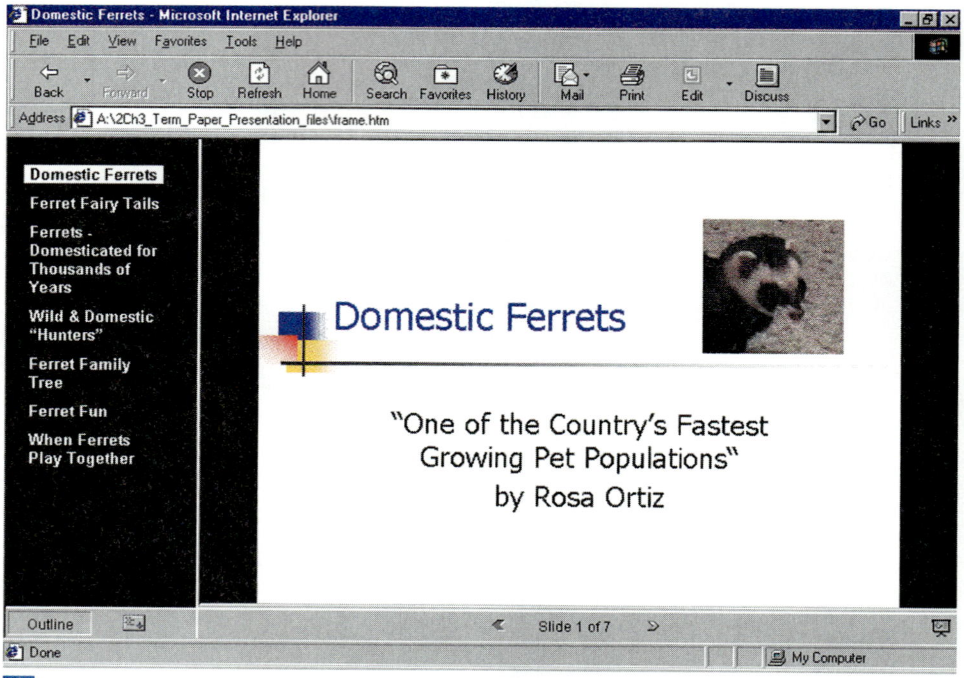

FIGURE 3.22 **The first slide of the linked PowerPoint presentation.**

13. Open the NotePad document with the various Web addresses that were trapped previously. You will be using the URLs contained in this document for creating your links to Web locations.

Click to invoke the Start menu.

Click to invoke the Programs menu.

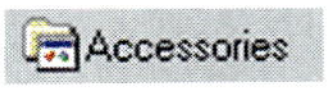	Click to invoke the Accessories menu.
	Click to start the NotePad program.
File	Click to open the File menu.
Open	Click to activate the Open dialog box.
Look in:	Change the disk/directory to the location where your Web files are stored. In this example, they are stored on drive A.
2Ch3 URL Addresses	Double-click this file name to load the document (Figure 3.23).

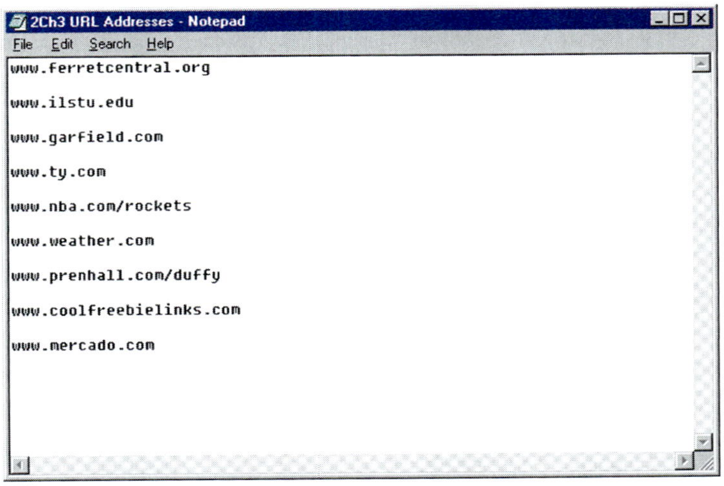

FIGURE 3.23 The 2Ch3 URL Addresses document with the Web addresses to be used in the home page document.

	Click to minimize the NotePad window.

14. Insert a second graphic image and link that image to a Web site. Once the link is created enter explanatory text.

CTRL + END	Position to the end of the Web document.
↑	Move up one line.
	Click the Insert Picture from File button to open the Picture dialog box. Use the Look in selection box to go to the disk/directory holding the Web files.
2Ch3_Ferret_2	Double-click this file to insert it in the Web page. A large image now appears.
Click	Click the image to select it. Click the lower right-hand resize button and size the image so that it appears like that depicted in Figure 3.24.

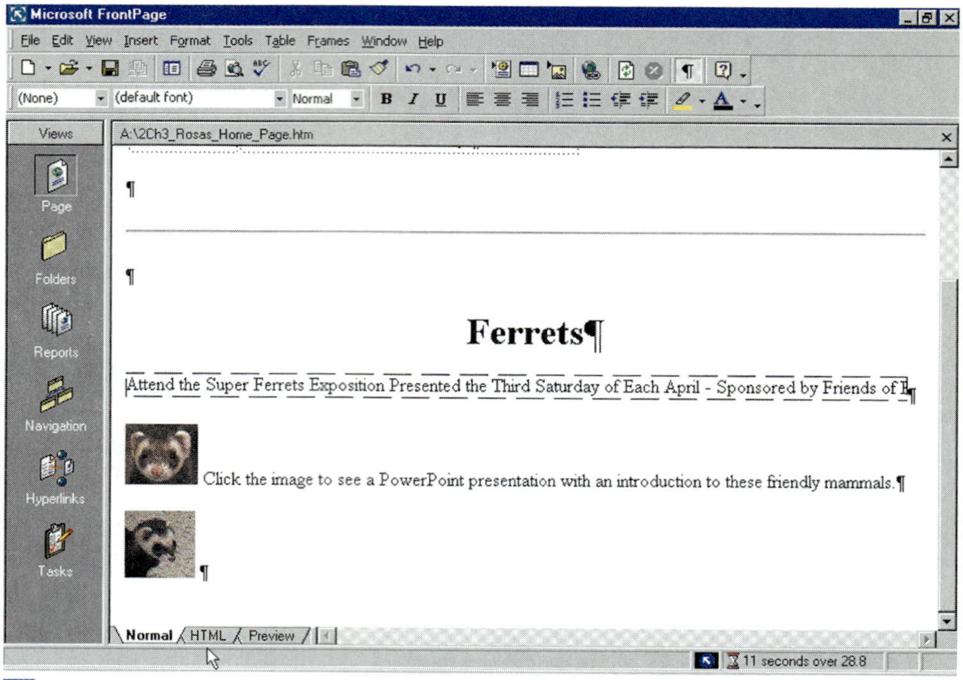

FIGURE 3.24 The second resized ferret image inserted in the Web page.

15. Link this image to a Web site.

Click Click the ferret image so that the selection handles appear around the image.

Click the Insert Hyperlink button on the Standard toolbar to invoke the Create Hyperlink dialog box.

2Ch3 URL Addresses - No... Click this taskbar button to activate the NotePad window.

www.ferretcentral.org Click-and-drag to select this text in the NotePad window.

CTRL + **C** Issue the Copy command.

Microsoft FrontPage Click this taskbar button to return to the FrontPage window.

CTRL + **V** Issue the Paste Command to paste the Web address in the URL text box. Your completed Create Hyperlink dialog box should look like Figure 3.25.

OK Click to create the link and return to the Web document.

→ Press to de-select the graphic image.

SPACE Press to insert a space after the image.

Type: `Click the image to visit Ferret Central.`

Enter this explanatory text.

ENTER Press to position to the next line. Your Web page should now look like that depicted in Figure 3.26.

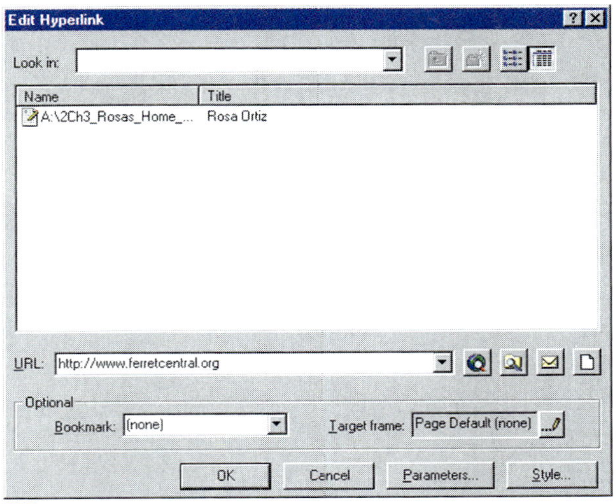

FIGURE 3.25 **The Web link for the Ferret Central Web page pasted in the Create Hyperlink dialog box.**

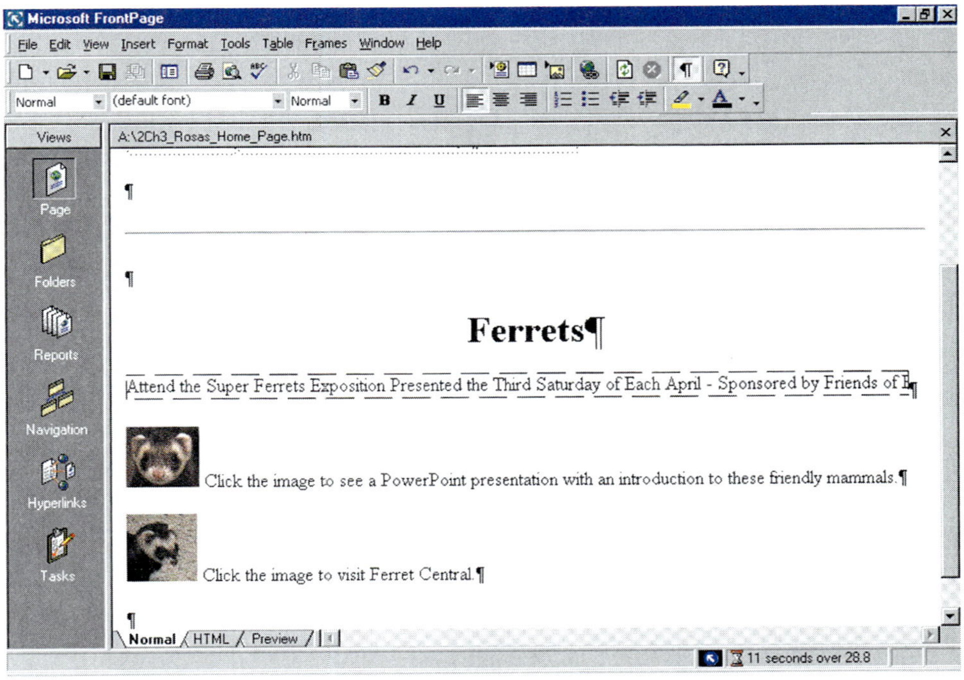

FIGURE 3.26 **The Web page with the two image links and explanatory text.**

16. Use the commands from the previous steps 9 and 10 to create the third link shown in Figure 3.27. The image filename is *2Ch3_book1* and the document on disk to which you are to link is called *2Ch3_Ferret_Web_Flyer*. Enlarge the image so that it looks like Figure 3.27. Insert the explanatory text.

17. Use the commands from the previous Steps 9 and 10 to create the fourth link shown in Figure 3.27. The image filename is *2Ch3_logo* and the document on disk to which you are to link is called *2Ch3_Term_Paper*. Enlarge the image so that it looks like Figure 3.27. Insert the explanatory text. When you are finished, test the links using your Web browser.

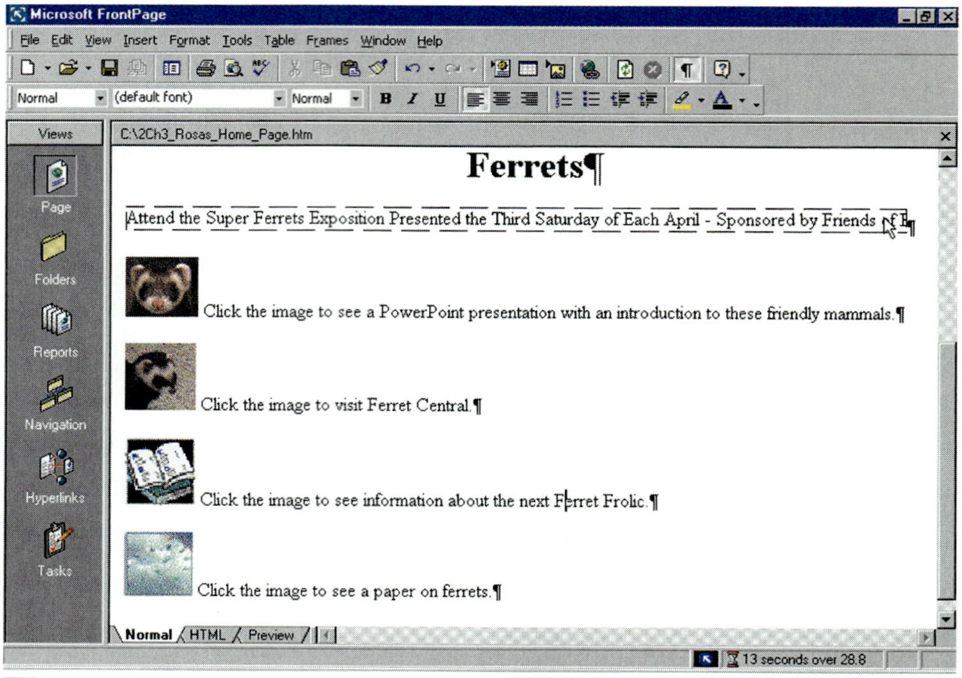

FIGURE 3.27 The Web page with the four image links and explanatory text.

18. Insert a horizontal line.

 Save the Web document.

(ENTER) Position to the next line.

Insert Click to open the Insert menu.

Horizontal Line Click to insert a horizontal line in the Web page.

(↓) Position to next line.

19. Create a centered heading line.

 Click to center the text.

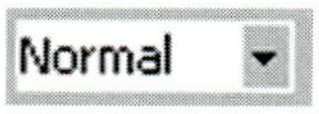

Click the Style button to invoke the Style menu.

Heading 1 Click this style.

Type: `Personal Information` Enter this text in the Web page.

(ENTER) Position to the next line.

 Click to left justify text.

20. Use the commands in step 2 to create another two-cell table. Once the table is created, make certain that the insertion point is in the right-hand cell of the table.

21. Use the commands from the previous steps 14 and 15 to insert and create the ISU link shown in Figure 3.27. The image filename is *ISU_Logo* and the Web site to which you are to link is *www.ilstu.edu.*

22. Enter the text in the left-hand cell. Center the text. Use the Heading 3 style for the text.

Type: **I attend Illinois State University – Home of the Redbirds – Visit that home page by clicking on the ISU Logo.**

Click Click outside and below the table to move the insertion point. Your Web page should now look like that depicted in Figure 3.28.

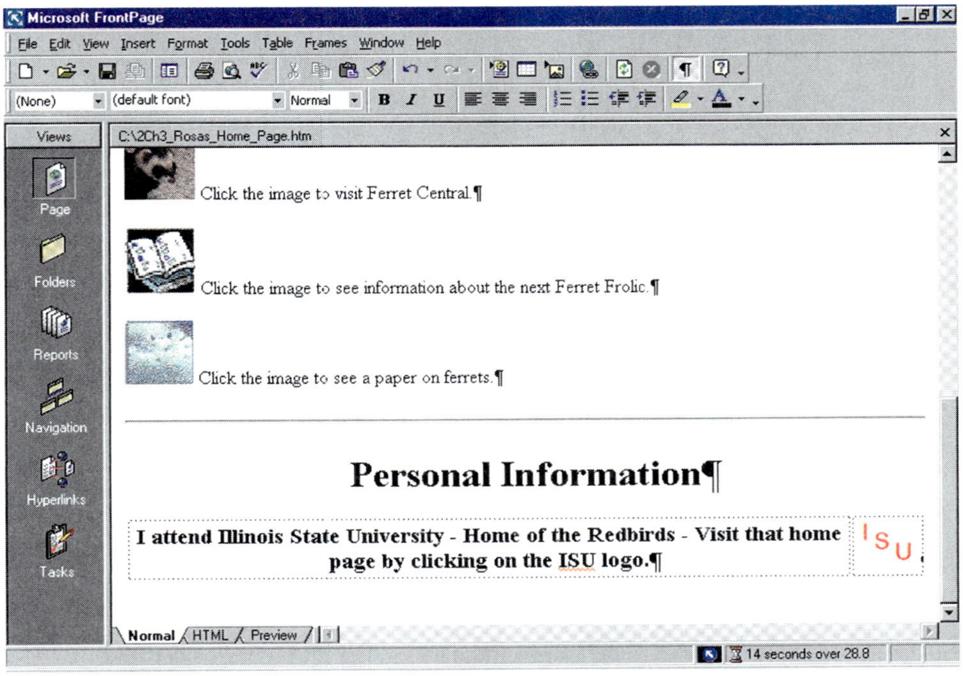

FIGURE 3.28 **The Web page with the beginning of the Personal Information section of the Web page.**

23. Insert the previously prepared RTF file with some autobiographical information. This file was created using Microsoft Word and then saved as an RTF file to remove any formatting characters used by Word.

Insert Click to open the Insert menu.

File . . . Click to activate the Select File dialog box. Use the Look in selection box to switch to the drive/directory where the Web files are stored. This example uses drive A.

Files of type: Change this selection box to Rich Text Format. Your Select File dialog box should now look like Figure 3.29.

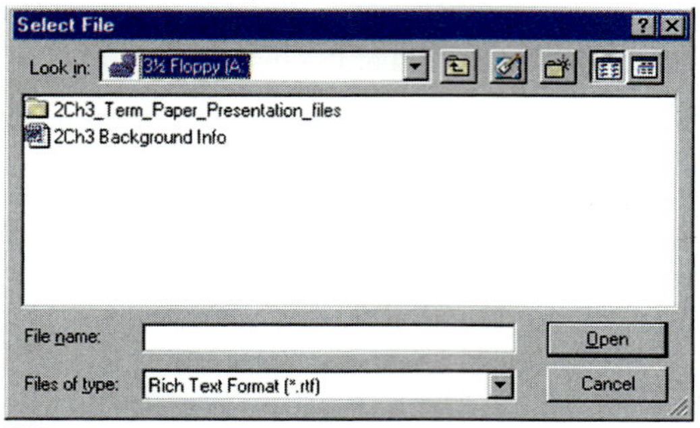

FIGURE 3.29 **The Select File dialog box displaying any RTF files.**

2Ch3 Background Info Double-click this filename to load the autobiographical information. Your Web document should now look like that depicted in Figure 3.30.

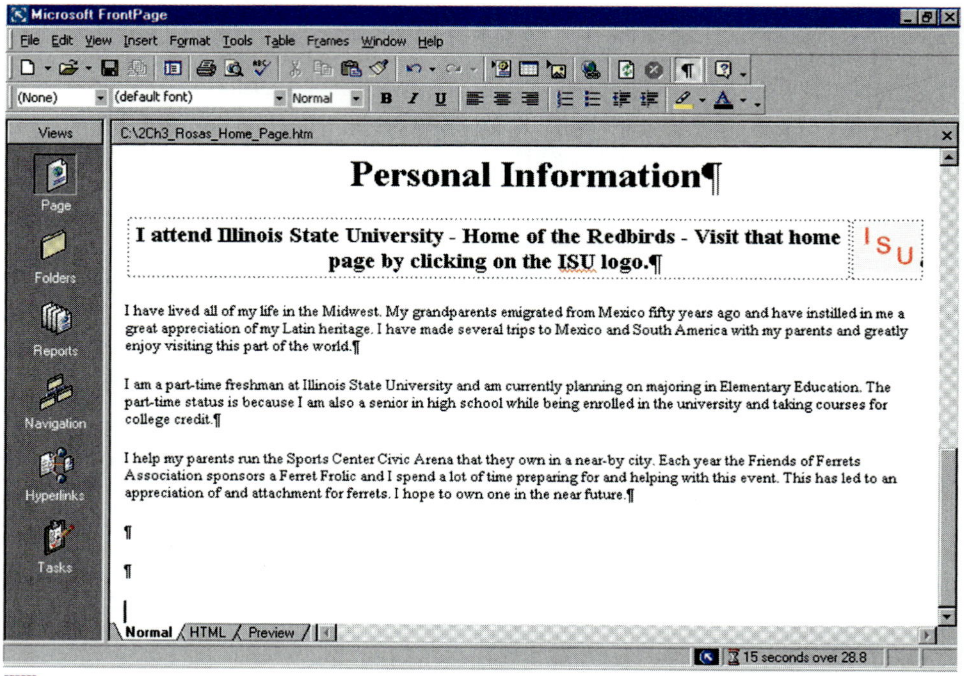

FIGURE 3.30 **The Web document with the text from the inserted RTF file.**

BACKSPACE — Press twice to get rid of the extraneous blank lines.

Save the Web document.

24. Enter the hobby heading. Select the Heading 3 style.

Type: `My Hobbies Include:` Enter the heading text.

ENTER — Position to the next line.

Click to turn on bulleted text. Enter the five lines of bulleted text shown in Figure 3.31.

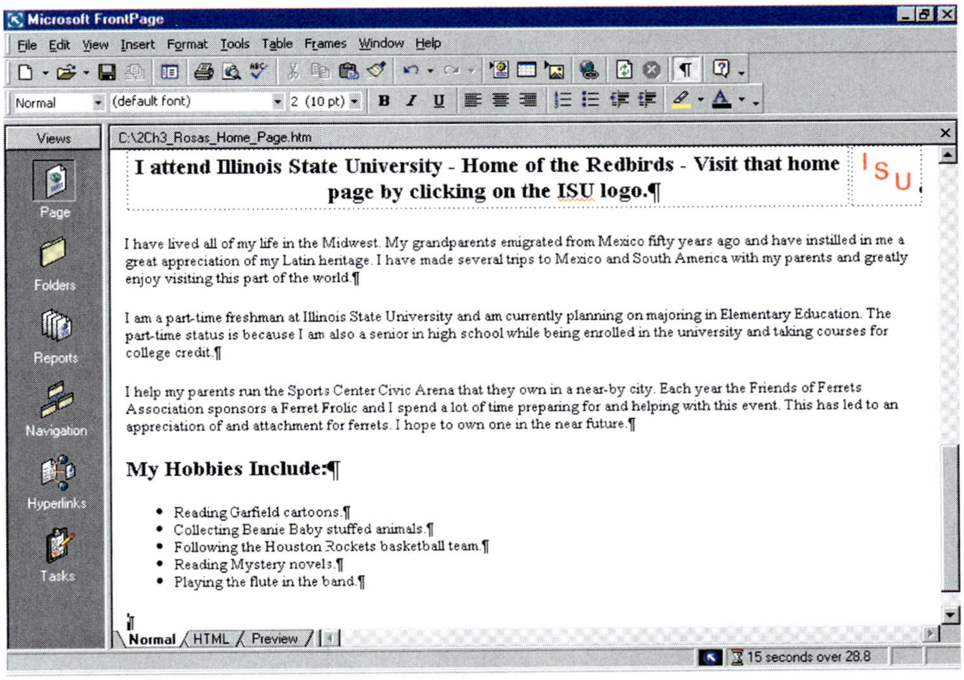

FIGURE 3.31 The Web document with the bulleted hobby text.

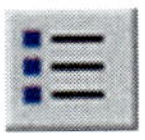

Click to turn bulleting off after pressing (ENTER) on the last line.

25. Create the first text-based Web link. If you have closed the NotePad window, open it using the instructions in the previous step 13.

Garfield Use a drag operation to select this text.

Click the Insert Hyperlink button on the Standard toolbar to invoke the Create Hyperlink dialog box.

Click this taskbar button to activate the NotePad window.

www.garfield.com Click-and-drag to select this text in the NotePad window.

(CTRL) + **C** Issue the Copy command.

Click this taskbar button to return to the FrontPage window

(CTRL) + **V** Issue the Paste command to paste the Web address in the URL text box. Your completed Create Hyperlink dialog box should look like Figure 3.32.

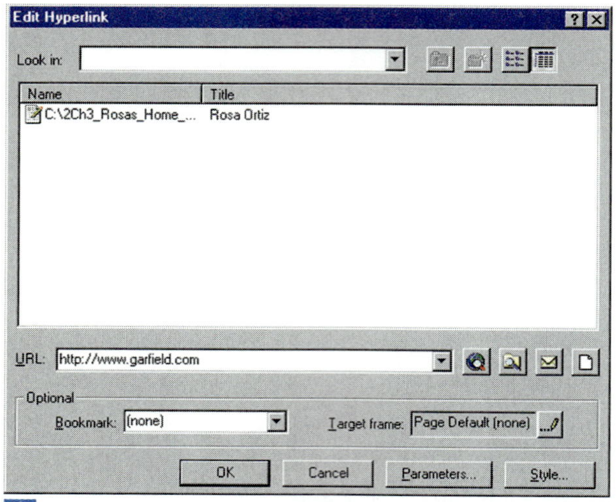

FIGURE 3.32 The Web link for the Garfield Web page pasted in the Create Hyperlink dialog box.

Click to create the link and return to the Web document.

Press to de-select the text. Your Web page should now look like that depicted in Figure 3.33.

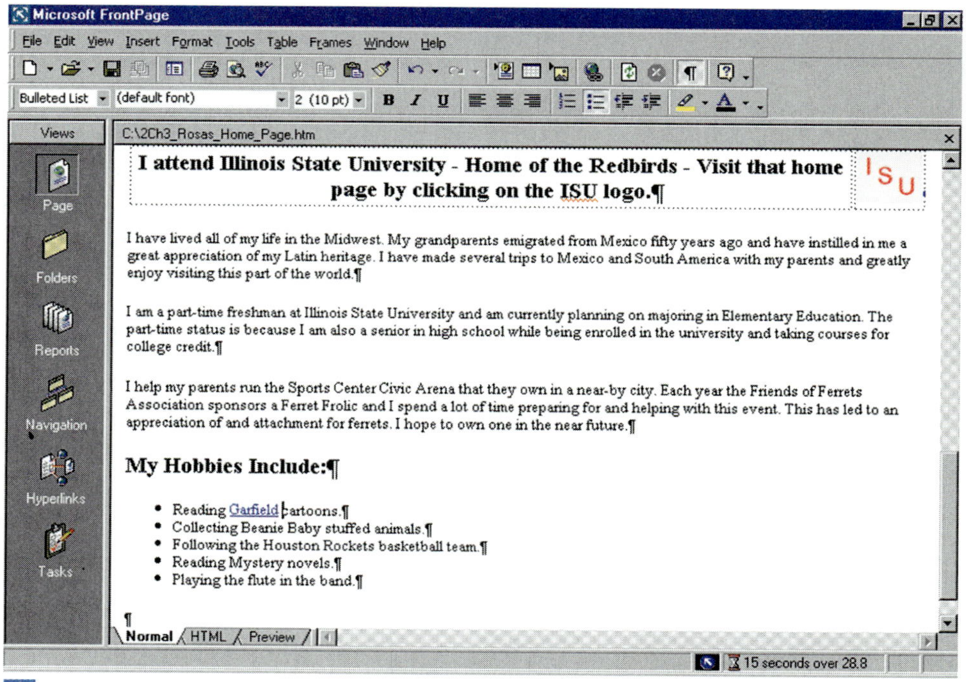

FIGURE 3.33 The Web page with the Garfield text link.

26. Use the following text and the Web addresses in the NotePad document to create the remaining hobby links:

Text	Web Address
Beanie Baby	www.ty.com
Houston Rockets	www.nba.com/rockets

27. Using Figure 3.34 as a guide, enter the Cool Sites text shown in Figure 3.34. Use the following text and the Web addresses in the NotePad document to create the remaining hobby links. Test all of your text links.

Text	Web Address
Weather Channel	www.weather.com
Office 2000	www.prenhall.com/duffy
freestuff	www.coolfreebielinks.com
Latin Music	www.mercado.com

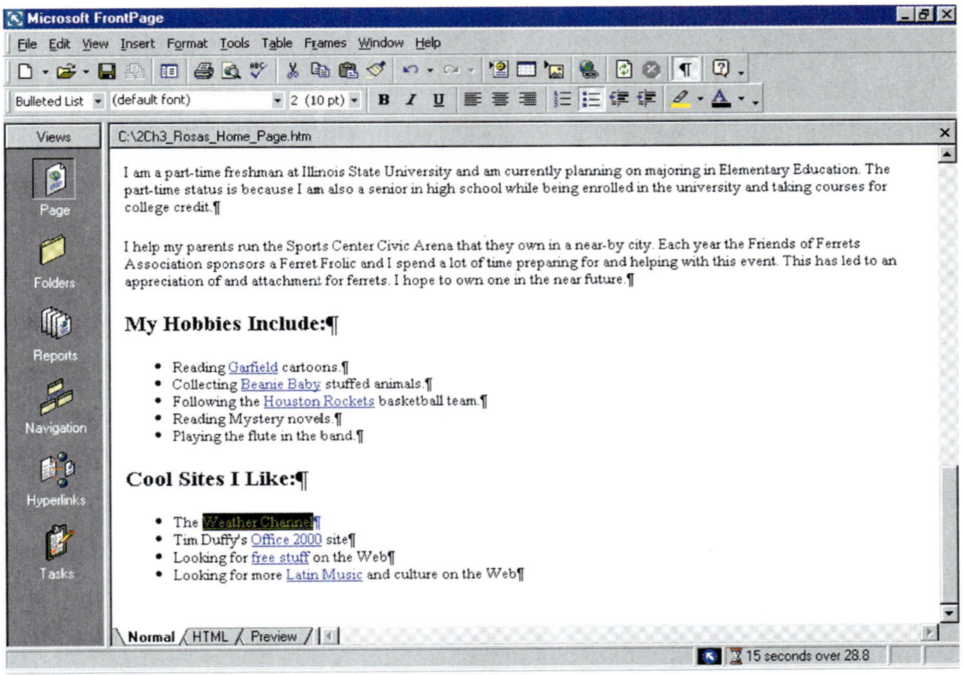

FIGURE 3.34 The Web page with the Cool Links text and created hyperlinks.

28. Create a horizontal line and enter the last heading line.

(ENTER)	Press to insert a blank line.
Insert	Click to open the Insert menu.
Horizontal Line	Click to insert a Horizontal line in the Web page.
(ENTER)	Press to insert a blank line.
	Click to center the text.

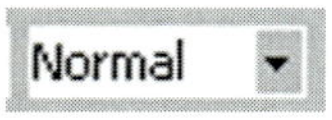

Click the Style button to invoke the Style menu.

Heading 1 Click this style.

Type: **`Contact Information`** Enter this text in the Web page.

(ENTER) Position to the next line.

Click to left justify the text.

29. Enter the E-mail sentence and create the E-mail link.

Type: **`You can E-mail me at Precision.net`** Enter the text.

Precision.net Use a drag operation to select this text.

Click the Insert Hyperlink button on the Standard toolbar to invoke the Create Hyperlink dialog box.

Click the Make a hyperlink that sends E-mail button. The Create E-mail Hyperlink dialog box now appears.

Type: **`rortiz@precision.net`** Enter the E-mail address. Your completed E-mail Hyperlink dialog box now appears like Figure 3.35.

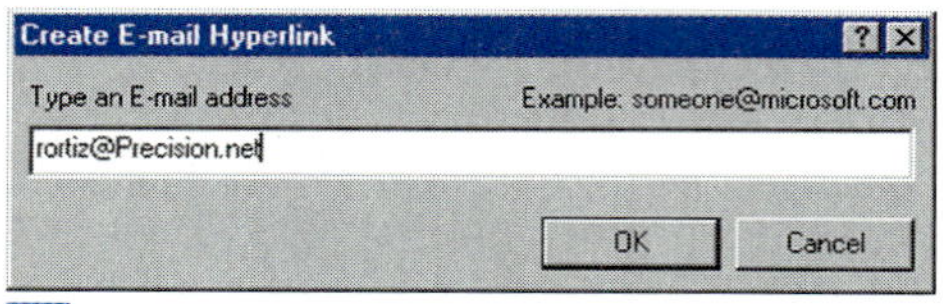

FIGURE 3.35 The E-mail Hyperlink dialog box.

Click to create the E-mail link and return to the Create Hyperlink dialog box (Figure 3.36).

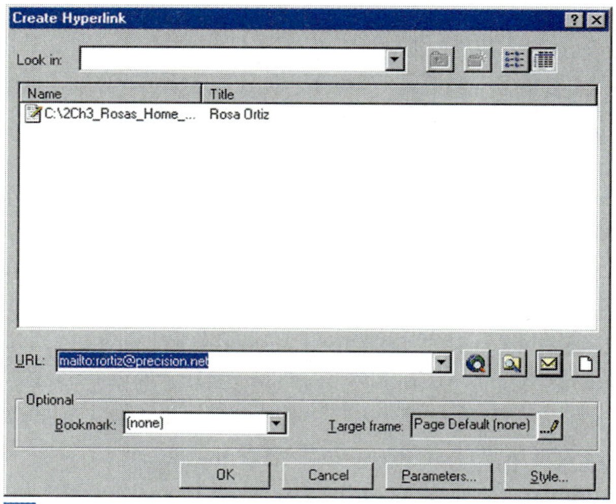

FIGURE 3.36 The Create Hyperlink dialog box with the mail to HTML E-mail link tag.

Click to return to the Web document. Test the E-mail link using your browser.

30. Add a theme to make the Web page look more appealing. A theme affects the background, font size, buttons for bullets, and so forth in a Web document.

CTRL + HOME	Position to the beginning of the Web document.
Format	Click to open the Format menu.
Theme . . .	Opens the Themes dialog box.
Sumi Painting	Scroll down and click this theme. The Themes dialog box previews the selected theme (Figure 3.37).

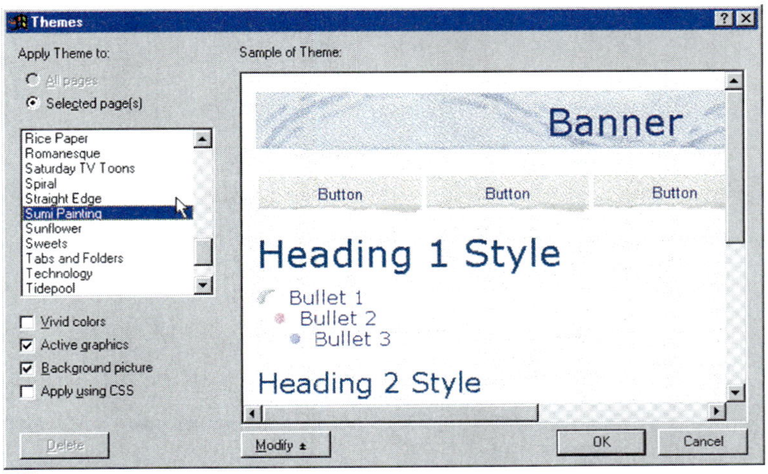

FIGURE 3.37 The Sumi Painting theme previewed in the Themes dialog box.

OK	Apply the selected theme against the Web document. Your Web document should now look like that depicted in Figure 3.38.

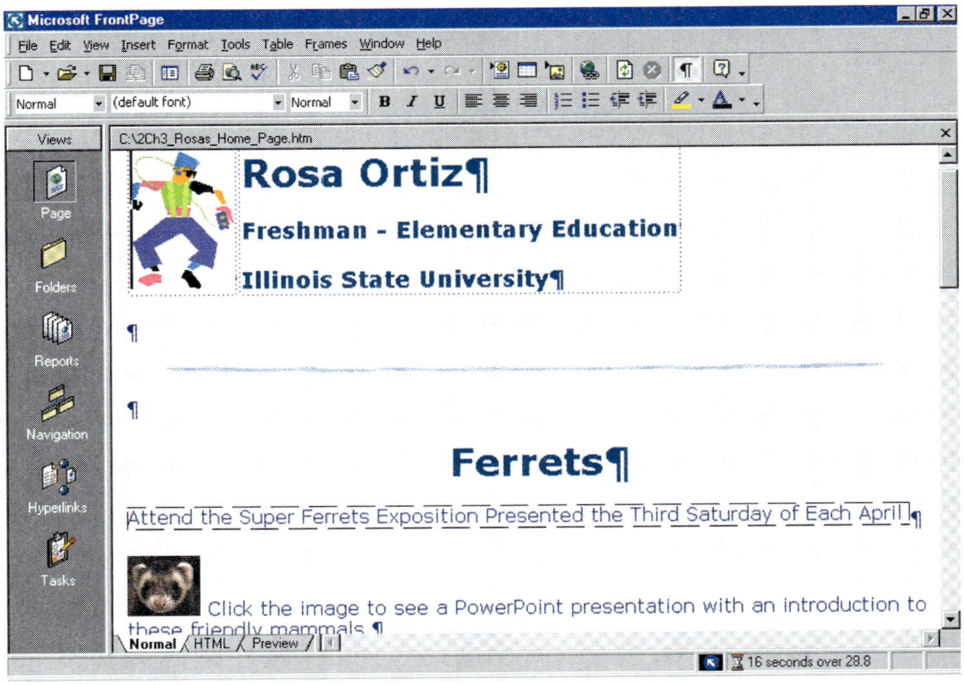

FIGURE 3.38 The Web document with the Sumi Painting theme applied.

31. Save the changes.

Click to save the changes. The Save Embedded Files dialog box now appears (Figure 3.39). These are files that are used in the Sumi Painting theme.

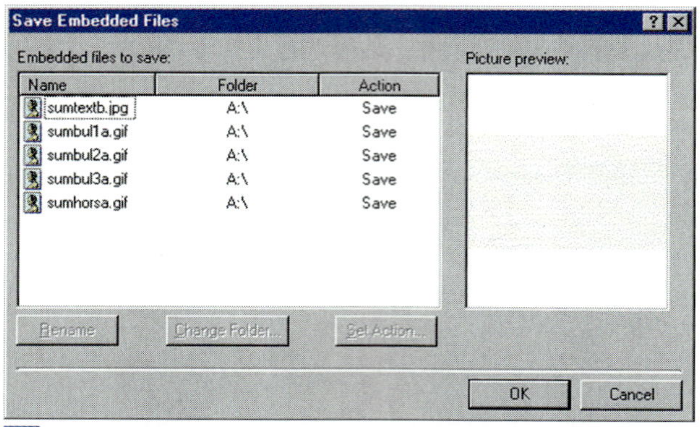

FIGURE 3.39 The embedded files needed by the Sumi Painting theme.

Click to save the theme files to disk.

32. View the HTML commands used to create the Web page.

Click this tab to view the HTML commands (Figure 3.40).

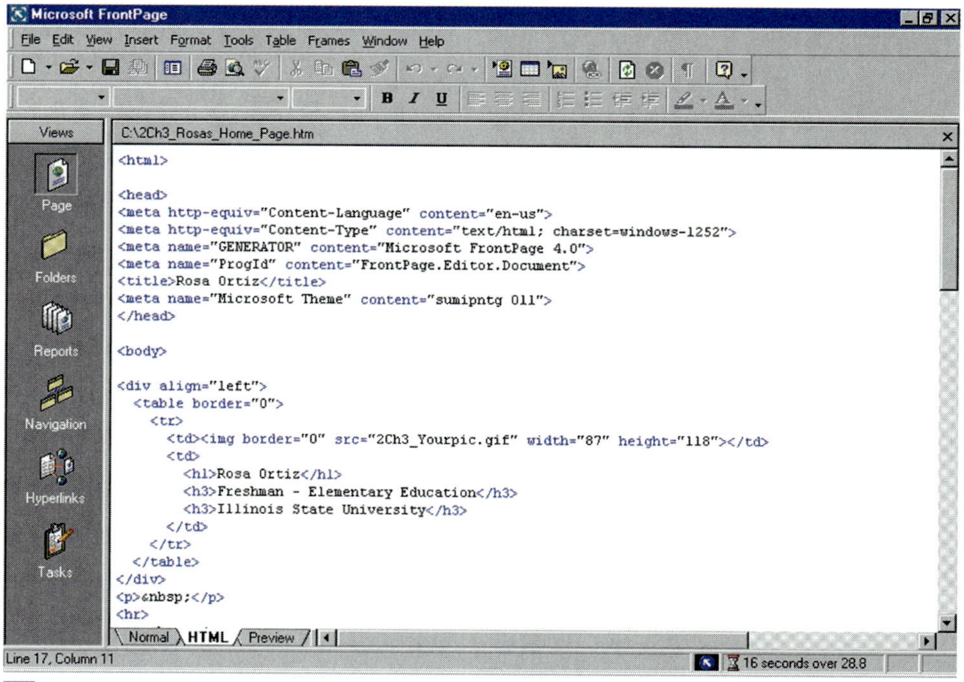

FIGURE 3.40 The HTML commands used to create the web page displayed in the HTML FrontPage tab.

Click to print the HTML commands. Use your printout and examine the various HTML commands in your document. Refer back to the tables at the beginning of the chapter to decipher any of the commonly used HTML commands.

33. Print the Web page.

Click to invoke the Normal tab of FrontPage.

Click to print the Web page.

34. Close FrontPage. Start Explorer and load the Web document you created (Figure 3.41). Make certain that all of the Web and document links on your Web document function properly. If you find any errors, you can correct them by using FrontPage or by accessing your Web page using NotePad and making changes directly to the HTML commands.

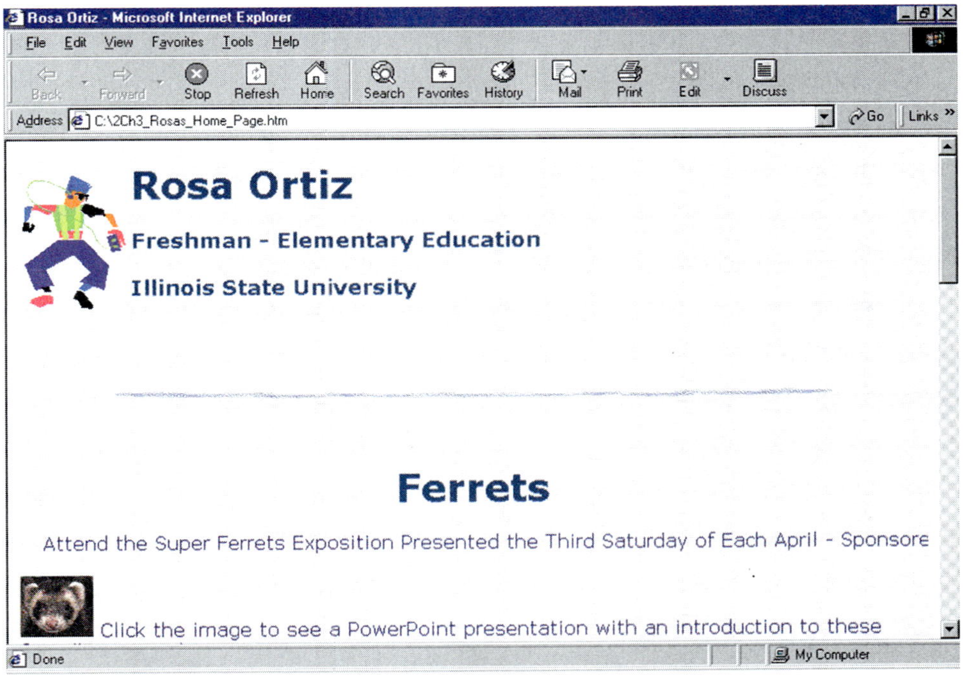

FIGURE 3.41 **The home page accessed using Internet Explorer.**

35. Once your Web page is working correctly, it is ready to be uploaded to your Web server. Your instructor will provide you with directions on how to accomplish this.

On Your Own

Find the following HTML commands that perform the following tasks.

1. The HTML commands that are used to create the *Ferrets* heading.
2. The HTML commands that are used to create the image link that links to the PowerPoint presentation on Ferrets.
3. The HTML commands that create the table for the link to Illinois State University.
4. The HTML commands that create a bulleted list of items.
5. The HTML commands that create the text link to the Weather Channel.
6. The HTML command that creates the E-mail link.

Reinforcing the Exercise

1. Tables make it easier to combine text and graphic images at the same location in a Web document.
2. The style controls the type of lines entered in a Web page.
3. Links can also be embedded in a graphic image or text.
4. You can create a link that accesses a document on disk, a Web site, or an E-mail address.
5. You can test a Web document by clicking the Preview in Browser button.
6. If you are making changes and testing frequently, remember to use the Refresh button of the browser.
7. Text can be pasted from a NotePad window or inserted from a Word RTF file.
8. A marquee consists of moving text that appears when viewed by the browser. Some browsers, however, do not support the marquee feature.

Session Review

The Web browser is the piece of software that translates HTML-based documents and then assembles the text, graphics, and sound files to create and display a Web page to the screen of a computer. An HTML document is a text document with tags that tell it where to find files and then where to place the files in a document for display to the screen. The text portion of a Web document usually appears before any other files appear.

A Web document is composed of HTML tags that appear between less than (<) and greater than (>) symbols. HTML tags are not visible when a Web document is displayed, but provide the Web browser with instructions about what to do with and how to display a document.

A Web page is usually one of many such components of a Web site. It may contain hyperlinks that allow you to indicate to the browser that you want to jump to another part of the same document, a different file on the same computer, a file on a different computer, or establish an E-mail link for sending an E-mail message.

A Web page should be planned before you start building it. Any images should be gathered. The layout of the Web page should be determined. Any text files that will be used to create the Web document should be created. You may also wish to place Web URL addresses in a NotePad file for easy inclusion in a link as you build the Web page.

Because UNIX-based machines do not readily accept spaces in filenames, filenames should not have any embedded spaces, rather, the spaces can be replaced with underscore characters.

Originally Web pages were built using solely HTML commands and a text editor like NotePad. Web editors have since been developed that allow you to use a WYSIWYG environment to build the Web page. Such editors do not require any detailed knowledge of HTML. Rather, as you enter text and perform other commands, the HTML commands needed to perform those tasks are automatically included in the Web page document. On such WYSIWYG editor is Microsoft's FrontPage 2000.

Key Terms and Concepts

application window 111
Formatting toolbar 114
FrontPage 111
HTML tag 106
menu bar 112
Standard toolbar 112
status bar 114
title bar 112
Views bar 112
Web document window 112
Web site 107
workspace tabs 115

Session Quiz

Multiple Choice

1. An HTML command/tag is enclosed in which symbols?
   - **a.** [ ]
   - **b.** < >
   - **c.** { }
   - **d.** ( )
2. Which of the following items is loaded first in a Web page by the browser?
   - **a.** Image file
   - **b.** Sound file
   - **c.** Animated clip art
   - **d.** Text
3. Which of the following tasks is involved in planning a Web page?
   - **a.** Generate an outline.
   - **b.** Develop any text files that might be inserted.
   - **c.** Gather image files in one location.
   - **d.** All of the above are involved in developing a Web page.
4. Which of the following HTML commands do not have to be used in pairs?
   - **a.** <b> </b>
   - **b.** <p> </p>
   - **c.** <u> </u>
   - **d.** <I> </I>
5. A hyperlink in a Web page can link to:
   - **a.** a different file on the same computer
   - **b.** a Web page on a different computer
   - **c.** the E-mail program to send an E-mail message
   - **d.** all of the above

True/False

6. The marquee feature of FrontPage might not work with each browser.
7. FrontPage treats a Web page differently from a Web site.
8. An RTF file is created using the NotePad program.
9. When you are creating a Web page using FrontPage, it is difficult to test your HTML document to see how it works.
10. FrontPage is a WYSIWYG HTML editor.

Session Review Exercises

1. Define or describe each of the following:
   a. hyperlink
   b. Web site
   c. HTML tags
   d. marquee
2. The language used to build a Web page is called ____________.
3. A ____________ ____________ is composed of a number of Web pages.
4. You can use the ____________ program to hold such text as Web addresses.
5. The ____________ ____________ HTML pair of commands is used for boldfacing text in a Web document.
6. The ____________ HTML tag is used to reference any item contained in a list of items contained in a Web document.
7. The ____________ HTML tag is embedded in an E-mail hyperlink.
8. The ____________ ____________ feature of the FrontPage window allows you to see different parts of a Web site.
9. A ____________ ____________ ____________ button of the Standard toolbar allows you to invoke your browser to test the Web page.
10. The ____________ button of the Formatting toolbar allows you to determine the type of line to be entered in a Web page.
11. The ____________ tabs allow you to enter your Web page in WYSIWYG mode, see the HTML instructions used for your Web page, or display the Web page as it will appear in your browser.
12. In a UNIX environment ____________ characters are used in place of spaces in a filename.
13. You can use the ____________ feature of FrontPage to have images and multiple lines of text side-by-side.
14. Use the ____________ ____________ FrontPage button to see paragraph markers and other items in the Normal tab.
15. The ____________ style is used to create text with the largest font in a Web document.
16. Use the ____________ ____________ button to create a link to a different Web location.
17. Text that is to be inserted in a Web document can be created by Word and saved to a file using the ____________ file format.
18. A hyperlink can be created so that you can click on either an image or ____________ to follow the hyperlink.
19. If you are using a browser to test your Web page, and you are continually switching back and forth between the browser and FrontPage, click the ____________ in the browser to reload any changes that have been made in FrontPage.
20. The ____________ feature of FrontPage allows you to add a background image, control the font of text, insert images for bullets, and so forth when using FrontPage.

Computer Exercise

1. Build your own personal Web page. You can use the hands-on sample in the chapter as a starting point. Look at the Internet Exercise below to help you prepare. In preparation for this project do the following:
   a. Plan what you want to include in your Web page and how you want it to look.
   b. Place all images in one location.
   c. Create any RTF text files that you want to include in your Web page (you can also use NotePad to create these files).
   d. Determine the Web sites for which you want to establish links.
   e. If you are going to link to any files, place those with your image files.
   f. What theme, if any, do you want to apply to your Web page?

Internet Exercise

1. Find clip art and background files for use in constructing a Web page.
   a. Open the Web page supported by this text (http://www.prenhall.com/duffy).
   b. Click the Sample of World Wide Web link and activate it.
   c. Click the Computers, HTML, and Internet link.
   d. Visit the various links that contain clip art and backgrounds.
   e. Download a piece of clip art and a background.
   f. If you have a color printer, you might want to print the Web document you accessed via the link HTML: Backgrounds and Color Notes.

GLOSSARY

account An individual's unique identifier at a particular location on the Internet.

address The location where the individual receives messages across the Internet.

application pane The location where the individual can create, view, and edit E-mail messages, maintain schedules, enter tasks, and access storage devices.

application window Contains the title bar, application control buttons, menu bar, document control buttons, Standard and Formatting toolbars, ruler, Office Assistant, split box, status bar, scroll bars, view icons, and a blank document window.

archive A storage area that can be used to store older messages to which the individual no longer has direct access.

Calendar A feature of Outlook that can be used to keep track of appointments and assignments.

categories Used for storing contacts, tasks, appointments, messages, and so forth.

Contacts A feature that allows you to store information like names, addresses, phone numbers, E-mail addresses, and so forth.

country (co) indicator The part of an Internet address that specifies a foreign country.

document window The area of the screen that displays the current Web page.

electronic mail (E-mail) Messages you can send and receive by using the computer. Also, the process of sending messages.

E-mail shorthand The brief, concise mode of communication used in composing E-mail messages.

emoticon A design created from the keyboard to help express an emotion in e-mail messages. For example, :-) is happy, :-(is sad, :-D is laughing, and :'-(is crying. An emoticon is also called a smiley.

FAQ (frequently asked questions) A file that contains guidelines for using a newsgroup as well as elementary information about a particular topic.

file transfer protocol (FTP) A method of using the Internet for copying a file from one computer to another.

flaming Sending a nasty message, or flame, across the Internet.

Formatting toolbar Usually located beneath the Standard toolbar, this toolbar enables you to format characters and paragraphs. Using this toolbar, you can select formatting styles such as the font, point size, text alignment, and bold, italic, or underlined text. You can also use the Formatting toolbar to apply predefined styles to text.

FrontPage A software program that is capable of developing large, complex Web sites.

Gopher A text-based, menu-driven program that allows you to access, view, and download files. Gopher was the immediate precursor of the Web and is still frequently used.

home page The first page of a Web site that includes links to other pages. Also called the start page.

HTML (Hypertext Markup Language) The hypertext language used to build a Web address or Web page. This language controls the appearance of a Web page.

HTML tag Text contained between less than (<) and greater than (>) characters.

HTTP (Hypertext Transfer Protocol) Software used by Web servers to transfer files through the Web to other Web servers.

hypermedia The means of communication on the Web that makes use of images, animation, and sound.

hypertext The means of communication on the Web in which you use pointers or links to navigate through Web sites.

Inbox The default pane/view that stores messages that you have received. The upper part of the pane stores the message header, while the bottom portion allows you to scroll through the selected message.

Internet A network of networks that allows you to communicate with people anywhere in the world and access information that you desire at any time.

Internet Relay Chat (IRC) An Internet service that allows you to communicate "live" with other users in Internet locations called chat rooms.

listserv A file that contains all e-mail messages related to a particular newsgroup topic.

login A procedure that identifies you to the host computer when you attempt to access the Internet.

lurking Spending a few days or weeks just reading newsgroup postings, not interacting, to see how the flow of a newsgroup progresses and to get an idea of the types of individuals who participate in the group.

menu bar Located under the title bar in a window, the menu bar contains the names of menus you can open to access commands. Windows is consistent in how menus are arranged from application to application, making it easy to learn various Windows applications.

modem Short for modulation/demodulation. A device that changes computer digital symbols to sound for transmission across telephone hookups. The receiving computer's modem then changes the sounds back to digital symbols.

network A set of hardware and software components that supports several people working together and allows these individuals to share hardware, software, and information with one another.

newsgroup Interactive discussion group accessed through the Internet.

Notes A shortcut that allows you to store short notes about items that might need your attention later. These notes can now act like electronic "sticky notes" and can be attached to various documents as reminders.

Outlook bar The large vertical bar in the left-hand side of the screen.

Outlook Today Allows you to preview the activities scheduled for today, any tasks that have to be accomplished, and provides information about any E-mail messages.

password A series of characters that verifies to the computer that you are indeed a valid user.

posting A message sent to or received from a newsgroup.

status bar Located at the bottom of the window, the status bar provides information on an object from the desktop that you select.

status indicator 1. Appears at the right end of the status bar and shows when particular program conditions exist as well as whether the toggle key is on or off

subdomain The part of an Internet address that indicates the name of the location and possibly the name of the server to which the message is to be sent.

TaskPad A feature that appears as part of the Calendar and allows you to create tasks that you or someone else is to perform.

Telnet A feature that allows you to have remote access to another computer, for example, to access the card catalog of another university.

thread A set of newsgroup postings related to a specific topic.

title bar Colored bar at the top of a window that contains the name of the open application and four buttons you can use to control the window: the control-menu, Minimize, Maximize (or Restore), and Close buttons.

toolbar The row of buttons that appears below the menu bar in an application window.

toolbox A floating palette that is displayed whenever you open the Design View of a report.

topdomain The part of an Internet address that specifies the type of organization that is to receive the message.

URL (uniform resource locator) The address of each location and file on the Internet. The URL consists of the protocol, host name, and resource.

Usenet An Internet service that started as a bulletin board and has expanded to include thousands of sites providing services worldwide.

Veronica An Internet service that allows you to perform searches easily by using multiple Gopher sites.

Views bar Allows you to select the desired view by clicking on one of its icons.

Web browser Software that communicates with other Web sites and transfers text, graphics, and even sound to your computer screen or speakers and displays and plays this data correctly.

Web document window The location where you create, view, and edit a document.

Web site A group of Web pages for an organization or some other entity.

workspace tabs Located at the left end of the horizontal scroll bar, these tabs control how the document is displayed on the screen.

World Wide Web (WWW or Web) Designed in 1989 to simplify telecommunications technology used for international research collaboration. Now the Web has tens of thousands of sites that any Internet subscriber can access.

INDEX